£5

Teaching Strategies
for the
Culturally Disadvantaged

Teaching Strategies
for the
Culturally Disadvantaged

by

HILDA TABA
late of San Francisco State College

DEBORAH ELKINS
Queens College of the City University of New York

Rand McNally & Company
Chicago

RAND McNALLY EDUCATION SERIES

B. OTHANEL SMITH, *Advisory Editor*

Broudy and Palmer, *Exemplars of Teaching Method*

Broudy, Smith, and Burnett, *Democracy and Excellence in American Secondary Education*

Burns and Lowe, *The Language Arts in Childhood Education*

Childress and Gauerke, eds., *Theory and Practice of School Finance*

Dupuis, *Philosophy of Education in Historical Perspective*

Evans and Walker, *New Trends in the Teaching of English in Secondary Schools*

Farwell and Peters, eds., *Guidance Readings for Counselors*

Foshay, ed., *Rand McNally Handbook of Education*

Haines, *Guiding the Student Teaching Process in Elementary Education*

Kaplan and Steiner, *Musicianship for the Classroom Teacher*

Kimbrough, *Political Power and Educational Decision-Making*

Krumboltz, ed., *Learning and the Educational Process*

Lewenstein, *Teaching Social Studies in Junior and Senior High Schools*

Lieberman and Moskow, *Collective Negotiations for Teachers*

Litwack, Holmes, and O'Hern, *Critical Issues in Student Personnel Work*

Michaelis, ed., *Teaching Units in the Social Sciences,* 3 volumes

Norris, Zeran, and Hatch, *The Information Service in Guidance,* 2nd edition

Parker, ed., *Rand McNally Curriculum Series*

   Ford and Pugno, eds., *The Structure of Knowledge and the Curriculum*

   Parker and Rubin, *Process as Content*

   Wellington and Wellington, *The Underachiever*

Perrodin, ed., *The Student Teacher's Reader*

Peters and Farwell, *Guidance: A Developmental Approach*

Peters, Shertzer, and Van Hoose, *Guidance in Elementary Schools*

Phi Delta Kappa, *Education and the Structure of Knowledge*

Phi Delta Kappa, *Improving Experimental Design and Statistical Analysis*

Rollins and Unruh, *Introduction to Secondary Education*

Shulman and Keislar, eds., *Learning by Discovery*

Smith, ed., *Aesthetics and Criticism in Art Education*

Smith and Ennis, eds., *Language and Concepts in Education*

Taba and Elkins, *Teaching Strategies for the Culturally Disadvantaged*

Trump and Baynham, *Focus on Change: Guide to Better Schools*

Vassar, ed., *Social History of American Education,* 2 volumes

Wolf and Loomer, *The Elementary School: A Perspective*

Zeran and Riccio, *Organization and Administration of Guidance Services*

Also published by Rand McNally

Gage, ed., *Handbook of Research on Teaching*—A Project of the American Educational Research Association

Copyright © 1966 by Rand McNally & Company

All rights reserved

Printed in U.S.A. by Rand McNally & Company

Library of Congress Catalog Card Number 66:19456

Second Printing, 1968

Preface

This book contains a series of sequences—call them sequences of curriculum, teaching, or learning, it does not matter. These sequences have been taught in sixth, seventh, and eighth grades to students whom today we call "culturally deprived." This term may be trival and overstated, but the fact remains that these students had in common meagerness of background, low economic and a minority status, and had learned relatively little up to that time. One was a group of second-generation American children. The program of this group was formulated nearly twenty years ago under the auspices of the project on intergroup education directed by one of the authors. This project was financed by the National Conference of Christians and Jews and sponsored by the American Council on Education. It was described in full in *With Focus on Human Relations* (Taba & Elkins, 1950).

The sixth- and seventh-graders were largely Negroes living in a slum area in a metropolitan center. Many of them were recent immigrants from the South. The sequences for this group were developed in the last three years by beginning teachers under the leadership of Deborah Elkins, who was also a teacher of the first group twenty years ago.

The purpose of both programs was to reshape qualitatively the curriculum, its content, and the way of teaching and learning in order to reach these students. These programs also endeavored to find a vehicle of content that would help these students to reshape their mental and emotional functioning and to establish a process of learning to learn.

Both groups, in differing degrees, lacked self-confidence, purpose, ambition, and many academic and interpersonal skills. Both had been used to considering learning as drudgery, a set of meaningless exercises, and had, either partly or entirely, given up trying to learn. Both needed an infusion of some excitement of learning and help in acquiring the skills that made successful learning possible.

The two sets of sequences have several things in common, although they differ much in content and in the level of ideas with which they deal and of the performance they require. All use content as a vehicle to develop certain powers and skills. They employ devices especially designed to kindle motivation in ways that touch the students. Both carefully program the steps in learning that students with certain incapacities must take in order to establish an autonomous, self-propelling pattern of learning. The curriculum content of both is partly traditional, but also, partly unconventional, because they are supposed to make a connection with the concerns of students. Both include diagnosis as an integral part of planning teaching and of teaching itself, and both pursue multiple objectives simultaneously. In both sequences fiction was used abundantly as a way of arousing the students' energy and motivation to learn, and to awaken them to an intuitive awareness of a concept or of an idea.

Tactically, these sequences employ comparing and contrasting as a means to generate ideas with minimum coverage and to encourage mental activity on the part of students. There is, however, a vast difference in the nature of the contrasts employed and the pacing of steps from the examination of detail to the generation of abstractions. These differences are not so much a function of age and intelligence—for both groups had about the same spread, irrespective of the grade level—as they are of the degree of educational deprivation and retardation that these students had suffered. They may have had also something to do with the differences in the severity of acculturation problems. The marginality of the existence and the educational deprivation of Negroes in a megalopolis seem to be more severe than the marginality of Caucasians of foreign parentage twenty years ago.

The content of the topics with which these sequences deal is almost irrelevant. The topics would and should be different with different teachers and different groups of students. They should vary to the extent that the concerns and interests of students vary, and also because different teachers invent different teaching devices and employ different details through which to translate their aims into classroom learning experiences. Even within limits of similar concerns and interests, there are still different roads to Rome: different sets of specifics can be used to bear on the same focus.

Because these sequences are intended as models of processes of teaching and learning, they are described in detail. The pedagogical comment is held to a minimum, appearing chiefly where it seems necessary to make clear the connection between the description of a procedure and the theoretical principle of learning or teaching that underlies it. These comments also attempt to show how to translate educational aims into a workable or learnable form.

These sequences do not constitute a course of study. Many other sequences that were part of the total program have been omitted. They do, however, constitute models for constructing units, interpreted as a collection of materials, devices, and procedures that hang together.

These remarks are not intended as an apology for the loose organization and concrete nature of the book. Perhaps descriptive cases and partial models are all that anyone is ready to offer at this particular point for this kind of education on this particular level. A greater degree of theorizing may be premature, for experimentation with, and exploration of, the particular kinds of concrete processes and devices on a fairly wide scale is usually needed before theorizing and tighter programming is begun, if we are to avoid pouring old wine into new bottles.

This book is for teachers and other educational workers concerned with pre-adolescents. The junior high school level tends to be a No Man's Land in education generally and in the education of difficult and retarded learners particularly. Pre-adolescence is a difficult period. In our urban culture, which induces expectations of sophistication quite early, being half child and half adult is perhaps even more difficult than the classical literature on that topic indicates. If there is one period of schooling where help is needed, this is it.

The chief impetus for exhuming a presumably "old" book is to offer it as an aid to the many people who are now struggling to make some sensible readjustment of programs for students who have already established a career of failure through the elementary years.

It is the hope of the authors that this book will serve as a guide in the process of building up a body of tested experience in curriculum construction and teaching which takes seriously the dictum of beginning where the students are and therefore regards whatever needs to be done not as remedial procedure, but plainly as a way of helping students to take the next step in learning.

Appreciation is extended to several teachers who worked with these sequences and helped to record them. The authors are grateful to Watt Long, who was at that time the educational director of the National Conference of Christians and Jews in San Francisco, and Earl Kalp, their director in Chicago, for negotiating the release of claims held by the National Conference and the American Council on Education on the original book, *With Focus on Human Relations*. Thanks are due to Virginia Palmer of San Francisco State College for the final shaping of the manuscript.

Hilda Taba
Deborah Elkins

San Francisco, California
Flushing, New York

Table of Contents

Teaching Strategies
for the
Culturally Disadvantaged

CHAPTER I

Cultural Deprivation as a Factor in School Learning*

Although the term "culturally deprived child" seems to be only a variation on the theme of problem children, retarded children, slow learners, the underprivileged, and the under-achievers, it is hoped that it will be more than just another euphemism—indeed, that it indicates both a new statement of the problem we are facing and an approach that examines possible causes rather than merely describing the difficulties of such children in school.

Four questions need to be asked about the theme of cultural deprivation: (1) What is the situation? (2) What are the social and psychological factors which account for it? (3) What factors in school experience contribute to educational retardation? (4) What is the task of the school?

THE SITUATION

Two developments seem to be responsible for the present interest in cultural deprivation as a factor in school learning. One, curiously enough, is a consequence of our approaching success in achieving the goal of providing education for all the children of all of the American people, as called for by the democratic ideal. As school attendance approaches 100 per cent of the school-age population, the school draws increasingly from the "bottom of the pile." The able, the adjusted, and the motivated, the upper 30 per cent in ability, have always been in school, and the schools have taught them fairly successfully. Extension of school attendance can only add to the number of students in school who are emotionally and physically handi-

* Part of this chapter is based on an article with the same title, Taba (1964).

1

capped, less willing and able, and less academically motivated. These students are not equally able to cope with the school culture and its expectations and may even be hostile to what school represents. The result is that the school population has become more heterogeneous and, further, that the schools are having difficulty coping with this heterogeneity.

The second development is the rapid migration to our great industrial cities, both from the rural areas of the United States and from other countries: Negroes and Puerto Ricans in the East; Spanish-Americans, Mexicans, and Indians in the Southwest; and marginal farmers and poor mountain whites everywhere (Jencks, 1962). The 1950 U.S. Census figures indicate that 25 per cent of these arrivals in the city have migrated from foreign countries or have foreign-born parents (U.S. Bureau of the Census, 1956).

This migration accentuates the disabilities of the migrant children in learning and socialization. According to Harrington, between 20 and 40 per cent of our population lives in a subsociety of economic, social, and educational impoverishment in the midst of a society of abundance. A portion of this impoverished population is concentrated in large cities where they not only face marginal employment and crowded and dehumanizing living conditions but also are the most displaced by rapid technological changes (Harrington, 1962).

Many of these migrants to large urban centers shift from living in the eighteenth to the twentieth century in one generation. It is a difficult adaptation, for it represents not only a shift from a simple culture into a more complex one, but also from a personalized culture into a society that is mechanized, anonymous, and alienated. To this has been added the debilitating effect of unemployment or the threat of it. In the impersonal culture of our urban life, individuals and families are cut off from familiar contact; there are few sources for advice, little support for one's identity, and little reinforcement for the values these individuals have brought with them. In addition, in urban centers, these migrants tend to be encapsulated in environments that deny them opportunities to familiarize themselves with the larger culture in which they exist.

Deutsch describes the conditions of life in the urban slum thus:

> Geographically, there are crowded and dilapidated tenements.
> . . . If the people are Negro, Puerto Rican, or Mexican-
> American, or poor mountain white, life is in a more-or-less seg-
> regated community. There are likely to be extremely crowded
> apartments, high rates of unemployment, chronic economic in-

security, a disproportionate number of broken families, and . . .
continual exposure to denigration and social ostracism of varying
degrees. The educational level of the adults tends to be quite
limited. . . . The result is a pattern of life that exposes a child to
a minimum of direct contacts with the central channels of our
culture. The conditions of social inequality, the absence of an
accessible opportunity structure, and the frequent non-availability
of successful adult male models create an atmosphere that is just
not facilitating to individual development. Moreover, the everyday problems of living, particularly those of economic insecurity
and a multiplicity of children, leave minimum time for the adults
who may be present to assist the child in exploring the world, to
reward him for successful completion of tasks, or to help him in
the development of a differentiated self-concept (Deutsch,
1964a).

The usual difficulties that plague the public school in large cities are
magnified among children who live in such conditions. These children show
a generally poor performance. They have a high proportion of failure, of
drop-outs, of reading and other learning disabilities, and of life-adjustment
problems. Sexton's (1961) tables of correlations between income and
education show that the members of lower income groups consistently
score lower on practically every index. They have lower IQs, achievement,
and grades; their health is poorer. They are beset with deficiencies in
reading and language, the two tools on which success in school depends.

The correlation of Merit scholars by family profession and income
levels dramatizes the discrepancy. The children of librarians and professors
produce 234 Merit scholars per 12,672 families, while the children of
laborers produce one Merit scholar per 3,581,370 families. Since it seems
reasonable to assume that potential merit is distributed much more evenly
than that, it appears that social rather than genetic factors are operating.

The problem is increasing quantitatively. According to Reissman in
1950, fourteen large cities had one culturally deprived child in ten; in 1960
there was one in three. It is predicted that by 1970, 50 per cent of
the children in schools in these cities will come from such environments
(Reissman, 1962).

Deutsch suggests, in addition, that at least in elementary schools,
anywhere from 40 to 70 per cent of the students will be from minority
groups (Deutsch, 1963).

These conditions also indicate the new proportions of the problem which confronts the public schools: the task of providing adequate and equal educational opportunities for the masses of students who do not or cannot respond to the traditional curriculum and instruction.

THE SOCIAL AND PSYCHOLOGICAL FACTORS IN CULTURAL DEPRIVATION

Recognition of difficulties does not build a theoretical understanding of their causes and of the psychological dynamics that underlie them. Educational programs for culturally deprived children will be sound only if they are built on a solid theoretical base and an understanding of the lives of these children.

The relationship between cultural background and school learning is neither simple nor well understood. It is generally known that there is a relationship between the social experiences of children and their development, even though it is obvious that this relationship is not one of a simple cause-and-effect type. The conditions of social, economic, and cultural deprivation usually produce many kinds of deficits. Some of these can be inferred from research available on social-class differences in values, behavior patterns, and aspirations. We know, for example, that low socioeconomic class homes have a limited educational tradition and, hence, that the children from these homes have little "know-how" about the school and its expectations. Uneducated parents who have a meager understanding of the requirements for success in school cannot help their children with academic content, teach them conduct expected in schools as they now exist, or kindle in them aspiration for continued education.

Generally, also, even if the parents of these children are educationally ambitious for their children, they cannot effectively communicate these ambitions, because they do not know how to, or else they lack the necessary means to prepare the child to avail himself of learning opportunities. For example, Negro boys frequently have no model of a successful male and, consequently, no psychological framework that suggests that effort can result in at least the possibility of achievement.

This phenomenon has been described in numerous studies. Kahl (1953) compared the college aspirations of the "common man's" sons with sufficient ability to qualify for college work with those of boys from middle- or upper middle-class families on the same ability level. Scarcely any of the parents in the "common man" group perceived college education as an objective for their sons. Those who had aspirations did not know what was needed to realize them.

In a lower-class, all-white, eighth grade in a large industrial city, the authors made similar observations. The parents who were interviewed about their ambitions for their children indicated interest in college, but their ambitions were vague and planless (Taba, 1955). Despite the recent rise in the level of aspirations, especially among Negroes, such observations are still pertinent.

Culturally disadvantaged children also lack the skills and the habits necessary for meeting the expectations of conduct in school. Observation in a first-grade classroom showed that the children did not distinguish one piece of paper from another, tearing out a page from one book to make a marker for another one, and then cherishing a piece of toilet paper. They have minimal training in disciplined group behavior. While the middle-class child acquires the norms of group behavior around the dinner table, lower-class families rarely have dinner together as a group. The consequences are illustrated by one teacher's bafflement when her children obediently sat down in their reading groups, but then stood and went about their own business. This was obviously a behavior learned in the family. The stories that the same children dictated about their families included recurring examples of withdrawal, or "running away" in the face of a conflict or difficulty: when father gets mad he "goes away and stays all night"; when brother gets mad "he goes to a baseball game"; when mother gets mad she "takes us to the movies and doesn't bring us back" (Taba, *et al.,* 1950).

Other well-documented difficulties include failure to exhibit the virtues cherished in school, such as cleanliness, punctuality, and orderliness. Often the teachers do not perceive behavior of this type as functional habits learned at home and in the neighborhood but interpret it, rather, as malicious conduct to be corrected by appropriate punishments.

But perhaps the most serious deficiencies occur in the area of cognitive functioning: in processes of thinking, in language skills and reading (Deutsch, 1964b). The intellectual inferiority of the children from lower class families and slum areas is evident from the first years of school. Children from such environments are apt to have various linguistic disabilities, such as poor articulation, limited vocabularies, and faulty grammar (Hunt, 1964a). School records indicate their incapacity in such cognitive processes as the ability to observe and state sequences of events, to perceive cause-and-effect relationships, or to group concrete phenomena into classes of phenomena. Presumably, individual potential is evenly distributed among all groups of people. If there are differences in the functioning intelligence, they must be caused by environmental conditions which inhibit or fail to convert the potential intelligence into a functioning one.

Recent studies of intelligence support the contention that the environment and the stimuli it offers have a great impact on the capacity to learn and on the development of intelligence. The initial research was carried on in the context of studying the influence of social-class status on the functioning of intelligence (A. Davis, 1952; Eells, 1953).

More recent studies of intelligence point out that intelligence is a product of a transaction between an individual and the environmental stimulation. For example, Miner (1957) describes intellectual stimulation as a product of the interrelationship of three factors: individual potential, motivation, and environmental stimulation. Environmental stimulation involves more than the degree of complexity and variations in the environment. It also involves motivation or selectivity in responding to the environment. Different individuals respond to different cues in the environment. The variations in responses are due in part to the individual's motivation and in part to the availability of adult mediators who help the child to develop concepts with which to interpret their environment. Therefore, a potentially rich environment may be functionally unstimulating and, conversely, a limited environment, if exploited to the fullest, may be highly stimulating. Variety in stimulation, combined with mediation, tends to sharpen the mental operations and to foster modifications in the conceptual structure.

Further suggestions regarding the nature of intelligence emerge from considering the theories about its development. Piaget (1950) and Hunt's (1961, pp. 258–259) interpretation of his ideas point out that the development of intelligence is substantially influenced by environmental conditions. According to data from these sources, the full development of abstract intelligence depends on the abundance of experience with concrete operations: manipulation of objects, processing concrete data, experimenting with spatial and time relationships and with the transformation of sizes and shapes. Cognitive potential is developed to the degree that such stimulation is systematic and has order, and to the degree that the transformation of concepts is "mediated" or helped along by adults.

Lack of opportunity for organized manipulation inhibits the development of conceptual schema with which to interpret that environment or to understand a symbolic representation of it. Deficiency of adult mediation decreases the child's capacity to convert the kaleidoscope of environmental stimulation into orderly perceptions and organized concepts.

According to this concept of intelligence, the greater the variety of stimulation and the more numerous the situations which initiate modification of conceptualization, the more mobile and differentiated the mental structure becomes. In other words, the more the child hears, sees, and interprets, or is helped to interpret, the more different things he will want to see and hear, and the more he will get from what he sees and hears. The greater the variety of reality situations with which the child has coped, the greater is his ability to cope with new stimuli. Any of these conditions—a limited environment, a lack of systematic and ordered interpretation and mediation, or a limited motivation—or a combination of them, may bring about deficiency in the development of intelligence.

These concepts of intelligence and ideas about its development suggest the possibility that children from the homes and neighborhoods described above may be potentially able, but developmentally retarded in intelligence and, hence, also in learning to read and to master the content of school subjects.

Research indicates that the conditions of life in slums tend to be meager in all these respects. Slum life provides a minimum range of stimulation and minimum opportunity to manipulate objects or to experiment with them in an orderly manner. Monotony of input limits expressiveness or the output and the ability to perceive precise relationships or other abstract qualities, such as size, shape, distance, and time. In addition, the lack of adult mediation reduces further the child's opportunities to link experience with its interpretation, i.e., the ability to convert objects and events into verbal symbols, to perceive causal relationships, and to form abstractions.

An examination of the diary materials of lower-class, eighth-grade, slum area children in a northern city confirms the lack of opportunity to interpret experience or to check such interpretations, if attempted. Typically, a day is characterized by a rapid shift from one activity to another, by lack of sustained attention to one thing, and especially by the scarcity of experiences with abstractions. For example, if parents and children eat dinner together, the time is spent in meting out punishments for infractions committed the day before and in allocating chores. In only one instance out of twenty-five did the members of a family use dinner time to discuss what happened to them during the day, that is, to express and interpret their experiences (Taba, 1955, Ch. 2). Further, as Bernstein (1960) points out, lower-class conversations tend to be limited to the immediate instant, and they generally do not include time sequences, relationships between concepts, logical sequences, or causal relationships. The records in subsequent chapters show that the speech sequences are limited and poorly structured. Yet they have an expressive quality, if one overlooks the poor structure and spelling. Thus it seems that the problem of linguistic deficiency is not merely that of lack of vocabulary or poor syntax. It includes, also, a low level of conceptualization and a low ability to perceive relationships. The combination of nonverbal orientation and an absence of conceptualization may very well account for what we call low intelligence in lower-class and slum children.

If a child's sensory discrimination, language, and cognitive skills are inadequately developed, he is not prepared to cope with the complex and confusing stimuli that the school offers. He is not capable of handling the many strategies of transforming information which make it usable: he cannot see sequences, reverse the order of events, group properties of objects and events into class categories, or develop generalizations from specific data. Yet success in school depends precisely on these cognitive skills: the ability to distinguish the meaning of one word from that of another; the capacity to handle the abstractions that organize the physical characteristics of the environment, such as direction, distance, location, scale, etc. This is the mental equipment upon which the performance in school depends.

The consequences of cognitive deficiencies in culturally deprived children are complicated by their pattern of motivation and attitudes. Psychologists describe the characteristic syndrome of feelings and attitudes of the cultural deviates as follows: such children have a feeling of alienation induced by family climate and experience combined with a debilitatingly low self-concept; they tend to question their own worth, to fear being challenged, and to exhibit a desire to cling to the familiar; they have many feelings of guilt and shame. These children are wary: their trust in adults is limited; they make trigger-like responses and are hyperactive; they are quick to vent their hostility orally and physically. In other ways they are apathetic, unresponsive, and lack initiative. It is difficult for them to form meaningful relationships (Krugman, 1956; Beiser, 1965).

These characteristics result in behavior that teachers, who are accustomed to other children, have difficulty understanding: a negative attitude toward school, teachers, and achievement; the tendency to seek immediate gratification rather than long-range goals, and to use violence in solving conflicts. Some of this conduct, such as fighting, plays havoc in school and is, therefore, a great cause for misinterpretation and disciplinary action. For example, Haystack, a seventh-grade slum child, said: "Teachers are funny, they are so afraid of a 'leetle beet' of fighting." What Haystack described as a "little bit" of fighting was a regular gang war. On the other hand, teachers seldom see the behavior of "Haystacks" as caused by a different concept of fighting, much less understand his concept of their behavior. For this reason, the treatment of "'Haystacks" tends to be inappropriate.

Further, achievement as a means of making continued education possible is relatively little understood. Thus, the teacher of culturally disadvantaged children who uses grades as an incentive to learning, because she expects them to value good grades so that they can get into college, is apt to be disappointed. Getting by rather than getting ahead is the rule. The discontinuity between the culture of the home and of the school makes it difficult to develop in these children the desire for competence in the school environment which is necessary for a continuing positive interaction there. The children have entered school without the skills on which the curriculum is founded, and, furthermore, they find it difficult to see the point in making an effort. Thus, for them, the school becomes a place which makes baffling demands, where failure is a rule, and a feeling of competence is rare. Their resulting "why try" attitude also renders ineffective grades, promotions, and other similar external incentives used by the schools. It is because of these factors that urban schools with a large proportion of disadvantaged youth become increasingly less conducive to the productive learning and positive relationships between teachers and students which is one source of the motivation to achieve.

FACTORS IN SCHOOL EXPERIENCE

Unfortunately, through the attitudes of the faculty and choice of curriculum, the school often increases the alienation of such children. Deviation in cultural background naturally creates a discontinuity between the cognitive, perceptual, and emotional development of the child and the school curriculum and expectations. This discrepancy is not merely a result of a deficit in academic skills. It is also a discrepancy in orientation to language as a medium of communication. For example, the difference between the linguistic style habits of students and teachers can be an effective deterrent to communication and, therefore, to learning. Slum children are not accustomed to attending to, or being an object of, the long, orderly, verbal sequences that teachers use in explaining subject matter. What is more, directions given in such language not only fail to elicit attention, they also cause these children to "draw curtains," as anyone observing classes in schools in disadvantaged areas has probably noted. The much-noted short attention-span is thus only partly a habit built in disordered and discontinuous home life. It may also be a consequence of the meaninglessness of much of their school work and of an almost allergic reaction to an overabundance of commands, prohibitions, and directions which have flooded the ears of these students both at home and in school. These youngsters probably spend the major portion of their time in repetitive and unproductive activities, such as putting commas between "similar" words when they either do not know the meaning of the term "similar," or cannot see what particular similarity is involved in the given example.

Perhaps the most serious obstacles to learning arise from the discontinuity in the meanings attached to verbal cues employed in teaching and curriculum materials and the meanings which these children have acquired in their out-of-school experience.

A considerable portion of the material that describes family life, homes, human relations, or the work of the world consists of content that is alien to the experience of culturally disadvantaged children. Consider, for example, the description of a policeman by a fourth-grader in a city slum:

> To tell the truth, I don't like policemen, because one day I was walking on Broad Street and I saw a police car on Western Avenue. There were no police there. I waited for a while. Soon the police came out of the house. They had a man and a girl with them. The man and the girl were put in the police car, and taken away to the jail. I don't know what they had done, but the reason I don't like cops is because they are so rough when they arrest people. They didn't have to push the girl down when they put her in the car.
>
> Yes, I would have run home if a cop had stopped me fighting in the street, because I am afraid of a cop. I did run away once and hid in my house. I was playing on the roofs of some houses with some other boys and the ball went through a skylight and broke it. The cops heard us and chased us. I ran home, but some boys must have told him, for he came to my house and rang the doorbell. I wouldn't let him in he was going to come in through the window and get me. I knew I had to open the door then. He said, "Why'd you break that skylight for?" "I ain't been out. I been right here like my father told me." He said, "You are lying, boy, because I saw you run." I kept right on lying and he left. I was afraid, just shaking, and I felt like busting out crying, but the cop didn't know that. He thought I was rough (Taba, *et al.,* 1950, p. 11).

This description conveys a meaning of a "cop" that is quite at odds with the definition the teacher used when talking about policemen as "community helpers," or what the reader contained on the same topic.

A similar discontinuity was revealed in a second-grade, semi-rural, lower-class area when the teacher showed the children the pictures of homes in primers and asked whether they knew homes like these. The class shouted a resounding "no." When asked to describe the homes they did know, their descriptions were both sensible and differentiated. They described a variety of homes, including trailers and shacks. They talked of large families who had to live in small houses, and the problems this situation created. They were, however, unacquainted with white houses with green shutters, where a smiling mother in a starched white apron welcomes father and his briefcase home from work. Naturally, the alien content in the readers made the mastery of reading skills by these children vastly more difficult.

It is difficult for any person to span two cultures. If the discontinuities in the demands of the two contending cultures are mild, they may only dilute the socializing power of the school. If they are severe, such as is the case when the problems arising from social isolation, race, language, and differences in standards of conduct are combined with difficulties encountered in mastering alien content and new skills, they may lead to disorganization or neurotic behavior (Allinsmith & Goethals, 1956).

For the first-grader from a culturally deviated environment, the spanning of the culture of his home and of the school may be sufficiently difficult to be described as a cultural shock which may affect his academic performance. Elam (1960) describes cases of severe acculturation problems resulting in a total incapacity to respond. Writing about Puerto Rican children in New York, she describes the acculturation shock that causes them to cease responding altogether, because they believe that to function is to fail. For them, it is safer not to respond. Milder cases have been observed in which children "tune out" when directions are given.

The school often compounds the psychological consequences of this shock by demanding too abrupt a transition in language habits, conduct, and skills. By doing this, it not only fails to facilitate the process of transition or acculturation, it also contributes to the making of the "non-learner" and "under-achiever."

Finally, there is the problem of the undiscovered potential, or the hidden IQ. Schools can measure only the functioning capacity of students. Further, the instruments used for testing intelligence identify only a particular, limited potential—largely, the capacity to manipulate verbal symbols and abstractions. These are precisely the accomplishments that are the least stimulated in the culturally deprived environment, as is reflected in the consistent correlation between low-income homes and low IQ scores. Guilford (1956) has attacked the concept of IQ as a single ability and points out that intelligence test results do not reflect either cultural or personal variations in expression of intelligence because they are compounded of too narrow a range of abilities. Sigel (1963) says that, because the "rightness" of the responses in intelligence tests is determined by the cultural conventions assumed by the test-maker, such tests have limited usefulness in discovering the potential of many children. For instance, when Mexican children, who have had no experience with saucers, pair the "cup" with the "table" instead of with the "saucer," the response is marked wrong, even though the pairing is perfectly logical according to their experience. The use of IQ tests that combine the culturally biased content of the items with an emphasis on a limited type of mental operation produces the phenomenon of undiscovered potential, the "hidden IQ." Further, Eells and Haggard suggest, by believing that the IQ measures potential and by acting on this belief, schools doom the individual to the class of his birth (Eells, 1951, 1953; Haggard, 1954).

To these arguments Hunt adds the criticism of the concept of fixed intelligence that underlies the intelligence tests. He reminds us that the nature of the encounters with the environment constitute the conditions of intellectual growth and that, therefore, the quality of the encounters that are open to the child is a powerful influence in determining his rate of mental growth (Hunt, 1964b, p. 212).

These deficiencies in the background and the problems precipitated by the school form a vicious cycle. Culturally deprived children come to school with acculturation problems, an ill-developed capacity to differentiate and to conceptualize experience, and—by school standards—poorly developed verbal articulation. The resulting low performance on ability tests leads to designating these children as slow learners or low achievers. This designation reduces their already low self-esteem and self-expectation still further. Meanwhile, they are required to learn the most crucial skill—reading—while their acculturation problems are at their peak. Thus, first-graders from culturally deprived homes carry a double load in their first school year—that of mastering a new skill for which they are not ready, and that of mastering a new culture. Predictably, it is impossible for them to master either task.

Moreover, the "socialization" process of the school induces conflicts with that of the child's home. Because teachers have insufficient sociological and psychological sophistication regarding the psychological consequences of cultural deprivation, the socialization processes practiced in the school require the children from these backgrounds to deprecate themselves, their parents, their way of life, and the values in which they have invested their feelings and emotional identification and upon which their self-esteem rests.

The net result of all the factors noted above is that culturally deprived children are often labeled uneducable and treated as such. Little is expected of them, and they, in turn, offer little. As a manifestation of the self-fulfilling prophecy, they expect little and get little. Comparatively speaking, these students "get dumber" as they grow older, and by the fifth grade they are three years behind. Their meager achievement further lowers their self-expectation and generates hostility to school, teachers, and the whole business of learning. The resulting dynamic turns children who in kindergarten are described as "curious," "cute," "affectionate," "warm," and "independent" into the ones described in the fifth grade as "alienated," "withdrawn," "angry," "passive," and "apathetic," and just "trouble makers" (Deutsch, 1963). Something has happened in this five-year interval for which the school itself is responsible.

Deutsch puts the problem as follows:

> Before we place the entire responsibility on the school. . . . an important fact must be noted. The overwhelming [opinion] of studies on the relationship between social-class learning [and] school performance . . . is that children from backgrounds of social marginality enter the first grade already behind their middle-class counterparts in a number of skills highly related to scholastic achievement. They are simply less prepared to meet the demands of the school and the classroom situation. Conversely, though, the school has failed to prepare to meet their needs. The failure of the educational institution to overcome the children's environmentally conditioned handicaps too often results in early failure, increasing alienation, and in increasingly greater gap between the lower-class and middle-class youngsters as they progress through school. In other words, intellectual and achievement differences between lower-class and middle-class children are smallest at the first grade level, and tend to increase through the elementary school years. It is here where the interaction between school and early environment, instead of having a facilitating influence, has a negative effect. While the school does not contribute to the initial problem (except through its effect on the previous generation), neither does it contribute to the overcoming of the initial handicap. (Deutsch, 1964a, p. 254).

THE TASK OF THE SCHOOL

The factors discussed above redefine the task of the school. It must be recognized, however, that the school is only one ingredient in the complex of causes responsible for the problem. The school is, however, the institution in the best position to affect the situation.

Current programs favor two methods of meeting the problem. One is that of early intervention, represented by such pre-school programs as Project Head Start. Such programs are based on the assumption that the pre-school years represent the appropriate time, and a critical stage, in child development—a time at which efforts to compensate for environmental deprivation will have an optimal effect. The age of three to four years coincides roughly with Piaget's "pre-operational" stage, at which time the child is focusing his attention on organizing his auditory and visual stimuli and begins to handle, through language, simple symbolic representations.

The other method is the program of remediation, such as classes in remedial reading and language skills. These programs concentrate on grade levels at which the deficiencies in these skills begin to seriously affect the academic performance.

Obviously, the school's task goes further than this, both as to the nature of the program and as to the ages of students involved. One can ask legitimately, with Hechinger, "Head Start to Where?" (1965, p. 58).

As the chapters that follow show, intervention to compensate for a variety of deficiencies cannot stop with pre-school-age children. It is necessary, moreover, to redefine many elements of the curriculum, instruction, and approach to learning.

First and foremost, the schools must develop a better understanding of the implications of the social and psychological dynamics of cultural deprivation and translate this understanding into educational programs, into the training of teachers and administrators, and into the planning of curriculum and instruction. Further, the schools must recognize the complexity and seriousness of the problem. If there is one single principle governing the program-building for the educationally and culturally disadvantaged children, it is that no single device will suffice to counteract or to remedy the complex of factors that produced the problem. One is distressed to observe the repeated efforts to "cure" the ills by crash programs which depend on some single device, such as remedial reading, counseling, or juggling the organizational structure of the school.

Educators also need to realize that they share the responsibility for the failure of these children. Usually, the efforts to diagnose the problems have overemphasized the cultural deprivation of the children's background and have overlooked the school's failure to respond to the needs generated by these conditions. Somehow, it has escaped our attention that our basic curriculum and instructional methods were formulated when only the most able and willing attended school. Therefore, instead of revising the fundamental approach to curriculum and teaching in order to make remedial measures unnecessary, most reforms tend to give priority to remedial measures.

If the double burden of dealing simultaneously with acculturation problems and school learning is to be avoided, providing early supplementary experience seems almost a necessity. Administratively, this may be accomplished by an ungraded sequence in the first few years, by the addition of a pre-school year devoted to the task of filling in gaps in the children's experience, or by postponing instruction in reading. These measures may prevent development of the negative attitudes toward learning and the lowering of self-esteem. Moreover, it is possible that by separating the tasks of acculturation, which involve acquisition of both the concepts and the language skills necessary for future reading, from the task of learning to read, schools may do more to improve the level of achievement than by any other single measure.

But unlocking the hidden potential also requires a radical change in curriculum and teaching on all levels. Both the materials and the methods of teaching need to be aligned with the psychological realities of culturally disadvantaged children. While essentially the learning processes of the culturally disadvantaged do not differ from learning processes generally, the particulars for generating these processes do. For example, while all children learn better when the content of curriculum is tuned to their own experience as a point of departure, for culturally disadvantaged youngsters this is a *sine qua non* if any motivation at all is to be generated. While attention to developing an adequate self-image is an important ingredient in developing autonomy in learning, or a "set to learn," in any child, in the case of the culturally disadvantaged this involves the additional task of helping them disassociate *their* selves from the crippling, inferior social role into which the social environment has cast them.

Further, research on the cognitive style and language patterns of culturally deprived children suggests the need to capitalize on materials and tasks that use the operational and concrete, rather than verbal, stimuli. To cultivate mental activity in children encumbered by poorly developed skills in both language and thought, it is doubly important to use materials and devices that provide for concrete thought operations through manipulation and experimentation with objects and processes. Provisions involving an emphasis on analysis, comparison, and precision in verbal description are needed to develop the mental structures needed later to understand the symbolic presentations in books.

The research on motivational patterns suggests the futility of emphasis on external rewards and the need for stressing the kindling of curiosity, the opportunities for experiencing one's own power over the materials, and other intrinsic motivating devices. Consequently, new motivational devices are needed.

There is considerable evidence that a sense of "belonging" in school life enhances learning and influences the children to stay in school. Surprisingly, little has been done in the current program for the culturally deprived to encourage greater participation in school life and to create forms of grouping and of learning that enhance interaction and a sense of belonging. Too often, the learning of the common culture is made difficult by the expectation that it can be accomplished across the social lines and with verbal exhortations, rather than by use of models and examples. A grouping to provide sufficient heterogeneity in cultural background and ability would permit some informal learning of the culture through direct interaction. Wisely designed cultural heterogeneity in classrooms would probably do much to reduce cultural deprivation by providing models for motivation, conduct, ways of thinking, and aspirations, as well as for language patterns.

In summary, it is possible to conceive of education as a countervailing force to overcome the deficits accumulated in culturally deprived environments. To do this, educational programs must be geared to the existing developmental stages, at whatever level they may be. The commitment to help the culturally deprived needs to be accompanied by an appropriate strategy that frees teaching from unrealistic assumptions, expectations, and sacred cows regarding what subject matter must be covered when and how. In today's climate, with its emphasis on "no-nonsense disciplined learning," the idea may not be too popular. It is much easier to assume that if Moore at Yale can teach three-year-olds to read, early reading should be attempted with all three-year-olds. Yet, for culturally deprived children, school must first both supplement and counteract their social learning if they are to have an equal opportunity to learn. School must also fill the gaps left by inadequate social learning at home and bridge the conflict between the culture of the home and that of the school.

The task calls for creative innovation all along the line. No society has as yet made the most of the potential of their children. Yet, the increasing role of technology in our society, combined with the ideal of optimal development for all youth, demands that we do better than others have done or than we have done in the past.

CHAPTER II

The Students

The programs described in this book were developed for two different groups of students. The first group, composed of sixth- and seventh-graders in the early 1960's, was in a large school located in a segregated community in an eastern industrial city. Most families were recent arrivals from the South. The families were largely lower-class with a sprinkling of middle-class skilled technical workers and a few professional workers.

The classes were relatively small, twenty to twenty-five students in each. All classes had a double period with one teacher.

Many of these students were typical of what one finds in an "average" class in disadvantaged areas. Intelligence scores were available on only a few of the students, and these indicated a median IQ of about 100. The children entered the sixth grade with an average reading score of 4.5. Actually the fourth-grade placement is optimistic because, in the feeder schools, the teachers felt that students should be promoted and therefore "jacked up" the scores. The statement was commonly made that "if he signs his name to the test, he gets a score of 3.0." Most students were a year or more retarded in reading, and a large number could barely read on the third grade level. The ages ranged from 12 to 15 in all classes because many students had been held back a year or two in the lower grades.

A small proportion of the students were not discipline problems, could carry on average school work, but lacked skills with which to put that ability to work. They had limited vocabularies, and their speech patterns reflected those of the encapsulated community in which they lived. They habitually dropped suffixes and used the tense of verbs incorrectly. Yet their speech was expressive, interesting, and occasionally even beautiful. Compared with students of equal ability in other areas in the city, they would be classified as under-achievers.

In general, these students carried the physical and emotional scars of deprivation and segregation. For many, the free lunch was the only meal of the day. At home, the meals consisted of peanut butter and bread, with no milk. In fact, the students very often rejected milk that came with the school lunch, because it was not exactly a familiar item in their diet and they did not "like the taste." For the most part, they lived in extended families in which the grandmother, uncle, or aunt was the guardian. Even in intact families where both parents worked, relatives other than parents were often in charge. Families were large and included children as well as adults of all kinds: people the family "felt sorry for," foster children taken in order to help defray the expense of owning a house.[1] Most children did not know what it meant to sleep with fewer than three other people in the same room. The children of professional and highly skilled personnel were from small families and enjoyed more comfortable living conditions, including a sorely needed bit of privacy.

It is not surprising, then, to find that these classes showed a high rate of emotional disturbance. Each class contained a number of problem children. In one seventh grade, seventeen students were classified as highly disturbed and slow learners. Three of these rarely came to school. Many students manifested serious behavior problems to themselves and others. For example, one boy was a stutterer, the butt of continuous teasing; a boy and a girl with blonde hair, blue eyes, and dark skin showed the consequences of a lifetime of persecution; one fourteen-year-old boy who had the frame of a mature man was constantly in trouble for molesting the girls.

Discipline problems were severe. Even in the "average" sixth-grade class, the majority of the students showed hostility and several were seriously disturbed. The "disturbed" classes—consisting of students who had met failure year after year, lacked sufficient food, and experienced neglect of all kinds, especially of affection—were very difficult to manage. As they entered the classroom, they slammed their books on the desks. Usually one boy approached another with his fist and soon became the center of a fracas. As the teacher entered the room after hall patrol, she yelled, "Sit down!" One or two did; after another try, two or three sat down. It usually took twenty minutes of such a procedure to settle the entire class. Even then, every sentence uttered by the teacher was punctuated with, "Jeffrey, mind your own business"; "Debra, stop talking"; "José, keep your hands to yourself"; "Gwen, you're not listening."

Tantrums were common, caused even by simple remarks, such as "She stole my pencil," or "He called my mother a name." Actually, the tantrums were often attempts to seek attention from the teacher and usually occurred

---

[1] Foster children referred to the guardian as "aunt" or "uncle," which made it difficult to determine whether this was the eighth home or the only home the child had ever known.

when a student felt overlooked because the teacher momentarily paid more attention to someone else.

The incidence of thumb-sucking was high enough to shock the adults unfamiliar with such classes in segregated schools. Children who gave up the thumb substituted a pencil or another object or managed to suck on an infant's nipple when no one was looking. A number of students, who disappeared suddenly for several periods, confidentially told the teacher that they were sucking a "baby bottle" in a hide-out within the school. These same students revealed that their parent or guardian pacified them with bottles and nipples during periods of stress.

A large proportion of the academically poor and the disturbed talked to themselves, evidently as a way of "tuning out" the class when bored or disinterested in the work. In many instances, these students were not aware of the fact that they were talking. If the teacher called on them in an attempt to bring them back, the usual response was, "I ain't doin' nothin'," or "I ain't botherin' nobody."

The pupils could not tolerate silence; it "made them nervous." There-fore, noise-making reached a high level in classes where the teacher had reasonably good control as well as in those in which the pupils had the upper hand. In the first type of classroom situation, the noise consisted of such things as pencil tapping, rhythmically drumming feet on the floor, paper crumbling, and muttering. In the disturbed class the students simply ran around, matched lunch money, yelled, or fought. Yet there was always at least one individual who sat completely removed, remote, seemingly un-aware of what was going on around him. In the academically able classes the conduct was close to the norm.

There were, of course, many problems with academic work also. Many of these students found it almost impossible to do schoolwork alone. It took a few months for teachers to discover that they could achieve much more if they organized classroom activities in such a way that pupils could work in pairs or in very small groups, and for new teachers to feel safe enough to try it. Teachers found that this method not only met the inces-sant need for help in every school task, but also allayed the insatiable demands for attention and affection, and thus freed them to aid more stu-dents with their work. As the teachers circulated among the groups, they could give a smile or a nod to three as easily as to one.

Because the majority of the students, regardless of ability, were lack-ing in language skills, the ordinary textbook in all subjects, especially social studies and English, was completely meaningless and useless. Students with three or more years of retardation in reading or "listening vocabulary" would not tolerate books labeled for lower grades, and they "went into fits" at the sight of them. One teacher recognized this early in her career and ordered the delivery boys to return them to the bookroom. Others tried to struggle on, unaware of the relationship of these materials to the discipline of the classroom. These classes and their teachers suffered ten weeks of sheer frustration before the textbooks were temporarily abandoned.

Tests caused pandemonium. The students took one look and screamed, "I can't do it. Ten pages!" Some wept, others yelled, and still others rushed from the room, to return no more that day.

These were the conditions that prevailed before teachers learned to develop learning sequences that were designed to involve students in the process of learning. These also were the behaviors that slowly disappeared as the students began to sense the sincerity of the teachers' efforts to meet their learning needs. Name-calling dropped off. Fighting gradually vanished, and the senseless screaming and hooting disappeared. The change seemed almost miraculous, yet it did occur in the course of a semester in some cases, and it seemed to demonstrate that the school can be an island, a place in which the lives of children can be measurably improved.

Another group was an eighth grade in a public elementary school in a lower-class neighborhood of an eastern industrial city. The neighborhood was divided into three rather distinct sections. One section, on the fringe of a middle-class residential area, was composed of fairly old buildings in which the owner occupied one of the two- or three-family units. The second section, in an industrial and business area, had many old six-apartment tenement buildings among a few poorly maintained, single-family residential units. The third was a low-cost housing project.

The class was composed of twenty-five pupils, heterogeneously grouped. Seventeen of them had been in the same school the preceeding year, and eight were new. There were nineteen boys and six girls. Thirteen were Protestant, eleven Catholic, and one Jewish., Most of the students had either parents or grandparents who were foreign-born. All were Caucasians. In terms of socio-economic status, most students were either lower middle-class or upper lower-class. Three could be grouped as lower-lower. Although the homes of these students ranged in size from four to eight rooms, the living conditions were generally crowded, since the size of the families ranged from four to ten persons. Several homes accommodated grandparents and other relatives. One-fourth of the pupils had bedrooms to themselves. Two-thirds of the pupils lived with both parents, three with mothers and stepfathers; one had a stepmother. Three had only the mother, and one lived with guardians.

The intelligence of these students was average; their IQs ranged from 75 to 121 (median 101). Their educational age and achievements tended to exceed their mental ability. Only seven students were below the grade norm in achievement.

Essentially, this class was like any lower-class group in any American city during the period 1948–1949. It had its quota of problem students. Three girls in the class were on the verge of running away from home; one boy was involved in a serious theft; several were rejected in the group and needed help with personal difficulties; the mother of one girl left her family, the father threatened to commit suicide, and the girl was in constant turmoil; the immaturity of another girl could be traced to cruelty at home.

May was an example of such a disturbed student. She needed help desperately. Her parents had deserted her soon after she was born. She was living with her paternal grandmother, who disliked her, often telling her that she did not know whether she was her real grandchild and constantly reminding her of how much she was indebted to her for bringing her up. May began to stay out late at night and was finally caught in a vice squad raid.

The principal and the teacher had long talks with May, and the teacher did all she could to help her find a place with other students. She talked to her about what she would be capable of doing someday to earn a living, but it was possible only to delay the troubles that were coming, as May began to steal. She was caught, taken to another town, and placed in a foster home.

Gladys's parents did not understand English, did not know how to manage her, and left the disciplining to an older son who beat her, knocked her down, and kicked her unmercifully whenever she went out with one of her "sailor friends." She came to school one day with the skin torn off one cheek by the spikes in her brother's shoes. A married sister, her husband, and their child lived with Gladys's family, and there was constant friction. The brother-in-law created a row every time Gladys wanted a glass of milk (that had been bought specifically for her) because the baby might need it. She could not have company because it would make her sister unhappy.

The teacher encouraged Gladys to tell her mother what was going on and to try to enlist her help. This eased the tension for a few days, but then Gladys ran away one weekend and was picked up by police in another town. She was placed in the Detention Home but reported to school each day. For a time she seemed much happier at the Home; she even refused to see her family unless the policewoman was present. After a time, she consented to go home, but conditions there became unbearable again, and once more she ran away. This time it took longer to catch her. Again she was placed in the Detention Home.

Evidently things were going on at the Detention Home that brought new difficulties to Gladys. She remarked to the teacher, "I'm the only decent one in our dormitory at the Detention Home. You should hear what the other kids do—and they're only fourteen or fifteen years old." Gladys made a genuine effort to do the right thing, but said that the others "wouldn't let her." Each night she took many books with her because "it's so boring there, and there's nothing else to do."

One Friday night she was in tears because the girls at the Home were planning trouble that she was sure she could not stay out of. Yet she was afraid to spend a whole weekend at home and had no other place to go. The teacher got permission to take her to her house on difficult days and continued to do so throughout the year. Things eased up a bit when, one by one, the "nomads," as Gladys called her relatives, moved out.

Personal talks with Gladys could do little to offset what was happening elsewhere. Students did more than the teacher could to make her comfortable in the classroom. When nasty rumors were spread about Gladys in her absence, her classmates became quite indignant and even worried. When she returned, they provided real protection for her against anyone who tried to hurt her.

In a few respects, this class was unique. There was little or no hostility toward the school or the teachers. The class worked hard and showed few signs of antagonism toward academic tasks. They were also quite responsive and open and readily described their problems, dilemmas, and wishes in a series of open questions and themes that were among their first assignments. The students also showed extraordinary sensitivity to each other, a high group morale, and ego-supportive attitudes. They were willing and capable of learning and only needed an approach that would awaken them and a teacher who cared about them. Evidently, despite violence in many homes, school seemed to be a place of relative calm and stability for this group of adolescents.

CHAPTER III

Diagnosis of Gaps and Abilities

The preceding chapter described the general characteristics of culturally deprived children and youth. An awareness of these general characteristics is of little use to the teacher, however, unless he also has ways to secure diagnostic information on his class which is at once more specific and more individualized.

A basic cause of defective teaching strategies, of ineffective selection of content and materials, of inadequate approaches, and of poor learning atmosphere is lack of systematic, all-encompassing, and continuing diagnosis. Just as a good physician administers treatment only after thorough diagnosis, a good teacher builds curriculum and instruction on analysis of data gathered by use of searching diagnostic procedures.

Teaching in the dark is a questionable practice in any case. This is especially true in teaching students whose background, motivation, learning styles, and habits deviate from the usual, and whose attitudes toward school and teachers have been distorted by years of frustration stemming from unsuccessful learning careers. It is important that this diagnosis encompass a wide array of types of learning: knowledge, cognitive styles, levels of cognitive development, emotional dynamics, self-concept, skills, attitudes, and interests, among others.

For example, if a teacher knew that his sixth-grade pupils had no concepts of "eastward," "westward," "riches of the Far East," and "short water route," he would avoid assigning them the following passage from a sixth-grade social studies text.

> Christopher Columbus lived at a time when many people
> still believed that the earth was flat. He knew that the merchants
> of Europe were looking for a short water route to the riches of
> the Far East. Columbus believed that this could be found by

23

heading westward instead of sailing eastward (Devine, 1961, p. 105).

After all, instruction is a vehicle through which the purposes of education are executed. If the vehicle is not appropriate, these purposes will not be served, no matter what is said about maintaining standards.

Continual diagnosis is also necessary to provide the information needed to determine the existing level of achievement and to permit the teacher to judge the readiness of students for the ensuing learning activities. Without this information, instruction can either under- or over-reach what students can do—teach what they already know or expect what is impossible for them. Such records as are available suggest strongly that, for students with an educational deficit, over-reaching has been the rule rather than the exception, partly because of the vicious circle generated by their experiences during the first years in school. To repair the resulting damage and erosion, a teacher of the culturally disadvantaged must know rather precisely what hinders the learning of his students. To have any success at all, instruction should be based on analysis of results of rather searching diagnostic devices.

The emotional and social factors that affect learning must be understood, also, in order to create curricular experiences that are meaningful and worthwhile for the students for whom they are intended. This understanding is essential to regarding students as individual and as human beings with positive qualities, instead of so many gaps and minuses. Such an understanding is also a prerequisite to finding ways to eliminate their blocks to learning. For example, a student who is subjected to ridicule by his peers may remain a nonparticipant in class, a fact that hampers his learning to communicate verbally. Because the student makes no disturbance in the class, the teacher may be completely ignorant of the causes of his inability to learn.

Diagnosis, of course, is never completed. Every contact with students reveals something that the teacher did not know before, something important for intelligent planning of instruction. Diagnosis should also be as systematic as possible. It is true that an observant teacher can use any contact with children to acquire knowledge about them, but sporadic diagnosis is not enough. A planned battery of special procedures is needed. If these procedures serve at once as teaching devices and instruments of diagnosis, so much the better. For example, when students write about "Things That Bother Me," they learn to write, to revise, and to correct. Sharing the writing provides information about the universality of the phenomenon and extends their perspective on it.

The preceding chapter indicated some usually troublesome areas where a teacher of culturally deprived children might begin diagnostic inquiry. This chapter will describe some of the informal ways of gathering diagnostic information. It will also quote extensively from the children's responses to describe in detail some characteristic behaviors and levels of mental function. The amount of detail seems necessary because as individuals and as persons the slum children, especially those from racial minorities or foreign backgrounds, are baffling strangers to most young teachers usually assigned to teach in these schools. The emphasis on informal devices is intentional, not only because of the possibility of their double use, but primarily because the needed formal instruments are either unavailable or of limited use in creating functional instructional plans.

The compositions and quotations come from two groups of culturally deprived students described in the preceding chapter. The first group was composed of sixth- and seventh-graders in the early 1960's. The second group were eighth-graders in the late 1940's and were Caucasians whose parents or grandparents had immigrated to this country.

It should be noted that the original punctuation and spelling have been largely lost in the quotations from the second group, but retained to some degree in the first group. Therefore, no comparison of their writing skills should be made.

OPEN-ENDED QUESTIONS

Open-ended questions are often used as a device to tap the ideas, concepts, and feelings students may have on certain problems or in certain areas of experience. Such questions are similar in effect to the more formal projective tests. They provide an unstructured stimulus in order not to cue the students to an expected response. The responses can be secured in a variety of ways: as written compositions, through class discussion and socio-drama. Students who are old enough and skilled enough can write. Those who cannot or will not write can dictate either to the teacher or into the tape recorder. In the case of young children, conversations with the teacher in very small groups yield equally good results.

The questions can be formulated around any pertinent point. The range of such questions is limited only by the teacher's ingenuity in inventing them, and her ability to discern the areas of pressing concern to students and to focus on points which are helpful in guiding her teaching. Some questions have centered on the worries of the students, the concepts they have regarding the community, and the way they feel about school and teachers. Teachers have experimented with topics that study self-concepts ("What I Like about Myself and What I Criticize about Myself"), pupils' attitudes toward their homes ("What I Would Like to Change about My Home"), and their wishes and aspirations ("My Three Wishes"), ("What I Would Do if I Had $———"). The topic "What Makes Me Mad and What I Do about It," has been used to diagnose skills of interpersonal relations and handling of conflicts (see Taba, *et al.,* 1951, Ch. 6). The technique, of course, can reveal more than is implied in the questions: what standards the students set for themselves, their values, the problems they face, the level at which they perceive causes of and solutions to problems, what concepts and skills they master. The main requirement is that they tap spontaneous responses rather than studied answers, thereby revealing the functioning feelings, concepts, and ideas. Because feelings are easily distorted, misrepresented, and suppressed, such questions should be planned to contain only the stimulus and no cue as to an expected response. The climate of the classroom must also be free of threat. Projective questions can be a successful diagnostic device only where there is trust and rapport between the teacher and the students.

Worries

Knowing what worries students provides a great deal of information about the erosive effects of the home and school and, hence, about the self-concept. It also suggests what topics or incidents to use as a vehicle for whatever is being taught.

Below is a partial list of worries secured from the Caucasian eighth-graders when the teacher asked them simply to list them:

> People don't understand me.
> Get jealous very easily.
> How to make people like me—they like me when I first meet them but after a while I don't know what happens.
> People think I'm unattractive.
> Have awfully big hands and feet.
> Have awful laugh.
> How other kids talk about me.
> I want to be at the head of my class, yet I don't like to have kids call me the "Brain."
> My boy friend won't talk to me and I don't know why.
> I am only thirteen, but I like to do what my friends fifteen and sixteen do, and I can't go out.

Whether my father will ever realize I am getting older.
What's going to happen to me when I grow up.

Although the teacher had emphasized that it was not necessary to sign their names, over half of them did. Furthermore, they responded eagerly to an opportunity to discuss their list privately with the teacher. In general, the girls worried about their appearance and various aspects of their personal relations; the boys worried over things connected with their masculine status.

The following year, she asked the members of her new class to write about what worried them and why they thought it worried them. She assured them that it was quite proper to write frankly about one's anxieties, and set the stage by sharing with them some of her own, selecting those which could not possibly be theirs. The themes were infinitely more revealing than the lists had been. The students worried about their peer relationships, about doing something "wrong" (and consequent punishment), about pleasing their parents, about their parents' health, about caring for younger children, the family finances, and their own chances to earn a decent living.

In their words:

I worry about what people will think of me if I do something wrong. I think people will judge me by this.

I am always getting yelled at like losing the slip to father's pants or forgetting to mark someone paid on my book or forgetting that I was supposed to do something or other or forgetting that my little sister is only four, so not to be rough.

There were references to being subject to the whims of their parents' moods:

I worry about my father because when he comes home I always get in trouble for things.

My father comes home from work and is cross, so he takes it out on me most of the time.

I worry a little bit about the way that my father will come home. I mean in a good, happy way or a grouchy way. But if he's grouchy I stay out of his way and he can't find anything to holler at me about.

When I get my first report card and it's bad I am afraid to bring it home. I know my father will get mad. If he says anything my mother will say, "It's only the first one. Give her a chance to start." When my second one comes out and it still isn't good, I am scared even more to bring it home.

My worst worry is my school work. By that I mean math and only math. My father wants me to get a good mark.

If my brother doesn't bring home a good report card my father yells at him. He is always talking about him going to college and being something. So I try to please my father.

Illness in the family, and home tensions because of it, were frequent concerns:

When my mother dies will I be able to take it? I'll still have my father and my sister, but my sister wouldn't take the place of my mother.

My mother has to have another operation and my father is just at his wits' end. He's always picking on me about why don't I do this and that, and I find it's better not to say anything because it'll just start an argument. So I keep quiet. I also worry about my mother and wonder if she'll get better with this operation and when she'll be home. I'm worrying about how long it will take to pay the hospital bill and what we will have to go without.

. . . Maybe [my mother] doesn't realize that I worry about her, but I do. When I go to bed at night is when I usually think about her.

Drinking fathers caused much anxiety among girls:

My main worry is my father's life. I don't rightly know why but it could be his constant drinking. The doctor once told him he had a bad heart, and if he kept drinking he would probably get a heart attack and die. That scared him a little while, but now he is drunk every night in the week. I think the devil walks with him and his bottle.

The students were concerned about money:

> My mother always has to give me a couple of dollars to pay my [paper route] bill. Well, this week she did not have any money to give me. She said, "I haven't any money to give you this week." "I know," I said.

They felt rejected:

> The reason that I feel I'm not wanted is that ever since I was a little girl about seven, I had to take care of myself and had to do things that I thought was right. Now I feel that when I was small I did something wrong. I don't know if I did. See, my mother works and so does my sister, so I had to stay alone.

> I don't think many people like me or enjoy my company. I'm not a very good athlete, but I'm good in my studies. Sometimes when kids are chosen for a team I'm afraid I'm going to be chosen last.

> I always feel that I'm not wanted.

Fears

Closely related to worry, of course, is fear. To induce the sixth-graders in the first group to be frank, the teacher described some of her own fears and invited them to write "private" or "confidential" on their papers if they wanted only her to read them.

The out-of-school fear priorities are fairly clear: being attacked on the street, death, accidents (the number of these references is surprisingly high), rats, drunken people, incidents on the road when the family went down South to visit relatives, and punishment for their own misbehavior. Physical violence topped the list of reasons. Evidently, in the lives of these segregated disadvantaged children, violence is a regular part of everyday activities such as shopping.

> (GIRL): . . . . But most of all I am scared of walking in the dark at night by myself. I think someone will jump me and take me away.
>
> What scares me the most is when I have to go to the store at night. I'll be thinking that someone might grab me in the dark and kidnap me. They might kill me.

When I am walking to the store and it is dark and there are only three people. I am in the middle. It is alright if someone walks in front of me, but not in back of me. I feel that they might come up and grab me. You have heard of people getting strangled. That's why I get so scared.

(GIRL): Today I was to go to the stor for my mother I could not see. A men was come up the street and I was go down I saw him and I cross the street and the man cross the street too. I ran and he was coming. . . .

(GIRL): . . . . After my cousin had finished her dinner . . . . she look on the porch and saw a man standing out there . . . . by that time the Man started towards the Kitchen My cousin ran up to the bathroom and locked the door my my sister got the butcher knife I ran out the door and ran Down the celer . . . . taugh us a lesson to keep the Doars lock at all times.*

(GIRL): When I was in bed one Sunday night my mother was calling me over and over again and when looked down staris my father was laying down and his head was bleeing and my father wasn't breathing and my mother had took up first aid and she was breathing into him. He had opened the wrong door because he though he was going to the bathroom but he fell down the stairs.*

(BOY): The most thing that frightened me was when my friend kept on hitting on my other friend and the he told who stoal the wllet and he said me. So the cops came and took all of us to the station in the place were the cops stay. So they took our names on a piece of paper and a card. And then they called my mother up and my friends mother and that is what made me frightened. Because I knew I was going to get a beating.*

(GIRL): It started like this when father was working at a bar. When he met another girl. He was suppose to be working that afternoon. My mother ask him to be home early so she could go shopping. So ask ma. Could go over my Aunt Bettys house she said yes. She said be sure to be home at 6:00 because have dinner. When I got back they are

* Marked "private."

fighting and beating and I was screaming.*

(GIRL):   It was 12 o'clock went my father came home. I was asleep. My father hit me and my mother. I got frightened. He beat my mother up with the belt. I was running around the pleac. I got the police He went to jail and I am still frightened when some one hit her.*

(BOY):   I was living in the pridget [project] I on the fifth floor I was visiting my friend . . . then my friend got maddest at me he then he took a knief a stab me in the sede I got five steders [stitches] the policeman he toad the knief slap out of his hand.

(GIRL):   When I went South last wek when my grandmother died I was scared because down there they bring the body to the house in the afternoon and they stay until the next morning. I remember when my mother was in an accident and the ladies on her job called the house and told me what had happened and told me to call my father on his job, I was so scared that I couldn't dial his number.

(GIRL):   The thing I'm telling you about is rats. When I see a rat I get scared because I think that might bite me. If I get bit I can die and I think if I meet a rat I will faint.

Another thing that scares me is drunk people. When they say something to me I feel like I'm going to jump out of my skin. If they touch me my skin crawls.

(GIRL):   There are a lot of things that scare me, like the time we were going down south by car and when it became dark my father stopped by the woods to sleep. I remember when we went down south last July and it got dark. My father stopped by the woods to rest and I was lying on the floor. When I was almost asleep I heard a noise. I was too frightened to get up to look. Suddenly I didn't want to stay there any longer. I jumped up to see what was out there. It was an old man with a white cat. My brother heard me and got up too. He saw the man and scared my parents more than I did. Then he drove till morning.

(BOY):   What really scares me is when I can't sleep. I lie awake
* Marked "private."

think what it's like to be dead because when you're alive and you look at a casket it looks kind of small but when you're dead I guess it makes no difference.

As mentioned earlier, these children fear punishment for their misbehavior, but their fear does not prevent that misbehavior. Again from the second group:

The things that scare me most of all are those that I know are going to happen. For example, when I do something wrong and I know my mother or father is going to punish me for it. One time I got in trouble for playing hookey. I thought my mother was going to punish me for it. Another time I got in trouble with the police. I had to go to court. I thought I was going to get put away, but the judge just put me on probation. That is the kind of thing that scares me most of all—when I know something is going to happen.

The themes on "Things That Frighten Me" helped the teacher not only to glimpse the shadowy, nameless fears that walked beside these adolescents, but also to diagnose their strengths and weaknesses in writing skills. This information helped her to develop a new plan for help with writing skills. Aid was given only on demand: help was given only when a child recognized his need and asked for it. This resulted in a number of words remaining misspelled in any given paper, but also in a renewed effort on the part of the students to improve their writing skills. Few at first, demands for help increased as time went on and as students began to recognize their inaccuracies.

Wishes

Wishes are perhaps more directly related to values, and to the limitations in the environment than are fears. When the Caucasian eighth-graders wrote about what they would wish for if they had three wishes, their papers demonstrated the toll on these students of crowded living conditions and broken homes. They reiterated the themes of rejection, loneliness, desire to be accepted, to make good. They wanted more privacy, places to do things, and beauty. Surprisingly they did not emphasize the desire for material possessions, money, clothes, etc.

I sleep with all four of my sisters and when I have reading to do I can't do it in bed because the light will disturb my sisters.

I wish I had a little room of my own with modern furniture, a victrola in it and my piano; a big table so I could draw or write or sew or anything.

I wish we owned a house of our own so that I could do what I want. The landlord locked my dog out and wouldn't let me put my basketball hoop on the garage.

I wish to live in the country for a while, not all the time, but live there in the summer and get away from the city where you are all crowded out.

I wish that my mother would get well so we could live together again. To live with your own mother makes you happier than living with someone else. [The child's father was dead and the mother was in a sanitarium.]

My first greatest wish is that my mother would come back live with me because I am gettin older and I have problems which if my mother was here she could solve them for me and I also miss her love. [This child's parents were separated.]

I wish my father were back. My father was the most wonderful person. He didn't have a temper like my mother. He was more lenient. But neither was a boss; they were together. [This girl's father died two years previously.]

. . . . to have my mother stop working so that she wouldn't be tired at night and she could have time to listen to me, or give me a hug. [The business of people not listening to them was a critical factor in both groups.]

I'd like to make good and give my mother the things she wants. This is what my father wanted to do.

One of my most important wishes is to get along with my stepfather and not to always be arguing with my mother over him. I just can't stand him but I think if I tried a little harder, I might be able to.

Another wish is to get along with everyone and for every single person that I know to look up to me like.

My first wish, to me, is very important. It is to be able to get along and be very popular with the other kids. This is important because I feel very left out when I am not invited some place or when kids talk about something and don't tell me what.

Some of these eighth-graders already knew that their ambitions would be thwarted; others had not looked far enough ahead to realize that it takes more than wishful thinking to succeed:

I'm afraid I won't be able to go to college. My father does not like the idea and also he does not have the money.

When I'm out of school I hope I will have money and not be a bum.

I want to have later on in life a substantial capital. I would like this because so far in my mother's life she has had to work harder to help us too. So, I figure that later on she deserves a long and well-earned rest. My second wish would be to graduate from high school with a scholarship. With a college education, I could get a better job and more money. Then maybe my first wish will be closer to reality.

Confusion about goals and the means of attaining them were revealed in the responses of the first group (the sixth- and seventh-graders) to the theme: "What Job I'd Like to Have." This topic had been assigned in order to collect information about their ambitions, because motivation and self-concept are so closely related to ambitions. The dominant response was the desire to help people. There was also the familiar concern with making lots of money and with being liked and wanted, though not necessarily by age-mates. College was mentioned frequently by aspiring Marines as well as by aspiring nurses.

I want to be a Marine. I like to help people who are sick and poor and blind. I would [bring] food for them I'll like to help blind people who can't see where they're going. . . .

I want to be a nurse . . . I want everybody in the hospital to be proud of me If I can. I want to be find [friend] to everybody. I want everybody to be well, not sick I love my people. . . .

I want to be a baby nurse . . . but I will have to go to school. . . . If I should change my mind I would want to take up beautician. . . . My mother likes me to comb her hair and the lady down the street likes me to comb her hair and her daughter's hair too.

I want to be a Marine because I like to fight but I don't fight too good. I think the Marines can make me tough. . . .

I don't know what I want to be. I never really thought about it.

It should be noted that there is a discrepancy between the level of aspirations and planning for realization, e.g., the student who says he wants to be a lawyer may be a chronic truant.

THE NEIGHBORHOOD

One of the characteristics of a disadvantaged area is that large numbers of families move around within it, transferring children from one school to another again and again during the year. Therefore, feelings about neighborhoods may provide information regarding rootlessness, frustration, isolation, acceptance of newcomers, etc. A teacher of the eighth-graders who asked the children how they felt about moving, received the following responses:

It's not easy to make friends.

I felt kind of funny not knowing anybody.

. . . . everybody look at so hard.

. . . . People wouldn't know me and I had to go to a new school.

It is like you are not wanted and it is bad to leave your old house and friends and it is usually hard to find new friends and when you go to a strange school you feel scared and you don't like that house and you wish you could go back to your old house.

I would feel lonely and strange and you want to have your old friends again. But after while someone comes and show you where the store or laundry store is.

The first group showed a certain ambivalence about the neighborhood in which they lived. They liked the neighborhood because they had friends there, but the habits of some of their neighbors made it not all together desirable. While they judged the neighborhood in terms of its cleanliness, they also seemed resigned to its squalor. Although some of them did recognize the possibility of changing it, they did not see themselves as involved in effecting that change.

My neighborhood is average; it has people in it that are nice and they have average houses and when they put their garbage out, on some days other people come and turn it over and then when you put it back up they come turn it over again. So I think every day about this lady that lives about two blocks from me. She throws her garbage out the window and uses it for a garbage disposal.

There is a man who lives with his daughter, and he owns this lot by my house and he has garbage and a dog and chickens, and all kinds of old things in this lot. And when I put my garbage out people take my tops off my garbage cans and put the garbage all in the streets. Bums walk around and throw wiskey bottles on the sidewalks, and children break old bottles on the street. The men that are building the new houses throw beer cans and beer bottles and paper in the streets and gutters, and they throw scrap wood all around and broken window panes are lying on the street and before they started building the houses people used to dump trash and garbage on the side of the street and the City had to send men to clean it up and put up signs, but the people kept dumping garbage there. That's how my block is.

(Boy):   It's not the cleanest or dirtiest one. It is a friendly one. It's an old-fashioned block, but everyone has a good house. In the summers the flowers are beautiful with the houses, and green grass, and across the street is a park we play and run and have pinnicks and talk about the old times. It's all fun and we go to the field and play, we get dirty and go home and watch T.V. or go to the center. We have an old family in the neighborhood who rides us in his car. We all keep our neighborhood clean. No one can say bad things about it because to me I wouldn't move for $100.

(BOY): My neighborhood is alright; almost all the people on the block have a dog. Some people let their dogs run in the streets: this causes a problem because the dogs do their mess all over the streets and on the lawns.

In my neighborhood there are a lot of improvements to be made. On my block there are too many dogs, they knock over the garbage cans and drag the garbage into the streets. Kids on my block play in the hedges. There's also some things that are good about my neighborhood. I like the way that the people take care of their gardens in the summer, and the way they always have the garbage on time.

My neighborhood was a nice neighborhood when we moved there. It is still nice. But some of the families moved in and some moved out. Some of the people who moved in did not seem to care about keeping the neighborhood clean. If the older people did not want to clean the yard, the children could, but they don't think about anything but playing. The neighborhood is clean, but there are some people who just don't care.

My neighborhood isn't very clean because people are very careless and lazy. They leave garbage all over the streets and in front of their houses. There are lots that people dump garbage and trash in. Unless someone starts doing something about it the neighborhood will stay dirty.

Girls tended to extend their discussion of the cleanliness of the neighborhood to include comments on a neighbor's poor housekeeping, poor personal grooming, and failure to keep young children clean.

In the summer some people have nice lawns and some people don't. There is one person in our neighborhood who spoils everything. Her house isn't clean, her lawn is dirty. Her yard always looks bad. On the fourth of July when everyone goes out and her family stays home and when we come back there is beer cans and whiskey bottles all over the place. Some of her children will come into our yard and pick some of my mother's flowers. Then my mother gets mad. The children shouldn't pick the flowers cause some people like to have their lawns looking nice. My house is a nice house. My mother's lawn is growing. She planted her garden and they are growing also. I would like my neighborhood to look beautiful.

There is nothing wrong with my neighborhood except half of the block is nice but the other half is dirty. The people who live in those houses have kids and they come out to play outside the whole day until the night, their mother doesn't wash them and put on clean clothes. Every time you pass by the odor is terrible. But on the other side, where I live, you see the green grass grow and it is very nice to sit out in the summer. But I think you can do nothing about those people because they do not care what you do for them. They drink beer and alcohol and are interested in nothing else.

INTERPERSONAL RELATIONS

When the first group, which lived in a segregated area, wrote about what hurt them, name-calling was a recurring theme. A great deal of resentment centered on detrimental references to their families, particularly their mothers, and to racial differences. The teacher selected this topic because she sensed that much of the explosive behavior was related to "hurts" and she needed to know their specific nature.

(BOY):   How it feels to someone to call you name. It hurts in your heart. It makes you fight. It makes you mad and makes you want to call name back. It make you feel like you do not want to be wonding [wanted].

(GIRL):   I don't see why anyone has to call anyone a name anyway. Just because someone is darker or lighter that don't mean anything God give us our color. and when someone calls me a name I just don't pay them any mind. We should be proud of our color.

(BOY):   When somebody call's you a name it kind of hurt you in side. And you know are going to fight. If somebody talks about your mother even you would feel hurt. And when somebody talk about my race it doesn't hurt me much because it is only one race and that the himan race and that is all.

(GIRL) : People hurt others by calling names or talking about somebody in your family When they talk about your color. They also hurt you.

(BOY) : They might be talking about their mother or father. The mother or father might have died and they don't like people talking. I don't care if people talk about my parent because sticks and stones will hurt but word want harm me.

(BOY) : . . . . IIe is hurt because this person may not have a family and they all dies.

(BOY) : . . . . You also feel hurt when a family secret is found out by friends. You feel hurt if you are dirty and ragged and people talk about you.

Despite, or perhaps because of, their awareness of how painful name-calling can be, the students indulged in it all the time. A game in which each player tries to outdo the other in name-calling and making derogatory statements is called "Playing the Dozens." For example:

CHARLES: Someone tole me you been walkin' with ugly stick last night.
DONALD: Who that?
CHARLES: You ma.
DONALD: You pa.
CHARLES: Step to the back of the room. (*Fight ensues.*)

* * *

CHARLES: You papa's Malcolm X.
JACQUELINE: Ain't no mama in it.
CHARLES: You TV come out of the junk yard.
JACQUELINE: Mine has a control on it. What you talkin' about?
CHARLES: You mama use blankets for pillow cases.
DONALD: You mama get dragged to the river and hit on the head like a iron pipe an git dragged through the mud like a flyin kite.

CHARLES: My mama ain't on the Mississippi with a whiskey bottle.

JACQUELINE: If you mama wasn't fishin' in the toilet bowl right now, she'd be up here to school.

CHARLES: Somebody tole me they rang you door bell and the toilet bowl flush.

JACQUELINE: Paul's did, with his mama's head in it.

DONALD: That water was dish water from the Mediterranean Sea.

In the following excerpt from a sociometric interview with a girl in the first group, references are made to name-calling and swearing. Note also the interviewee's strict sense of what behavior is proper in school and her anxiety when the offender is not properly punished according to her lights.

Jalna call everybody names and be cursing at the teacher and calling them names too, 'cept Mr. M. cause he be strict on her, you know, like the other teachers when she calls them names they don't do nothin'. Sometimes they write a card. She don't care. Sometimes she be good in school and quiet, but the other times she be bad. She always curses. I choose Arlene, Helene, and Maria, but they don't go—they don't walk home my way—I don't live their way.

In culturally disadvantaged areas, siblings are generally intensely loyal to each other, presenting a united front to the rest of the world. That does not mean, however, that there is no rivalry or hostility, but when it does occur it often has more the quality of peer rivalry among middle-class teenagers. Consider the following from a 14-year-old sixth-grader.

(GIRL): .... My sister come home from school one day and she came first when she got [home] a few minutes later there was a knock at the door so she was home by herself. And then she went and open the door and it was my boyfriend at the door he asked for me but I wasn't home yet so my sister told him why, he said because he want to take me out that night so my sister told him that I had something to do that night she said to him if he can take her out instead of me because I wasn't home then. So he said all right so when I came home she to me that he was by and he wanted to take her out and instead of me so I go so mad that called him on the phone and asked for him but he wasn't home at all so when he came over he saw me and start talking to me, and so I pull my sister back in my room and told her please don't go out with him and she said why and I told her she didn't know what this means to me. And so he called us and he and my sister said goodbye to me.

RELATIONS WITH PARENTS

Despite the alacrity with which these students defended the honor of their mothers, examination of diagnostic material indicates that their homes were far from serene. For instance, one teacher of the first group, who was about to launch a study of the executive branch of the government, asked them to write about the head of their household, who it was and what that meant.

(GIRL):   My mother is the boss when my aunt is gone. My mother likes order and for us to obey. And we do. If we don't she beats us and puts us on a punishment for three or two weeks. If we are *real* disobedient she puts us on a punishment for one or two months.
   My mother looks after the family and my father can take care of hisself. . . .

(GIRL):   My mother is the executive in our house. She works in a toy shop. She works to help pay the bills and she brings me home some toys. She likes her job very much.

(BOY):   The boss of my house is my father and sometimes my mother. My father and my mother work. My father gets paid before my mother. He buys our books and clothes. My mother buys our food. She gives us orders and if we don't do it we get a beating and stay in for one week.

In interviews with the teacher, punishment was discussed easily and readily whether it amounted to "having to stay in" or to whipping. Punishments tend to be both harsh and arbitrary, as one boy's account shows:

(BOY):   . . . . My father came home and saw that the window was broken and my sister did it. And she didn't have nobody to blim it on so she blimed it on me. Then my father said why did you do it. And I said I didn't do it. And then he said go up to your room and he'll be there. And when he came up stair you know what happen that he took his belt off and told me to turn around, then he swung and hit me. And the next day I said to myself why shouldn't I tell my father that she did it. And when my father came home that night I told him so. He didn't want to beat her because she was a girl. . . .

In most cases the "stay in" punishment was violated—or at least there was an attempt to escape it. Usually, mothers forgot whether they meted out a week or a month. Fathers rarely forgot and were usually more definite about the conditions.

The children retaliated by such means as "finding" money at home or by "forgetting" or "losing" it. The following quotations are from the first group:

(Boy):   I found a ten dollar bill on the floor and I did not know who it was so I pull in my bank and latter on I when to the store and brough me some candy bar, I gay some to my brother and my brother tell my mother so me . and got a beeting together. I did not think I oughth get a beeting because I did not know I was to give the money to my mother if I found it in the home.

(Girl):   One morning I went to the laundry mat I had $3.11 of my mother . . . . when I got to the lanundry I put the clothes in the michien. I Look for my $3.11, I could not find it. . . . I went back home. My mother said to go blak to the laundry and get the money. I did not find it. I did not get poised [punished]. At around 3:00 that day I went to the store I found the mony in my coat poket. I gave it to my mother that I was absent mined. In a way I think I sould have god punished.

An especially revealing theme in regard to ability to handle interpersonal relations and conflicts is "The Thing That Made Me Maddest." Most of the children from the first group wrote about their home situations. Some students unleashed their fury on the school and, where they felt secure, focused their anger on their teacher.

Broken promises were another frequent cause of hard feelings and misunderstanding between parents and children.

(GIRL):　. . . . It was on a Friday morning my was cleaning up she said hey Sam let's take out today. . . . So he ok. Then my mother came in the kitcen hurry up and finished you work because we going other Aunt Mamie house. So when we finished we got dress. Wc got upstrier and outside. My [father] said wait here I'll be right back because I'm going to the gas station. We waited for half hour. . . . So my [mother] told me to tell my brother's to unddress. And they could go out and play. Soon as everyone is unddress and comfortable my father comes walking in. So he [says] why aren't you dress. . . . Thats what makes me my father always says he coming right back and never does.

(GIRL):　One Christmas when I was ten years old my mother said she was going to get us all bikes. So when Christmas came and we woke up on Christmas there were no bikes anywhere. I asked my mother where are our bikes. She said here take your candy and when I went outside my friend kept picking at me saying you didn't get your bike. I felt like breaking here neck and everytime I would go outside she would kick on saying it and I would get so mad.[2]

(BOY):　Thc Thing that got me the maddest is whcn you the teacher of cause tell me to do things I don't even understand. And like now I didn't even know what to write until Stephen came up to me and said you're mad now.

(BOY):　The thing that got me mad was Being in [number of section] I like the class bot, I don't like the class number . . . wiat [wait] around and do nothing I hate to heai nonsent by Kig's [kids] and I hate don [dumb] kid's who talk slow word's.

Such papers offered the teacher a chance to learn about the relationships in families, the place of children in them, the values parents hold, and the punishments they mete out, as well as the rationale (or lack of it) for them. Evidently most of the children keenly felt a lack of security and

---

[2] It should be remembered that parents often make those promises in good faith. They may begin payments, and then have to default without the child knowing of the genuine effort made to keep the promises.

affection in their homes and revealed the deep frustration and disappointment this caused them. There was no one to talk to. This lack of affection was also responsible for their constant, insistent demand for the teacher's attention and affection. If situations, especially those at home, could not be improved, help was needed in facing and adjusting to reality. While these students disliked certain situations, they seemed unaware that it was often within their power to change them. Both groups of students were drastically handicapped in their life at home and at school by inability to understand the behavior, motivations, and desires of other people and by their lack of skills in the area of human relations. There was little evidence that they had any concept of teamwork as a feasible means of achieving ends which would otherwise remain dreams.

DISCUSSIONS OF INCIDENTS AND UNFINISHED STORIES

Like open-ended questions and themes, group discussions can serve a number of purposes simultaneously. Providing that the teacher has selected an appropriate stimulus and has mastered the techniques of conducting these discussions, they can offer considerable information on the general tenor of feelings in the group. When such discussions are conducted in the context of larger topics, they are especially valuable in clarifying certain perceptions and concepts, or in uncovering the feelings and problems of the students.

In the following example, the teacher of the first group was seeking information on the students' feelings and concepts on racial differences as well as introducing the unit, "The Family of Man," discussed in Chapter V. The students were Negroes and the teacher was not. The teacher displayed three large photos, one of a Negro child, one of an Oriental, and one of a Caucasian. She led the class to discuss what was happening in each picture, noting the physical similarities and differences. After this the teacher asked, "How many of you were ever sick enough to need a blood test?" The class responded eagerly. Evidently this was a topic that stimulated them. Then she asked, "What color was the blood?"

Boy: Red.
Teacher: And yours?
Girl: Red.
Second Boy: Mine was a rich red.
Third Boy: Mine was dark red.
Fourth Boy: Real dark red.
Teacher: Mine was red, too. It seems that all of us who saw

our blood in the tube have red blood. Could you describe
the color of the faces and arms of the children in this
picture?

FIFTH BOY: Italian.

FIRST BOY: Tannish. And this one is pinkish and this one
brownish.

TEACHER: Does everyone agree? (*Class nods agreement.*)
Then what do you think is the color of the *blood* of the
child in this picture?

SECOND BOY: Red.

TEACHER: And the second picture?

SECOND GIRL: Red.

TEACHER: And the third?

THIRD GIRL: Red.

TEACHER: That's interesting, isn't it?

FOURTH GIRL: (*In tone of amazement and wonder*) All the
children in all the pictures have red blood but their faces
are not the same color.

FIFTH GIRL: Yes! And they have the same kind of bodies.

SIXTH GIRL: No! Their bodies are *not* the same.

TEACHER: Do all have arms and legs and feet and ears and
eyes and mouths?

SIXTH GIRL: (*Bitterly*) If they are lucky. If they didn't lose
any.

FIRST BOY: They all come from a different country.

A special variant of group discussions is the eliciting of responses to
an incident in a story or in real life. The procedure of this technique is to
read a story up to the climax, cutting off the ending or the solution, or
to describe a sequence of events that arouse feelings, or an incident that
involves a dilemma, such as an interpersonal conflict. Naturally, the selections should have some pertinence to the problems that baffle the students.
The reactions can then be probed either in an unstructured way or more
or less systematically. In both cases, however, the discussion questions
need to be open-ended so that a variety of reactions are possible and
acceptable.

The excerpt below is taken from a discussion held when the teacher
of the first group was introducing the Triangle Fire sequence, discussed
in Chapter VIII. The discussion was triggered by the reading of a chapter
from Sholem Asch's *East River*. In addition to creating involvement and
motivation for the study, the discussion enabled the teacher to diagnose
the children's misconceptions about religious differences and their lack of

knowledge about money and salaries (equalled only by their interest in them).

In the chapter it was mentioned that a character was paid $12.00 a week. The children protested the low salary:

> (BOY):   I know a lady who makes $16.00 a week and my father works on the waterfront and makes $800.00 a week.
>
> (BOY):   My uncle, he make $100.00 a year and he work on a ship. And anudder man I know makes $90.00 a week in New York.
>
> TEACHER: In the story, one girl was Catholic and the other Jewish. Which girl do you think was Catholic and which Jewish? See if you can also tell us why you think so.
>
> (BOY):   I think Mary was Jewish because Jewish, they pray a lot. . . .
>
> (GIRL):   I think Mary was Jewish and Sara was Catholic because that day when Mary went to go home she had to go to church.
>
> (SECOND GIRL):   Jewish people are not rich and most people, Catholics, are rich and she had to work hard. So, I think Sara was Jewish.

Such a discussion can also be developed more or less systematically, in which case a sequence of questions such as the following is useful:

1. What happened in this story or in this incident? This is a question of prime importance in discussing any story because children often do not know what happened even if the teacher reads the story to them. If they don't understand this to begin with, they cannot deal successfully with the questions that follow. This one is asked to get a picture of the level of sensitivity and of perception. Some students may only restate the surface facts, while others may perceive the crux of the situation. Some may discern the motivations and causes of behavior and others may not.

2. Why did these things happen? The replies to this question suggest the level of the rationale of which the class is capable: whether they discern causes for behavior and what kind of causes they see.

3. How did those involved feel? This question diagnoses the capacity to put one's self into another person's shoes and reveals the gaps in sensitivity. For example, in situations involving children, adolescents, and parents, students find it hard to identify and empathize with parents; they are much more realistic about the feelings of other children or adolescents.

4. Has anything like that happened to you? This question probes the level of abstraction students can reach and therefore the level of transfer

that is possible. A low level of abstraction leads to searching for examples that are like some detail in the described situation, such as the fact of being spoken to in a harsh voice. A higher level of abstraction would produce examples on a more sophisticated level, such as that of meeting rejection in an entirely different situation, or difficulties encountered because the same situation is interpreted in a different way by different persons.

5. What would you do to make this situation come out better? The replies to this question reveal the extents to which the perception, feelings, and understandings created are applied. It is often necessary at first to break down this question: "If you were ——————————, what would you do to make things come out better?"

SYSTEMATIC OBSERVATION

In addition to the kinds of information that a student will give about himself, a teacher needs to know much that can be perceived only from an adult perspective. Observation yields this kind of information.

Observation is an especially necessary tool with students whose skills in writing and in self-expression are immature, as, for example, those in the primary grades, or defective, as is frequently true of culturally deprived children. Observation is usually directed toward recording visible behavior, such as work habits, performance of a skill, or the behavior of a committee chairman in action. Observation can also provide a multi-dimensional and longitudinal description of a few students: one can gather evidence on reactions to study, to stress, to other students, on attitudes toward school, interaction in classroom discussions, and participation in ongoing activities.

It is difficult for even the most conscientious teacher to observe every child in a class of over thirty, while at the same time teaching all of them, controlling the behavior problems, and keeping the bright ones busy. Almost inevitably, there are children of whom the teacher must say, "I don't even remember whether or not he was in class today." Systematic observation is necessary to get information on unobtrusive and withdrawn students.

One method is simply to select in turn three or four children to observe closely during a full day. Another method is for the teacher to select a characteristic and to note all behavior that might be symptomatic of it. This depends on knowledge about significant symptomatic characteristics of a particular group. Thus, a teacher looking for behaviors symptomatic of a shattered self-concept might notice that two minutes after an assignment of a page in a workbook one student slams down his pencil and puts his head on his desk. A bit later two or three additional heads and pencils go down. In the meantime George still has his thumb in his mouth, and his faraway look testifies that George is not "with it." In fact, his copy of the workbook lies unopened on his desk, bottom side up. No pencil or pen is to be seen. No one has bothered to hand him a sheet of paper nor has he even noticed this neglect.

Because so many culturally deprived children come from broken or foster homes, and because they move so frequently, it is often fruitful to focus observation on symptoms of alienation and withdrawal. A tall adolescent who is fully developed physically may be seen quietly sucking her thumb all day, withdrawn from the class. A boy reads novel after novel, occasionally pausing to glance disdainfully at classmates who struggle with beginning reading. A girl sobs to herself, "I don't like this class; I don't want to be in this class; it's a dumb class; I was told I wouldn't be put in a dumb class."

The teacher may also concentrate on noting situations that make the students apprehensive and fearful, and the students who are consistently on the alert, watching instead of concentrating on their tasks. Students know which of their peers "yuh gotta watch," and the teacher does well to heed their fears. Their fears are often entirely realistic, as the teacher's account of the following incidents show:

> Ross and Edmund wouldn't do anything alone. Edmund would say, "What's this word?" and Ross, the perennial truant— he really has a good mind—would tell him. Everything was fine for a while with those two anyway. And then suddenly one day a horrifying thing happened. Walter went berzerk with a great big wooden rifle. Three teachers tried to restrain him. He attacked Ross and clobbered him over the head. The kid is standing there, bleeding all over, with blood on his paper and desk. Blood all over him, all over his shirt, all over the room. I wrote a pass to the nurse and gave it to him and said, "Go." Later, when I talked with him, I realized that one big reason for his truancy was that he was afraid of Walter, the one who went berzerk. He was in mortal terror of him, but he wouldn't or he couldn't tell why. He's a funny kid, you know, Ross is. I think he's bright. He's in school so few days and yet he catches on fast whenever he is here. One day I asked him why he doesn't take off his jacket. He said, "I can't, it makes me feel secure." I said to myself, "He's like Peanuts in the comic strip." When Walter went after him that day, it was the climax.
>
> The kids tease and torture Walter so much that he had

taken all he could take. . . . He went after another boy, crying, tears streaming down his face. The kids restrained him. . . . I was upset no end about the way he beat him. It was pathetic. Walter was so hysterical. . . . He could have killed Robert. Robert deserves a good beating for what he does to others, but I didn't want murder in my room. . . . This is a fight that started outside of school and they carried it into the classroom. . . . They're very interesting kids. When it's something they want to watch as being *fun* . . . they'll watch it, especially when two girls fight. That they love to watch. And the only one who will break it up is another girl. When they sense real danger, they'll get into it and try to break it up. Also, if there's a fight and I want to go near, they'll pull me away and say, "No, Miss————. You'll get hurt. Don't go near." Somehow they know the difference when something is really dangerous and when it isn't.

A child who must be constantly alert for his physical safety cannot afford to concentrate on academic work; no sane person could. Unless the children know that the teacher can protect them from overt hostility and aggression in the classroom, they will not even remain in their seats to become inviting targets for bullies.

Two teachers who were friends and taught the same class at different times decided voluntarily to share observations. During his free period one teacher would observe the agreed-upon members of the other's class. Thus the active teacher was relieved of the burden of recording observations for that hour, and the observing teacher viewed the students from an entirely different perspective than he had when teaching them. Shared observations provided fuel for intriguing sessions on interpretation and, of course, added immeasurably to both teachers' fund of information. Such a technique is particularly useful to get information about the less conspicuous, quiet, or apathetic pupils, as demonstrated by the following observations about pupils in the first group.

Deena does her work standing up. Does not look at her book or at the board. Acts very tired . . . . Sits passively until reminded to do her work . . . . Eager to volunteer her answers later.

Attentive but yawns as though sleepy. Volunteers correct answer. Reads a book. Stops listening. Continues to read book throughout the lesson . . . .

Doesn't have or can't find homework. Walks around a little.

Is uninterested in lesson. Looks tired. Volunteers to take the wrong word off the board. Volunteers to answer dictionary question . . . .

Copies quietly. Does the work but doesn't listen to explanations . . . .

Copies quietly, but doesn't understand the work . . . .

Talks loudly. Stands up while copying from the board.

*   *   *

. . . . Charles is well dressed. George waits until teacher is not looking to throw paper plane at Charles. Charles is on point of throwing it back. Teacher steps in, gets the usual, "He did it first," from Charles. As lesson continues, Charles persists in communicating with George; as teacher steps in Charles apologizes to teacher. When teacher leaves his desk, Charles continues on his merry way. In writing business letter, Charles asks Chamber of Commerce for a "right-side-up backwards, upside-down cake." Asks teacher to read it. Beams with pride when teacher reads it to class.

*   *   *

Gladys sits in rear of room. Takes pre-test. Says nothing to anyone. Very well-behaved. After pre-test question sheets and a rexographed copy of spelling list are given out, Gladys sits; does nothing. After five minutes, goes to front of room to tell teacher she has been given the wrong sheets. Sure enough! . . . Always goes to front of room to ask question, as if a raised hand would constitute an imposition, forcing teacher to walk all the way to back of room . . . extremely shy and withdrawn. Does ask questions, give answers, but always characterized by tone of apology, subservience . . . afraid of offending; speaks in subdued quiet voice . . . her own personality seems to have been buried under a bushel . . . would take guff from anybody and always thinks herself at fault . . . she *has* come alive when praised for her work . . . had her hand raised constantly during discussion, but still with the attitude of, "If you call on me I promise not to be any trouble."

It is, of course, necessary to record observations. Otherwise, teachers unconsciously modify them during the course of the year, and it becomes difficult for them to recognize the changes that have occurred. Further, recording observations sharpens both the capacity to "see" students and to interpret objectively what one sees and directs attention to the fact that often the content and the teaching strategy are the causes of negative student behavior.

Recognizing that there is a relationship, and sometimes a negative one, between the teacher's teaching and the student's response is a critical factor in becoming a good teacher. If the teacher records his observations, he then has a reliable guide when he wishes to study the relationship between his teaching strategies and the students' behavior. This relationship will be dealt with more fully later in the chapters that describe instructional sequences.

SOCIOMETRIC TESTS

Diagnosis for the purpose of guiding instruction is incomplete without information about conditions that either enhance or impede learning. The social climate of a classroom, particularly the nature of interpersonal relations among the students, are among such crucial conditions. The structure of interpersonal relations affects the atmosphere of the classroom, determines the communication lines, affects the frequency of discipline problems, and controls the amount of energy that an individual can put into learning tasks. It determines the roles they can play in the group and, therefore, their access to the sources of learning and of stimulation.

A sociometric test is one method of diagnosing the patterns of interpersonal relations in the classroom. In effect, the sociometric test reveals the structure of the student society (Jennings 1959; Taba, *et al.*, 1951). The test itself is simple. It consists of asking each student to select three persons with whom he would want to sit, to be on a committee, to go to a movie, or to do any of the things that can be done in a small group. It also asks each student to name persons with whom he would *not* want to do these things. In order to get valid results, the situation must be realistic; the arrangements implied in the question must not only be feasible, but they must also be carried out. For example, if "With whom would you like to sit?" is the test question, the seating must be rearranged in consideration of the choices indicated.

These choices can be tabulated and studied systematically to discover the nature of the interpersonal networks: what the patterns of choices are, which subgroups exist, what cleavages there are, what degree of isolation prevails, etc. The data can then be examined and the reasons for these phenomena inferred from the data, such as whether the cleavages occur along lines of differences in racial background, because of lack of skills in interpersonal relations, as a result of culturally conditioned variations in characteristic behavior, or as consequences of certain school practices, styles of teaching, or methods of grouping. The means employed to improve the relationships will depend on what cause is indicated. It may be necessary to help individuals to change, to modify the values of the group, or to alter school practices. Such measures may include reseating the group, if formal seating is the practice, using new criteria to compose group activities, such as committees, training the pupils in group processes, or changing instructional practices.

Because the record of sociometric choices describes only the surface of relationships, it is useful to inquire into the reasons for choice and rejection in order to detect the values that control the choices. This can be done by sociometric interviews, either oral or written. The simplest way is to ask the student how he happened to choose the individual he did choose.

The interview can be introduced rather easily by the teacher telling the class that he is having some difficulty in making seating (or committee) arrangements and that it would help if each child told him privately the basis for his choice. Although interviewing the class is time-consuming, the teachers reported that students were eager to talk, and that it was well worth the time spent on it.

In general, teachers found that involvement of students and an expression of genuine interest on their part were enough to keep the class talking. At times, of course, it was necessary to elicit clarifying information. For instance, when a student said, "I just like him. He's a good sport," the teacher looked interested and queried, "Good sport?" The student replied with a functional definition of "good sport." "Yes, he is. If I'm on his team and I lose the ball he never gets mad."

Once the responses to the interviews are classified, it is possible to describe the values that prevail in the group. Information on the prevailing values enables a teacher to judge whether these values are congenial to individual growth and to learning, or are characterized by brittleness, division, and social distance. It also enables a teacher to judge the degree to which the classroom climate enhances or thwarts learning, the development of adequate self-concepts, and feelings of performing an appreciated role in the group. Sociometric data enable the teacher to judge to some extent whether the classroom climate fosters acceptance of diversity and of individual autonomy, or whether it supports the tendency to reject individuals, to dominate, or to indulge in ego derogation.

Further, possession of such information has a direct strategic value. It gives the teacher a more adequate basis for grouping the students in study groups, committees, teams for projects, etc. Many teachers have found that smaller face-to-face groups encourage openness and participation which are impossible to obtain in the total class group. If, in addition to being small, such groups are composed so that psychological cohesion is enhanced, conditions are created for far more productive work than would be possible otherwise. Sociometric data also help to identify natural leaders and to open up a wider range of leadership roles than are usually recognized and used. They are invaluable in determining what the communication lines in the class are: why remarks by some students instigate constructive follow-up by others, while the same type by others are occasions for arguments; why the class attends to what some say, and fails to hear the remarks of others.

Groups vary in the kinds of behavior that are accepted, cherished, or valued, and in the characteristics that cause rejection, isolation, or cleavage. Some individuals find it hard to explore and experiment with new relationships, and they seek the security of long acquaintance. In some classrooms, or groups within a classroom, ability and achievement bring recognition and status. In others, individuals are sought because they are outgoing, friendly, and fun to be with, or because they are helpful, thoughtful, and considerate of others.

One teacher made a sociogram of a class in the second group in order to discover leadership patterns, having concluded from observations that there were few or none. For example, there seemed to be no particular pattern as to where the students sat in class. The sociogram demonstrated that there was leadership. This teacher accurately predicted the unpopularity of certain pupils on the basis of disparaging remarks made by others, the pupil's own irritability, aggressiveness, or marked communication difficulties. He had a greater difficulty predicting popularity. However, in all cases, well-chosen children from both samples ran the gamut of desirable characteristics. Their behavior was flexible enough to mean many things to many people (Elkins, 1955). The leaders, however, seemed to concentrate on being helpful.

The teacher will find it especially illuminating to make a record beforehand of his own judgments as to who is accepted or rejected and why. A teacher who tried this on a class of the eighth-graders found some startling discrepancies between his judgments of peer acceptance and actual acceptance among the students. Estelle, who seemed outstanding to the teacher because of her helpfulness both to the teacher and her peers, did not receive a single choice. Agnes, who seemed unremarkable to the teacher because she was not particularly attractive and was quiet in class, received a very high rating. The teacher had accurately predicted that

Emily, a little girl with a childish hairdo who went around hitting others when she was unhappy, would be rejected by the more sophisticated teenagers. It was not surprising, either, that Patrick was unchosen, because he was almost totally deaf, and communication with him was difficult. Earlier, the students had commented scornfully about May, "Oh, she's never in school. In the seventh grade she was always absent," so the teacher did not expect her to be popular. The high number of rejections she received was a surprise.

In personal interviews their reasons and values began to emerge. Of Estelle they said:

> She comes to school early, and we don't see her much. If she doesn't like somebody she comes right out and says it to their face. But usually she won't say anything unless they jump at her first.
>
> Bridget and I are like old maids, and Estelle likes boys. When she's around Freda she swears. She hasn't got a very good disposition. She gets awful mad at things. We'll be fooling with her, and she'll get awful mad and yell and everything.
>
> She'll look mad all of a sudden, and she'll say nothing is wrong, but we know there is. When we're together she's uncertain about things. She doesn't know whether she's wanted or not. I always ask her to come with us, but when we're discussing where we want to go and she doesn't happen to be there and she doesn't hear about it, she says, "Oh, I guess they just don't want me." She says we never ask her, but we do. But sometimes she's not around, and we can't tell her about it. She wanted to go to Lewiston, and we didn't because it was too cold, and she had a sad face and tears in her eyes.

Thus her peers perceived Estelle as a child frustrated in all her attempts to join a group of teenagers, disturbed and upset because she knew she was unwanted, displaying a "bad disposition" as a result of her frustration, joining in friendship with another girl who had a "bad reputation" because no one in her own group would accept her, and bringing upon herself further condemnation because of that very friendship. Further, the teacher realized that he had not ameliorated the situation by constantly asking Estelle to assist those who wanted no assistance from her. Graceful obscurity was called for so that Estelle might have a chance to adopt more acceptable behavior.

Agnes, whom the teacher found unremarkable, proved to be a leader because she found it easy to relate herself to other students. She was available to them whenever there was a personal problem to be solved, consoling them, and giving counsel and assistance. Of her they said:

> She can take criticism without getting mad over it. That's one thing I can't. She's not snotty-like; she doesn't hang around with you and with no one else.
> You can always tell her things and she won't go around telling everybody else about them.
> She knows my faults, but she doesn't hurt me. In fact, she tells me my good points. Bridget said I look awful in shorts in gym, and I cried, but Agnes said my legs aren't so big and fat as all that, and she makes me feel better. She knows everything that's going on. She helps me more with outside problems. When I got my report card and I was crying and my mother says I can't go out with boys, Agnes comes over and says, "Don't worry and you'll pick up and then you'll go to Miss———— and she'll write a note home and tell your mother you're improving."

In some instances where the teacher had an accurate idea of the child's social status, the comments of his peers gave rise to deeper questions in the teacher's mind: questions about a child's home situation, his dependent actions, and about what could and should be done for him.

While analyzing the interviews, the teacher looked for values that controlled the children's interpersonal relations. What were the criteria by which peers were accepted or rejected? Which were reasonable and which were immature and in need of modification? What kind of planning and teaching was needed to make those modifications?

The following values suggested themselves as being in need of modification. First, the students rejected girls who were considered "boy-crazy." They needed to understand that an interest in the opposite sex is a normal part of growing up, and that it begins in some girls earlier and more intensely than in others. Second, they rejected as "not nice" children who "didn't fix their hair nicely," whose "house isn't clean," who were "loud," and who "picked an argument." They needed to learn that in rejecting a person for such superficial reasons they might be depriving themselves of a rich friendship. Third, they shied away from a person who was seeking new friendships, preferring one whom they had known for some time because "he sticks by you." They needed to see friendship as an inclusive instead of an exclusive association, particularly considering their transient milieu. Fourth, they rejected a person who could not take teasing. They needed to become more tolerant of hurt feelings and to inquire into the causes of such sensitivities. Fifth, they rejected a person purely on the basis of a third person's opinion, whether that person was their mother who "said so" or a peer. They needed to formulate their own opinions of individuals. Admittedly, the teacher was faced here with a delicate task of encouraging the students to think independently without losing respect for their parents.

Among the disadvantaged Negro children, three criteria for choice seemed to dominate: being able to borrow money, to share food, and willingness to help out a friend in a jam. In this group, an innocent party, especially if his current misbehavior was a trifle in the light of his total behavior record, would frequently take the blame for his friend's action, feeling that he had nothing to lose.

Reasons for rejection were also related to money. People borrow and don't return the loan. They dislike peers who "bother when they are not repaid." "Bothering" may range from mere annoyance to a bloody fight. Often it means teasing and getting other people into trouble. These students are not particularly fond of peers who "cut up" in class, yet they join the fray once it has started. Through it all there is a yearning for order, to "have someone patrol." Being "boy-crazy" was not a cause of rejection in their group.

The disadvantaged Caucasian students also placed a high value on helping a friend in a jam, but their manner of doing so was different. They tended to organize the class on behalf of the offender, as in one case when they circulated a petition against demoting a certain student. In other cases they interceded directly with the teacher. (Evidently, certain authority figures were not as threatening to these children as others and were perceived as being helpful.) Also, the children knew each other over a period of years; the Negro children had fewer opportunities to build permanent relationships.

GENERAL INTERVIEWS

Another diagnostic technique is a general interview. The general interview goes beyond the sociometric in that it is not focused solely on a child's relationships with his peers. An example of the questions asked of the first group of students follows.

1. How did you happen to choose——————? (Ask supplementary questions about the three choices.)

2. How did you happen *not* to choose——————?

3. What do you do after school until bedtime? With whom? (Ask supplementary questions like "until supper," etc.)

4. What do you do weekends? With whom? (It may be necessary to break this up: "before lunch," etc.)

5. Who lives in your house? What ages? Relationship to you?

6. What do the grown-ups in your house like most about what you do?

7. What do the grown-ups in your house wish you didn't do?

8. What do the grown-ups tell you about yourself? (Things you like to hear? Not to hear?)

9. What stories do they tell about things you did when you were little?

10. What do you want to be? Do you know anyone who does this?

PARENT INTERVIEWS

Students' home background, especially the emotional atmosphere, has much to do with learning and behavior in school. Hence, parent interviews, appropriately conceived, have yielded much information that is useful in understanding the students.

The eighth-grade teacher used the following schedule of questions, which was especially devised to reveal parental attitudes toward children, their ambitions for them, and the nature of contols they exercised. The questions provide only the skeleton, and must be supplemented with others as needed.

1. *Opening*

"How do you feel ——————— is doing?"

This lets parents discuss what is uppermost in their minds and leaves the choice of what to say entirely to them. The things that are mentioned will often give clues to what the parent is aware of and what he overlooks entirely.

2. *Aspirations and goals*

"What plans do you and your husband have for ——————?"
or, "What are your hopes for ——————? What are your husband's hopes?"

These questions permit the parent to express any differences of opinion in the family. The responses will tell whether the parents' aspirations are too high, whether they are related to financial realities, or whether the parents have thought of future goals at all.

3. *Association with other children*

"How do you arrange for ——————'s friends?" or, "How do you try to select your child's playmates?"

This wording permits the parent who imposes controls on his children to say so freely, because the controls over the child's comings and goings, his associates or intimate friends, are usually accepted.

4. *Neighborhoods*

"You know the neighborhood better than I do. Are there opportunities that you would like your child to have?" or, "How do you like this neighborhood?" or, "Do you think this is a good neighborhood for boys and girls?"

This type of question gives a chance to express almost anything about the neighborhood: what facilities it has for living, as well as how the parents feel about it as a place to live.

5. *Worries and pleasures*

"What gives you most pleasure about your child? What worries you most about ——————?" or, "What are some of ——————'s best qualities and habits? and, "What do you think are ——————'s worst faults, faults we may not see at school?"

These questions permit the teacher to see what bothers and pleases parents in their children, and how reasonable parents' expectations of their children are. These expressions of favorable and unfavorable characteristics also usually reveal parental attitudes toward their children and, hence, the emotional atmosphere in which they live.

6. *Closing the interview*

The opening question, "How do you think—————is doing?" permits a completely free, unguided response. In closing an interview it is well to give the parents a similar opportunity to express any ideas or thoughts that may have been left unsaid during the interview. Two good closing questions are "Is there anything you would like the school to do for you?" "What suggestions do you have for ——————'s program here?" These questions also close the interview on the note on which it was introduced, namely, the problem of how to plan better for children, and how to do it with the help of the parents.

Below are records of interviews with two parents of the eighth-grade class. The teacher used the occasion of having to plan high school programs for students as a specific reason for having interviews and told that to both parents and children. Her own purpose was to find out as much as she could about family and sibling relations, because those were the areas in which she was developing her program. She was anxious also to compare her data on association patterns in school with information about peer relationships outside.

INTERVIEW WITH MRS. T

This was an unplanned interview. Mrs. T came into school demanding to know, "What is this all about?" [my wishing to see her]. She came in when I had a class, and not wishing to leave the children to talk to her for any length of time, I asked if it were possible for her to make a definite appointment. "I work, and my time is taken up too," she said. So the teacher left the class and spent the period with her.

She didn't know "how C is doing." She doesn't see her enough. How should *she* know? Her report card wasn't good, though. All she knows is that her mother sees C more than she does, and they [C and the grandmother] don't get along and she [Mrs. T] is sick of the fights.

Apparently, the situation at home is quite a strain on all members. C claims the grandmother "hates" her. C tells her so at least a few times a day. C and she clash at all times. She complains about the grandmother to Mrs. T as soon as Mrs. T gets home from work. Then the grandmother complains about C to her. She knows her mother doesn't hate the child, but can't make C see that. C feels that she cannot even go to the icebox for an extra snack of food; she does not feel as if this is her house and she a part of it. Mrs. T has fruit and candy in their room upstairs and always tells C to take some even though she has bought it for her own lunch. C had a fight last week with her grandmother and refused to talk to her for four days. Her mother came to Mrs. T and said, "What am I? A dog to be treated that way in my own house?" Mrs. T talked to C, but it did no good. She still isn't talking.

Mrs. T didn't know what C should take in high school. She does want her to graduate from high, but hasn't discussed occupations with her at all. It's up to the child and her teacher.

She doesn't have anything to do with choice of her child's friends. She doesn't even know who they are. She's never around enough. She has to go out some evenings and "live a little" for herself. No, C doesn't have any friends come up to the house. The grandmother won't permit that. She doesn't like extra children around. After all, she's a woman of fifty-four, and she likes to walk around the house in bare feet, etc., etc. She can't do that with strangers around. Mrs. T doesn't have any friends over either. She has to go out to see other people. If she could get a three-room apartment, she could allow C to have friends visit her, and she herself would stay home evenings more often. She had heard her mother complain about C's friends' reputations, but she knows nothing herself about that. She demands that C be in the house at 8:30, and the grandmother sees to it that she is in. She told C that she had to be a good girl because of all the awful things that can happen to girls—like being "put away" because they're "not nice." C said, "Don't worry, mother, I won't do anything wrong."

She knows C hangs around the game room at night, but doesn't know where else she goes at night. She knows she plays basketball after school.

She doesn't like C to be late to school so much because she doesn't like to write notes for her tardiness. "What's the idea of notes anyway? When I went to school, if you were late, you were late, and that's all." C goes to bed late—11 o'clock very often. She just mopes around downstairs all evening.

C has an "awful" temper, is not easy to manage. None of her other children are. One boy is in a foster home, living with a teacher who has done a great deal for him. She "watches his language and manages him better than I could do, but he'd rather live with me." One boy is in the County Home and he cries everytime she goes to visit him. She'd take her three children to live with her if she had a place. But how can she keep up a place and support them? Anyway, wouldn't there be an agency like Juvenile Court which should be interested enough in kids to get her an apartment for $25 a month? If she could get one, maybe she'd manage. It's hard to manage, though. C is always kicking about how she doesn't have any decent clothes. The grandmother thinks the mother buys the child too many. But Mrs. T thinks that they are important [she was well-groomed, herself, as is C]. And then, too, she tries to give C extra little luxuries in food. She likes bananas and Mrs. T buys them for her cereal. She has to buy extra food like that, because even though she pays her mother for board for herself and C, the grandmother does not buy those "extra" items, and if she does, they are not for C. C earns $1.00 a week babysitting. Mother doesn't have to give her an allowance unless she earns no money.

After much thinking, Mrs. T finally remembered that one nice thing about C was the way she takes care of her when she is ill. She's a very nervous woman—she says—was treated at the clinic when she was having trouble with the kids. They told her then that she needs lots of recreation and "not to worry about things." She has gone to pieces many times. She doesn't know why she does, but things "get" her.

Here is a mother to whom her girl is a bother. She knows little about her, and her own concerns crowd her so much that she cannot spare any for her daughter. Meanwhile, the daughter is anxious to get out of the house as much as she can and needs help both in facing her family problems and in having a healthy life in school. What kind of school program would help C? How can she be made more a part of the school group so she can find opportunities for healthy relations so completely lacking at home?

INTERVIEW WITH MRS. H

Mrs. H is a friendly, well-dressed, nice-looking young woman. She was most willing to talk about P and about her family.

To the question, "'How do you feel P is doing?" she said, "Well, we want him to do right, but we don't want to push him too much." She and her husband expect the best he can give, but no more. When she was in school, she left her homework till the morning, but not P. He even does his on *Friday* night. She says to him, "Why don't you leave it? You have two whole days this weekend." But he refuses; he has to get it off his mind right away.

She called herself a "lucky mother" several times during the interview. She has never had to spank P because "I can always talk to him and make him understand." She's glad she has two boys instead of girls because "I like boys better. They're easier to manage." She taught piano years ago, and enjoyed her boy pupils more than the girls.

She's not quite sure what she wants P to be. It's pretty much up to him. Both parents, however, are anxious to send him through college. She did not graduate from high school, though the father did. She went to music school instead. Mr. H went to our school as a boy, and was glad to move to this section two years ago so the boys could go here too. "In the other school, they taught you to read by looking," and the boys had a terrible time with reading. When they came here, the methods were different. "They sounded out the words," and they "got along better with their studies." P wants to be an engineer, though he doesn't know what kind, and he has heard about M.I.T., so that's where he'd like to go—unless he changes his mind.

She lets him pick his own playmates. There was only one instance when she interfered. P was chumming around with a high school lad who she felt was a "bad influence," and she asked him not to go with him. She never "orders P around"; she *asks* him to do things. He usually does.

When they first moved here two years ago, she told P not to go into the schoolyard at night with the other boys. She found out that he did do it nevertheless. She brought the subject up one day, and he lied to her about it. "That was the only time he ever lied to me. And really, he didn't lie then, either. He was just evasive." She talked to him some more, and he promised her he'd never do it again. He has kept his promise. Now she realizes he did it because he was new in the neighborhood and wanted to make friends by doing whatever the gang does. "But I told him it takes more courage to say 'No' than to do what the rest do, and they'll admire you for it." Now he has his own gang, and seems content. [In this setting, "gang" simply means any informal group.] Recently the only boy she has objected to is J. He "beat up" her younger son D who is only in the fifth grade. Mrs. H demanded that J come to see her, and all P's friends went looking for him. Before she knew it, there they were—five of them pushing J ahead of them until he went into her house. She told J she'd not have raised one single objection if D had been his size and the fight equal, but he was taking advantage of a smaller boy. [She says J had him on the ground and stuck three fingers in his eyes.] She threatened that if he ever touched D again, she'd go right over and talk to his parents.

The trouble with the neighborhood is that there's no place for the children to play. She is lucky that they have their own home and often there are "ten kids in our living room," but every time they go into someone's yard the police cruiser gets a complaint and goes chasing the neighborhood kids away. Their chief need is a big open place to play—"football or anything."

The thing she enjoys most about P is the "way you can talk to him." She hopes he doesn't change. "Of course, you never know how they'll be when they get a little older, and drive a car." She's anticipating trouble here—afraid that he'll become too cocksure of himself behind the wheel. But right now he gives her no trouble, causes her no worry. "You can talk to him the way you can talk to an adult." That gives her much pleasure. Her only slight concern is that he "doesn't stand out enough" in school recitations. She wants him to be less shy, but not aggressive. She wants him to learn to speak well because, although you may not plan your life that way, many times "you find you have to speak before a small group at least." Her husband finds that true. He has to instruct forty men at a time on the use of certain machines, and wishes he had greater command of English and of himself in front of a group. She was amazed at the poise of the children who spoke at Parents' Night. She realizes P is shy. That is why she stopped teaching Sunday school. She felt that perhaps he'd talk more if *she* were not the teacher. Except for her knowledge of this, everything about her boy is a joy to her.

The father apparently is away on business trips quite often and she feels lucky that her boys are easy to manage. Otherwise she wouldn't be able to manage without a man home all the time.

P has a chemistry set and filled the house with smoke one day. Evidently it didn't upset the mother very much, and she encourages his interest in it

If Mr. and Mrs. H disagree as to how the children shall be disciplined, the children are never aware of that disagreement. Each upholds the other's decision.

The attitude of this parent is a complete contrast to the preceding one. The mother is pleased with her children, feels she can manage them, and has hopes for their future. In spite of a fairly difficult condition in the neighborhood, she seems to manage to safeguard her boy from "bad" relationships without resorting to harsh rules about associations and reasons with children instead of imposing arbitrary controls.

It should be noted that in segregated communities the parents had high expectations for the school's role in helping their children overcome their historical deprivation. One mother wanted the school to "help him grow up to be responsible and to be somebody worthwhile" because the school could "give him an education and a steady mind." The insistent cry of mothers, "BE somebody, BE somebody," is heartrending to the teacher who is sensitive to the needs of the children and to the plight of parents who in desperation turn to the school for help. A father, pleased that his boy was learning manners in school, could only add, "There's so much. I can't explain it all. And please teach him to read, because I can't read too good myself. . . . When I go to work and he is in school he can't get into trouble."

Yet the students often are not in school; many of them are truants. If the school does not alleviate the human needs that prevent these children from learning, it fails in its teaching task. For the school to fail them is to consign them to years of growing despair and frustration, and to fail as an institution in accomplishing its task—preparing thinking citizens for a life in a democracy.

In the following chapters we will discuss curriculum theory and teaching strategies that attempt to meet both the human and academic needs of these students. While the theory applies by no means exclusively to culturally deprived children and it has been successfully practiced in middle-income schools, all of the examples and accounts of attempts will be drawn from experiences with the same two groups of children encountered in this chapter.

CHAPTER IV

Some Guidelines for
Instructional Strategies

There is more to be said about the principles of teaching the culturally and educationally disadvantaged than can be said in any book. It would be presumptuous to pretend that one chapter can suffice even to introduce these ideas. This chapter is intended primarily to give the reader some kind of perspective for interpreting the descriptive learning sequences that constitute the bulk of this book.

It is recognized rather generally that conventional instruction does not reach adolescents with cultural and educational deficits who have already established a negative attitude toward their own capacities, school learning, teachers, and the rest. The kind of experiences that are offered, the motivational devices used, the content, as well as the approaches to teaching, seem somehow to miss the mark, either because they are incompatible with the needs of such students and therefore represent meaningless drudgery to them, or because some links in their education are missing. The severe retardation of such students that shows up in the junior high is an eloquent testimony to the lack of success of such programs.

This suggests also that remedial measures on higher grade levels that only repeat what these students have already failed at are not the best answer. Perhaps a qualitatively different program is called for. This book is devoted to examples of qualitatively different instructional approaches. It is also a tentative effort to re-examine the several elements of curriculum and instruction in the light of the specific needs of such groups of students.

Basically, of course, there is no difference in the way in which culturally disadvantaged students learn. Their learning processes are subject to the same general principles of learning as are learning processes of the normal run of students, but with a difference. For example, all need to

65

proceed from the concrete to the abstract, but there is a difference in what is abstract and what is concrete to students who have gaps in their cognitive and verbal development and whose life experience may be limited in certain areas. Possibly, less verbal students need a different kind of concreteness than do those with normal linguistic equipment. Verbal explanations may communicate more to the latter than to the former. All students need certain basic cognitive tools to process information and to develop insight into relationships between facts and concepts. But the students from limited environments may lack the concepts which children in a normally stimulating environment have already acquired. Some of these now in the sixth or seventh grade may be working with the intellectual motor of a seven-year-old, at least in certain aspects of their encounters with school materials and the world. All students need to be motivated to learn anything at all. But *what* motivates them may be totally different. All students need to practice skills, and all learn these skills more easily and more willingly when such practice avoids rote drill, concentrating rather on repetition in a new context, but culturally deprived children may require more numerous repetitions in a more visible and inviting context.

What then, are the requirements for the instructional patterns?

A CONTINUAL DIAGNOSIS

A continual diagnosis of these needs and gaps and a continual appraisal of progress are almost an absolute necessity. As Chapter III has demonstrated, diagnosis is a continuous and a perennial task. Like spring plowing, it is never completed. It has to be done over and over again, at every step of instruction. For this reason diagnosis must be made integral to the very process of learning and teaching; otherwise it would absorb an unreasonable amount of instructional time and possibly provide less effective guidance to teaching.

Diagnosis also needs to be comprehensive: assess the background of experience, the way students feel about school and themselves, the values they hold, their basic, emotional, human needs which are not met and which therefore retard learning, the interests and areas of concern which offer clues to motivation for learning, the ideas and concepts they have, and how they think. The list is endless, and each teacher can extend the diagnosis to what seem to be the most urgent requirements for her particular group and the program. If the teacher, for example, wishes to make a transition from walls as material objects to the abstract concept of walls as psychological barriers, she needs to know whether her students can make the transition. She needs to know who is ready to examine a situation deeply and who can only scratch the surface, who can express ideas with ease and who finds it extremely difficult. Diagnosis via feedback thus becomes part of every teaching act and a basis for planning the next learning experience. This daily feedback and diagnosis are especially needed to help a teacher reared in one subculture to tune into the learning process of children in another subculture and, thus, to permit her to translate what is to be learned into appropriate experiences, instead of being forced to bend the students to conventional learning patterns.

A SIMULTANEOUS PURSUIT OF MULTIPLE OBJECTIVES

It is a widely accepted fact that acquiring knowledge and skills is not the only objective of education. Balanced instruction must provide also for increasingly effective ways of processing and thinking with that knowledge for attainment of desirable attitudes and sensitivities. If instruction is to be effective, these four areas of objectives—knowledge, thinking, attitudes, and skills—need to be pursued simultaneously.

However, most of the machinery of instruction is mobilized mainly to the end of acquiring knowledge and mastering the basic skills. The acquisition of information, rather than processing it to convert it into ideas, is the chief target of most instructional materials and of the techniques of teaching. For example, schools stress telling and reading—absorbing—instead of questioning, searching, and analyzing; reproducing generalizations instead of generalizing, hypothesizing, and making inferences, or differentiating which facts and ideas are relevant or irrelevant for a given purpose.

Because these students are unlikely to be well read or to have high IQ scores, and because it is further assumed that thinking is a product either of much knowledge or a high IQ, the cognitive component of the education of the culturally deprived is usually either underplayed or completely neglected.

It is important for all students to master certain cognitive processes and intellectual skills because they are a cornerstone for many other types of achievement from reading to solving mathematical problems. This need for basic conceptual tools has been obscured because the life experience of so-called normal children usually provides them with sufficient practice of these skills to enable them to succeed in the ordinary school tasks.

The case is different with the educationally disadvantaged youngsters. They come to school with a severe deficit in ability to abstract, to see relationships and other cognitive processes. It is not uncommon, for example, for the sixth- and seventh-graders in disadvantaged areas to operate with the cognitive motor of a seven-year-old: they cannot restate sequences of events in a story, have not yet acquired even the simplest forms of categorizing, do not have a model for connecting causes to consequences, etc. These deficiencies prevent success in all kinds of learning tasks. Students who lack the concept of similarity have no idea what to do when workbook directions call for putting commas between similar words. Inability to restate or even to recognize sequences of events renders meaningless certain passages in novels or historical accounts in texts. Inability to discriminate between main ideas and their specific illustrations creates barriers to comprehending what books or teachers say. Difficult abstractions leave them confused, indifferent, or helpless, as the descriptions in Chapters V and IX will show. These examples could be multiplied ad infinitum.

Because there is a serious deficit in the development of cognitive tools in their earlier socialization, emphasis on developing a capacity to conceptualize, to generalize, and to abstract is an objective of prime importance for students from culturally deprived homes. Their low academic performance is not necessarily an indication that they cannot master these processes. Students who currently show low academic performance can learn many of the cognitive skills, provided a beginning is made where they are, and provided account is taken of the existing level of their cognitive tools. The accounts in the chapters that follow, as well as evidence from other sources, suggest that this emphasis is perhaps the most potent single way of upgrading the rest: of mobilizing motivation, of generating autonomous learning, and of catching up with the deficit in knowledge and skills.

Sensitivity training and the development of attitudes toward self, other people, and to the gamut of democratic values and human relations are another important area of emphasis. These qualities and powers are the necessary ingredients of self-development as well as of school learning. For example, needed group skills are derived from responsiveness to and contact with peers, and both are necessary ingredients for receiving from peers the support for effort and ego-fulfillment these students fail to receive elsewhere. Among these students there is a greater than usual insensitivity to the feelings of others and to what might be called the moral criteria and democratic values, an insensitivity they have developed to protect their own feelings in an environment that includes hostile adults.

The lack of ordinary skills, such as reading and writing, among the culturally deprived has been subject to so much comment that it requires no elaboration. Name an academic skill and you locate a deficit. But there are other less frequently noted, but perhaps even more crucial, skills, such as the complex of skills related to impulse control, solving interpersonal conflicts, and listening to each other or to directions. Because the problems of interpersonal relations, especially those of handling rebuff, misunderstanding, and criticism, are a regular part of the lives of these students, the skills relevant to coping with these situations are important aspects of becoming a person in their own eyes and of preventing a sense of failure.

Productivity in group situations requires a variety of skills: doing orderly and focused thinking in groups, planning for group goals, controlling egocentric drives of dominance and self-interest, managing conflicting ideas with some degree of objectivity. For example, committee work flounders because individuals are energized by their own needs and are insensitive to the requirements of the group task or do not know how to further group goals or cannot identify with them.

Implementation of the platform of multiple objectives described above sets several new requirements for instructional planning. First, it is important to keep in mind that selection of content implements only one of these areas of objectives, namely the acquisition of information. The kind of content one deals with does not help develop thinking, attitudes, or even particular skills; these are learned from the type of learning experiences that are provided. This means that the planning of learning sequences must proceed on two tracks simultaneously: planning content and planning the learning experiences and activities. In planning instruction, teachers must think of the scope and the sequence of the learning experiences, as they now think of the scope and sequence of content.

Teachers must also be aware that a different learning strategy is needed to achieve each of the four areas of objectives noted above. The way of learning facts (knowledge) does not automatically produce a way of thinking with facts. For one thing, facts are learned instantaneously and can be acquired by passive absorption. Thinking is learned only by active process, by doing it, and it takes time and repeated performance to master the skills that are part of it. Learning of attitudes usually requires experiences and materials which have an impact on feelings. Skills are learned primarily through practice and, if possible, repeated practice in different contexts.

A DEPTH STUDY OF CONCEPTS AND IDEAS

Coverage is the bugaboo of an instructional program for the educationally disadvantaged. Because of the many deficits in content background, in reading and language of these students, their power to absorb new content is slow.

A better program for such students is one which emphasizes a number of important concepts and ideas and which judiciously limits the coverage of detail in order to provide time for depth study of these ideas and concepts. If the program is to be productive of learning, these ideas should be both significant generally and capable of being made important to these students. This approach amounts to emphasizing fewer aspects of durable knowledge on behalf of a wider coverage. A clearer understanding of an idea can emerge from studying a few instances in depth than it can from covering many lightly. This way of organizing content and learning experiences should be especially suitable to students with a host of learning difficulties.

Further, this concentration on durable knowledge, accompanied by a reduction in coverage, permits instruction to be focused on meeting the important intellectual and social needs of students and gives greater freedom to use content and materials that are appropriate to these needs.

Understanding of complete ideas can be achieved with limited coverage of detail, provided that the concrete instances selected are contrasting examples and provided that these instances are studied in depth. It has been demonstrated that the technique of comparing and contrasting sharpens the perception of ideas and enhances the cognitive functioning of students at the same time (Taba, *et al.,* 1964).

Focusing study on concepts and ideas involves students in complex thinking processes: perceiving relationships, making discriminations, relating concrete illustrations to generalizations, making inferences, and hypothesizing. Many teachers feel that this is an impossible task for students who have academic difficulties. This is far from the truth. The basic problem has been that teachers of the slower learners have offered far too few experiences in concept development on the assumption that these students are incapable of thinking and that much knowledge must be covered before anything resembling conceptualization and generalizing can be attempted.

In order for the depth study of a concept or an idea to be productive, certain requirements have to be met in organizing the instructional plan. First, the central organizing idea or concept of any topic or area of study must be one which can be translated into learning experiences that are within the capacity of the particular group of students. In other words, the ideas and the details necessary for understanding them must be both significant and learnable.

Constructing a psychologically valid sequence of learning experiences is another, and a rather crucial, requirement. Learning experiences need to be organized in a sequential order in which each preceding step develops a basis for the subsequent one, and each subsequent step capitalizes and builds on what preceded. This continuity and sequence are especially important in the development of abstract ideas and concepts and of the skills required for processing information. These are learnings which cannot be acquired instantaneously in one lesson or sometimes even in one unit. H)wever, as long as the interest span remains short, the sequences to d(velop a concept or an idea must also be short. But they should build upon each other so that the depth study represents an accumulation of shorter sequences. In other words, it is necessary to plan learning sequences both in terms of short-term and long-term goals.

To discover or to arrive at an abstract concept or an idea requires a sequence of numerous and varied learning activities, through which students systematically examine the various elements from which to compound the concept or the idea. The learning activities must start with concrete instances with which the students are already familiar or which are related in some way to their experience or to the experience of people they know. For example, if the idea to be learned were that "germs have a significant effect in the history of man," students might first describe what they know about germs, diseases, and protection against germs. As they listen to each other, they gain a rudimentary perspective from the exchange of their differing experiences. Next they can read and discuss accounts in books and newspapers about water pollution today, learn about health regulations in large cities, interview someone from the city board of health, read biographies of scientists like Pasteur, see movies of people suffering from disease in tropical and populous nations as well as in our own country, read about the bubonic plague, yellow fever, malaria, etc. If all this is related to the focusing idea of controlling the work of germs, these varied activities do not simply build up aggregates of information, but represent a process of examining the central idea from several perspectives and of building insight into the basic concept.

It takes time to pile up these varied experiences, which many teachers often consider a waste of time. However, if each learning experience is designed to contribute to multiple types of learning, this time is well used. For example, a sequence of activities may develop a series of skills these students need to master, provide many new insights, create new models of thinking, and even help them learn how to work together. This means, of course, that each learning activity has a specified and identifiable target or targets and that the teacher knows precisely what students are supposed to learn from it. It means, further, that the use of these skills and processes is built into the sequence so that they are natural parts of the activity in the sense that they are needed to carry it on. Developing a booklet on aspirations (see pp. 116–118) is an example of such natural requirement for a massive effort at writing, spelling, reading, and listening, all activities not normally enjoyed by these students, but in this case performed cheerfully, conscientiously, and even eagerly.

PROVIDING FOR HETEROGENEITY

The learning experiences or activities must also allow for and even capitalize upon heterogeneity of ability, skill, and background of knowledge. Perhaps the greatest stumbling block to learning in the traditional scheme of instruction is the lack of individualization of learning: the imposition of standardized expectations regarding performance, the uniformity of materials and of pacing. Planning for heterogeneity implies more than individualizing the rate of covering a given topic. It requires provision of varied activities related to the same topic, such as self-selection of diverse books to be read to find answers to common questions, and opportunity for different students to find their own way into new content and ideas. Primarily, though, it involves an organization of instruction around ideas and concepts large enough to permit an open-ended and varied approach (Elkins, 1963) so that each individual can respond to the task in terms of his particular concern and according to his level of perception, performance, and skill.

If each learning task is open-ended in the sense that it not only permits but encourages responses and contributions that differ in depth and sophistication, in actual content, and in ways of thinking, true flexibility and individualization of instruction can become a reality—and an exciting reality at that. For example, topics and study questions can be developed so that there is no *one* right answer but many ways of answering. There is no one right answer if students are to identify the purposes that walls serve, or to examine the consequences of conflicts in the family.

Part of the strategy of providing for heterogeneity is the use of a greater range of materials and of means of learning, such as stories, pictures, films, and tape recordings to supplement or even to supplant the textbooks, and of observation, manipulation, and experimentation to extend the means of learning beyond reading. The teacher needs to assemble a variety of such material, and much of it will have to be produced by teachers. Some can gradually be produced by students and then used by subsequent classes. Fortunately, the textbook stranglehold is being broken, and a greater variety of study materials from short selections of raw data to maps and pictures are becoming available. Somehow, the idea is spreading that an exclusive diet of similar, uniformly phrased, and predigested study materials is not the most adequate way of nourishing productive learning.

PACING OF LEARNING

Just as the content of instruction moves from topic to topic, so it should also move from one cognitive skill to another. Both movements need to have an appropriate psychological sequence, and the movement of both must be in accordance with the readiness of students and the level of difficulty. The teacher needs to know whether the students can handle the new concepts and the processes required by the new task.

Of special importance to students with learning difficulties is the adjustment of pacing to their performance level. While the sequential steps in learning sequences must be incremental in the sense that each step requires performance on a higher level than the preceding one, the crucial problem is to determine how long a group must remain on one level of performance before a transition is made to a more demanding level. However, the successive learning tasks must be "bite-size," namely, they must require a performance that students can manage on their own, challenging enough to require them to improve, but not so difficult as to ask more than they are capable of at that time. For groups with meager skills, this programming of bite-size steps which are at once appropriate to the task and to a given group of students requires of teachers a great deal of awareness and judgment. Each learning step must match the powers of the students. When the task is too complex for them to master on their own, not only do they lack a feeling of success, but learning tends to be less autonomous and effective. To calculate what is bite-size for a given group and to break the learning tasks down accordingly, it is necessary to take into account not just content facts, but also the difficulty of the concepts that organize these facts and the intellectual processes with which to process the data. Decisions must therefore be made regarding the time needed to master the content, concepts and cognitive processes before transition can be made to the next and more demanding steps. This is conceivably the problem of pacing (see Taba & Hills, 1965).

Furthermore, it is important to keep in mind the fact that each new learning technique requires many new skills that must be mastered before they can be used under circumstances in which formerly the weakness of skill prevented the learning of the information or the ideas. For example, working in committees saves time and allows comparing and contrasting a greater variety of data and of interpretations, but poor skills of organizing committee work may produce less learning than does reading a common text (see Chapter XI, "The People of America," pp. 206–240). Transition from reading a single text to the use of multiple materials requires selective reading, interpretation, and note-taking. These represent new ways of assembling and organizing information as well as new ways of thinking. Students need help and time to acquire these new modes of learning. The pacing of learning experiences, therefore, requires a consideration of a whole range of "prerequisites" beyond those of content alone.

CREATING APPROPRIATE MOTIVATING DEVICES

As was indicated in Chapter I, the motivational patterns of culturally disadvantaged students differ markedly from those of other students. A middle-class child responds to rewards such as grades and report cards because his family regards good grades as a value and he knows that they constitute a passport to success in entering college and.finding a job. Often the teacher has only to say, "If you hand in a sloppy paper once more, I'll take five points off your final mark" to get results. Such devices are ineffective with the disadvantaged youth. A substantial number of them greet such a statement with a stony stare and a shrug of the shoulders. What difference does it make anyway? No one at home considers grades as a value, and in many homes there is no one who cares about school work. When parents talk about what they hope the school can do, they rarely mention "marks." Reward is a stranger to these students, for whom even a simple thing like having someone pay them a compliment is an unusual experience.

Punishment as an incentive for doing what the school demands is equally inappropriate. Students are inured and indifferent to such acts as being "kicked out" of the room for inattention, being sent to the detention room, being "yelled at." These punishments may be less unpleasant to them than what they are escaping from in the classroom.

Too many students have already acquired a negative or an indifferent orientation toward learning by the time they reach the upper elementary grades and junior high schools. Therefore, motivating devices are needed (1) to break this orientation and to engage the students in the learning process, and (2) to keep them learning once the process has been started.

To engage students with an already weakened or nonexistent drive for learning, the use of experiences with strong emotional impact is an almost essential device. The chapters on learning sequences which follow illustrate several ways of making an impact on feelings in order to mobilize attention, motivation, and energy for learning.

One example of the use of dramatic literary description to arouse feelings and command attention was the Triangle Fire incident (Chapter VIII). The initial motivating force was not curiosity or interest of the students in understanding the situation but the sheer drama of the fire, together with the fact that fire hazards are well known to them.

Another important device is the use of the novel and the unexpected, in place of the usual media, at least for the time being. For example, to immobilize the previously acquired negative attitudes toward books, teachers, and directions, such devices as reading stories to the class instead of having students read them, or better still, recording them on the tape recorder for students to listen to either individually or in groups, are useful. As transitional devices to break established responses, such reversals of the usual and the use of the unexpected are quite successful.

Whatever the nature of these initiatory experiences, their content must have a close bearing on, or connection with, the experiences and concerns of the students if these experiences are to evoke a response from them. For example, discussing school walls as a way of introducing the study of blocks to communication and understanding "catches attention" because a school wall as a way of enclosing one "in the prison" is and has been irritating. To these students, aspirations as a topic has no meaning or interest, but a study of ads for jobs—a good beginning—hits a lively concern. The same is true of topics like peer relations and family problems. They permit the instructor to capitalize on existing interests and prevailing concerns and thus to mobilize motivation to consider the more relevant, but for the time being less interesting, aspects of human relations.

For a continued energizing of learning, other devices are needed. Knowledge of the characteristics of lower-class students who are educationally and culturally deprived suggests certain necessary features for these devices. For example, tangibility, concreteness, and overt activity are necessary ingredients of the learning experiences if curiosity is to be kept alive and the habit of short attention span is to be overcome. The learning experiences also need to include overt activities, which in themselves are either intriguing or rewarding to students. Writing in order to develop a booklet is such an activity, because being authors of a book is considered an accomplishment, the requirements for developing the ideas that go into it and the making of it set the pace, and because peers will read what they have to say. Introduction to drawing to scale through measuring their own apartments to determine where the walls are and discussing the function of these walls are another. Analysis of story incidents or of the conflicts in the family can be effected by creating plays to be performed in class, because dramatizing is an activity that these students can take part in—and will take part in over and over again. Motivation and the driving power are inherent in the overt activity. Eagerness to carry on the activity helps the student to perform the other difficult and "not yet enjoyable" tasks of writing a script, perfecting the mechanics of writing, correcting the spelling, using the dictionary and, of course, attending to something a sufficient length of time—all tasks that these students are poor at and loath to perform.

Finally, learning experiences must allow success to be experienced fairly immediately. This suggests that long-term sequences must be broken into smaller units which can be punctuated with some tangible, rewarding product or outcome, and which are selected so as to contain the possibility or even the certainty of success.

All this is not to suggest that the possibility of eventually capturing the intrinsic motivation is to be overlooked. Even the more retarded, deprived students have a potentiality for curiosity in learning per se. They *do* want to know something, to feel masters of some processes. They *can* be intrigued with performing such intellectual processes as discovering the causes and consequences of events, of putting facts together and making inferences from them. The problem is how to get them started so that they can experience the pleasure of performing these processes. The devices described above must be seen as transitional measures. Eventually the motivation of the students must spring from the task itself, and from the satisfaction that comes from being able to manage, to perform, to cope with, and to master things which hitherto had defeated them.

THE USE OF LITERATURE

The chapters that follow make a great deal of using literature (novels, stories, etc.) as starting points and often as means of learning almost everything else: to introduce new ideas, to provide material for analysis, to develop new concepts, etc.

Literature can serve many purposes in the education of the culturally deprived. First, it is a means of sensitivity training, a way of extending their limited experience with human behavior and the problems of human relations. Cultural isolation and alienation are the chief facts of life of the culturally disadvantaged. Each individual grows up in a cultural shell because his immediate socializing group, the group in which he grows up, is culturally unique and hemmed in. The avenues to the mainstreams of culture are usually further closed by segregation of residence areas, by a marginal existence, and by social isolation. Experiences in such hemmed-in cultural climates tend to cultivate ethnocentricity, in the sense of a tendency to interpret all behavior, values, and motivations in terms of the limitations of these settings, to develop a limited self-concept and either a defeatist or aggressive-hostile orientation toward the future. The fact that the socializing power of the families in urban slums particularly is diminished aggravates the problem of transmission of values, mores, habits, and behaviors that are essential to the development of mature, intelligent, responsible, and self-sufficient human beings and citizens.

These limitations impose on schools a special task of acculturation, of filling in the gaps left by defects in family life and the neighborhood. The use of literature is one means of filling this gap. Fiction is a potent source for extending experience, for internalizing values, for creating identification with people and problems unlike one's own. Because of the content of their lives, their difficulties in communication, and the general tendency toward a weak control of impulses, these students also need nonthreatening occasions that develop in them insight into the behavior of other human beings as well as their own. Reading and discussing stories that are relevant to their life problems also give them a perspective on their own feelings, help them see the universality of emotions and something of their causes and consequences. Literature also helps them identify with other human beings. In other words, literature takes a student out of his own limited and confined existence and helps him to become acquainted with the larger world. The chief contribution of literature, however, lies in its use as a motivating device to focus attention, and as a way of engaging students in the study of an idea, a problem, or a topic.

Emotional content—if it *can* be divorced from the intellectual—is of great import in the lives of all youth and especially of youth whose cognitive development is retarded. For such students especially, material that speaks to feelings provides the initial impetus to learning other things, such as skills. Reading stories that fascinate them motivates these students to want to learn how to read for themselves. The very act of reading brings the teacher and students, as well as the peers, together emotionally. The story provides a shared experience and evokes common emotions and, if discussion follows it, intensifies the shared experience.

Literature also offers these students a handle with which to open doors to bygone eras and faraway places. As was suggested in Chapter I, the concepts of space and time are conspicuously absent from their cognitive framework, as can be seen in the discussion of the Triangle Fire (Chapter VIII). These students have few criteria for determining when things happened or where. It is not easy to build these concepts by tackling them as concepts per se, but experience suggests that it takes a significantly shorter time to do it by using literature in conjunction with social studies.

For example, students gain a sense of and a "feel for" the ways of making decisions, clues about wages and conditions in factories and mines in another era if the teacher reads "with expression" excerpts from such books as *Sister Carrie* (Dreiser, 1960), or "Mother" (Paddy Chayevsky, 1956), or *How Green Was My Valley* (Llewellyn 1940), or *The Valley of Decision* (Davenport, 1942), making a few changes in vocabulary as she reads. Sections from Dickens' *Little Dorrit* and *A Tale of Two Cities,* and stories of Siberia give clues to the ways of life in other, very different, places. After the children have *felt* these differences, the factual material in the social studies text becomes meaningful. In other words, the introduction of an idea, a concept, or an insight through literature before beginning study of the text increases the possibility of understanding, and this also increases the mileage of learning from the text or other expository sources.

To do this, literature for use in the classroom must be selected by criteria other than those usually employed. The stories and novels need to be connected with and reflect the problems and experiences of the students; they should be selected, in addition, on the basis of whether they provide an opportunity to extend the perception of these problems. To be capable of engaging these students emotionally, the content must be mature and engaging, rather than diluted and didactic. Stories, novels, and biographies that meet these criteria are not too easy to find, nor do they always fall into the category of the "best" of literature, though recently the flood of paperbacks has considerably increased the available supply of useful materials.

A different technique of handling the stories is indicated also. The "readings" must be appropriate to the skills and perceptions of the students. For example, students who cannot read well enough on their own must be read to. Defective reading skills should not prevent them from hearing fine descriptions, rich language, and good vocabulary.

Discussions calling for response and analysis of the stories are another matter. First, the excerpts chosen will be more useful if they allow each student to respond on his own terms, with whatever sensitivity he can bring to it, and in terms of whatever meaning the story has for him. It must be remembered that among the so-called culturally deprived students there is as great a range of levels of perception and sensitivity as there is in any other class. The methods of discussion need to accommodate this heterogeneity by using a technique of open-ended questioning which permits each student to contribute his particular perception or his particular interpretation.

Naturally the quantity and the quality of responses to a story differ according to what experience an individual brings to it. In the eighth-grade class Don had a lot to say whenever the subject turned to a comparison of the roles of men and women or relations with younger siblings. Amy, the strongest objective generalizer in the class, indulged in quite a few self-references when stories touched on interpersonal relations or psychological consequences of being left out. Amy was also an inner-oriented child. Principles mattered to her. Sturdily she defended and applied moral principles, no matter how unpopular her position was. While tending to be judgmental and even compulsive, she was also objective, systematic, and rational in spelling out the reasons for her position. This is illustrated by her reaction to the story "The High Hill" (Deasy, 1948). While others responded selectively, she went systematically down the list of characters and appraised each one:

> I thought the story was beautiful. I think what the teacher in it wanted was to have Elvie have friends and that they accepted her just like she was, but did not worship her because she was daring. The kids did not like her until they thought she had dared to steal the ring. I think Margot was just spiteful and jealous because Elvie had gained Sisley as a friend in the story, and she thought Sisley just liked her because she thought Elvie was daring. When Margot found out Elvie was not daring, she thought that Sisley didn't like her [Elvie] any more and didn't respect her, but Margot was proved wrong by Sisley's act in the end.
>
> It proved that Sisley didn't like her for her daring, but I think she liked her because Elvie showed a fondness for her. When Elvie gave her the valentine and the way she kept staring at her, you could tell she wanted her for a friend. I think Elvie thought the only way she could get her as a friend was to show that she dared to steal the ring, but found out at the end that that wasn't the reason Sisley liked her. Miss Janiek thought only of herself and didn't think of the people of the future, who were these children. Miss Farrell tried to do what you're doing now; to teach not only what's expected of you but try to teach us brotherhood and understanding, so we'll be better people when we grow up. Miss Janiek said something (I forgot the statement she made) that proved she didn't think of these pupils in the future [Taba, 1955].

It is essential to follow the reading of stories with discussion. For one thing, discussion sharpens the insights gained by individuals. Pooling the different perceptions and sharing differences of opinion and feelings extends everyone's perceptions of the issues and problems presented in the story. Further, for many students it provides their first real opportunity to learn that it is all right to disagree because reactions to literature are legitimately unique and individual. These discussions also permit the raising and airing of issues, which could become subject for further study.

For all this to happen, especially with students used to silent treatment, a teacher must create an informal, nonthreatening, and inviting atmosphere. Asking open-ended questions, questions to which all students can respond in some way, is the chief instrument for creating such an atmosphere. Questions such as the following have been used with some success: "What seems real to you, or unreal? What do you like or don't you like about this story? What makes you feel this way? Which characters in the story do you like the best? and least? What do you hope will happen? What do you wish hadn't happened? What do you think the story is trying to tell you? What would be different about this story if ————— had not done —————? Which character would you like to be? What would you do differently or in the same way?

Often the teacher can simply invite students to decide what they would like to know or have discussed. This procedure gives the teacher an opportunity to see just what it is that the students notice or fail to notice about a story, or what puzzles them. Such open-endedness invites the students to express their opinions. Since there are no right or wrong answers, listening to the responses of his peers may lead a student to discover that not everyone feels the same way about the same things. He may become aware that he has more "authority" for his beliefs, can give sharper "proof," etc. Since the teacher does not force him to change his views, he is free to change them when he is ready. This process also encourages students to ask questions both of the teacher and of their classmates and eliminates the predicament of teachers who feel that it is their job to teach, but who don't actually expect students to have the answers. By following this procedure the teacher in effect is saying: "What you need or want to know is the crucial thing." The realization of this intent of the teacher rarely fails to produce an air of eagerness and anticipation of the next story even on the part of the most reluctant learner.

These remarks should not be construed to mean that teachers need give no guidance to the discussion. They do need to help students "move" in their thinking, to verbalize some of the problems for future study, and to help them plan the next steps. Sometimes they may actually need to list on the board the questions that emerge from statements made by the students either because they require further emphasis or need re-examination.

Always there is the task of seeking extension and explanation of ideas expressed. Queries and remarks such as "What makes you think that?" "May we have some more comments about this idea?" "May we have some more ideas on this point?" need to be used repeatedly. A perennial role of the teacher is to keep track of the strengths, inadequacies, and misconceptions and to jot them down for future reference.

In discussions of this sort, the strategy is to accept all ideas and comments even if they seem irrelevant, because at this stage evaluation tends to stifle further contributions, though students *will* challenge irrelevant or incorrect statements. If these challenges are premature or fall on students who are not yet ready to cope with them, the chief role of the teacher is that of a mild mediator: "Can we jot that issue down for treatment later? We'll have a few more minutes to give it then." As these postponed issues pile up, each is detached from its author and this relieves him of the "burden of proof," of defending his statement if he is not ready emotionally to do so.

After having extracted the essence of the students' ideas during the open-ended phase of the session, the teacher helps the discussion to move to more precise analysis. This means developing a systematic sequence of questions addressed to the points that require analysis. For example, one teacher planned to focus the questions on what individuals can do or say to build bridges for peace. The incident used to launch this discussion was from *Caddie Woodlawn* (Brink, 1963), in which the father helps Caddie understand why the mother had punished her. After the initial open-ended reactions, the teacher helped the students pursue ideas with questions that followed an inductive order of learning difficulty: "What did Caddie do that brought punishment?" "What was the punishment?" "Why did her mother punish her and let the boys go?" "How did Caddie feel?" "How do you know?" "Do you think the punishment was fair?" "What did the father do?" "Why did he do it that way?" "How do you think Caddie felt?" "How do you think the father felt?" "In what way did he change things?" "What seems real in this story?" "What would you do if you were Caddie? Father? Mother?"

In this question sequence the *what* questions come first. The *whys* and *hows* follow because they are more difficult and require an understanding of what happens first, what follows second, and why the order of events cannot be changed. Feelings are even more difficult to analyze and verbalize and, therefore, come later in the sequence. What is real or unreal is less difficult to deal with than is putting oneself in Father's, Mother's, or Caddie's place. The question, "In what way did he change things?" pinpoints the basic issue of what people can do and say to build bridges to peace. Students could not deal with this issue or its relationship to the idea of bridges without answering the preceding questions.

A still more controlled movement of analysis is represented in the following question sequence. This sequence carries the discussion from descriptive response through analysis of causes of behavior and of feelings to appraisal, as follows:

1. Opener: What does this story show – tell – suggest?
2. Some explanation to induce analysis of behavior: "Why do [people in the story] behave as they do," or "Why do you think these incidents or events occurred?"
3. Exploration of the feelings: "How do you suppose the [people in in the story] felt?"
4. Induction of identification to clarify the central meaning of the story, and to diagnose level of perception and of transfer: "Has anything similar ever happened to you?" Answers to this question allow the teacher to diagnose the points at which students connect with the story, what level of abstraction they are capable of, and, consequently, at what level of transfer they can perform.
5. General conclusion regarding the major message of the story, or an appraisal of the situation described, and action application: "What is the main conclusion you would draw?" "How would you change the situation to make it come out better?" or "What would you suggest people in the story might do?"

It is, of course, not easy to control the sequence of discussion, especially with volatile students who have difficulty with abstract thinking to begin with and who are not used to following sequences. The tendency is to focus on any point that strikes a personal chord, disregarding the relevance of the point to the central issue. Further, teachers who are sincerely interested in releasing free and autonomous expression are often in a quandary at first about the extent to which to control the discussion, where to enter it, and at what points to let it go. In general, teachers talk too much. Therefore, when they first adopt free discussions, they tend to say virtually nothing. Neither extreme is helpful.

Control of the discussion sequence is an important factor in structuring the development of ideas so that a cumulative heightening of perception and insight becomes possible. Control of discussion sequences is also necessary to create freedom of expression. A melee of non-sequential remarks creates a chaos: it does not open up avenues of association and it builds in students neither respect for varying opinions nor the disposition to listen and to respond to each other. Finally, to set the stage for an inductive and psychologically appropriate pattern, the teacher has to see to it that many feelings are expressed and many issues raised before a detailed consideration of any single one is undertaken. Such control does not mean holding a tight rein on discussion, and especially not on the content of what is said. Nor does it mean adherence to the "teacher questions, pupil answers" format.

ROTATION OF INTAKE AND EXPRESSION

An additional point might be useful not only in the general conduct of discussion, but also in the planning of learning sequences. That is the role of rather systematically rotating the experiences that require a reorganization of the very concepts with which information is interpreted.

Studies of cognitive development have established the idea that the dynamic of growth in intellectual operations is produced by a systematic rotation of (1) assimilation of intake of new information with (2) demand to synthesize the information and to express it in some way that is different from that in which it was acquired. The principle on which this rotation is based is that whatever the students assimilate, they organize and interpret according to the concepts they have at the time. If these concepts are inadequate, defective, or misleading, the meaning students get from information is also bound to be defective or misleading. Since it is impossible to "give" a student a new concept, it is necessary to use devices that force him to alter, reorganize, or stretch the "filing system" in his head. This is usually done by introducing a discrepant event, a question that raises a new issue or proposes a different angle.

DRAMATIZATION, PLAY-MAKING, AND ROLE-PLAYING

As has been pointed out elsewhere in this book (pp. 107–110), the "play" is a way of creating, identifying, and clarifying conflicting views and feelings. Because the performance of a play means having an audience, pupils will practice endlessly in order to make a good showing. This gives them an incentive to acquire the necessary skills of reading in a fraction of the time it would take in a remedial reading session. They will, for example, practice reading lines with appropriate expression over and over again. The process of trying out plays also requires much discussion before and after each attempt to discover what the central meaning of the story line and of the character is and how to convey this meaning most appropriately.

After the character is established and events discussed, the students can read the lines with far greater insight. Meantime they gain in understanding human behavior.

The same is true of poetry. The students in the first group liked poetry that they could understand, generally ballads and other narrative poetry. These poems can be dramatized and they lend themselves to choral reading, which adds another element of interest. Should the voice be that of a girl? Why? What is there in the poem that makes you feel this way? Should the whole class say *these* lines? Why do you think several voices are necessary? Should the chorus be male voices only? Why? Pupils learn interpretation because they *need* it for their performance. Analysis made in this manner seems meaningful and exciting.

Making up plays from stories is another intriguing and useful device for infusing reading with meaning and purpose, and for practicing skills in writing. One boy created a play for the whole book *Quarterback's Aim* (Lord, 1960), working evenings at home as well as in school. The most interesting chapters of *Squanto and the Pilgrims* (Anderson, 1953) were turned into plays by whole classes working in teams. This play-making and acting produced many types of training. The students had to read and re-read the stories they used in order to decide what to include in the play, and parts had to be copied and rehearsed. They created something of their own, a rare experience for students generally regarded as incapable of anything except routine work. Since everyone in the class had read *Squanto,* the whole class could serve as a critical sounding board for help in interpretation of characters and events in the Squanto plays, for establishing a relationship of the incidents portrayed to whatever idea was being studied at the time. Many occasions were created for critical evaluation because the "play-making" activity was intriguing enough to be repeated over and over again.

Role-playing has similar virtues but serves still other purposes. It creates a situation in which immediate problems can be tackled directly, without putting individuals on the spot. Students can express personal feelings and deal with sensitive personal problems under the guise of representing someone else, of "taking a role." Shy and reticent individuals, who rarely take part in a large group, can find a place in the endeavor of a small group involved in sociodrama. Since role-playing usually focuses on real life situations, the discussions of the scenes provides ample material for analyzing problems, for assessing motives and values, and for discovering the causes of human behavior. As such, these discussions are also a rich source of diagnostic information.

Role-playing is also useful for skill-training. For example, the pitfalls and problems of small-group work can be acted out by having one such group conduct its first meeting in full view of the rest of the class. Their procedures can then be analyzed by having the entire class discuss such aspects as how the decisions were made and who made them. Such skill sessions usually improve the planning of the subsequent group meetings.

Role-playing can be used further as a follow-up to reading of stories, especially if the stories are selected to represent the problems, events, or characters the students know. In such cases the stories are cut off at the climax, and students are asked to supply the endings. This engenders discussions of the logic of the events, motives, and characteristics: "Why would a character behave this way?" "If the events so far move in this direction, the conclusion should be thus and so."

OBSERVING AND INTERVIEWING

For students who find reading a relatively meager source of information because of reading difficulties, observation and interviewing are important additional sources of information. For one thing, for young people who live in a chaotic environment, systematic observation is a means of bringing some order into a seemingly uncontrolled pattern of events. Observation brings to their concious attention some important aspects of the environment which otherwise might escape their attention and thus corrects selective perception and the resulting distortion.

The content of observations also lends itself to scientific treatment and thus affords first lessons in such processes as tallying in order to discover patterns, and comparing and contrasting. For example, tallying ways in which young people, babies, and adults react to certain situations or to people in general and comparing the results bring home the need for considering behavior in terms of developmental sequences and differences according to the maturity of the individuals.

The results of observations thus treated provide the content for class work and help students to see the connection between school and the other aspects of their lives. School work becomes significant to them because it helps make meaning out of the way they function in other areas of their lives: a student can learn to look upon a younger sibling as an object of interest rather than merely as a nuisance or usurper of attention; the activities and emotions of adults take on meaning and may even become tolerable; and he may become intrigued enough to study his own reactions.

Observations of human behavior also enhance the meaning of the stories, plays, and poems he reads, and they help him to interpret the various activities that surround him with more insight. "What is being a bully?" "Why do some people behave this way?" "How do the bully's actions affect those around him?" "Whom does he pick on as a victim?" "Why?" "How do the things they see differ from the story?" "How are they similar?" "Why?" Thus, literature helps one interpret life, and, in turn, daily experiences carefully observed and evaluated help one to interpret literature (see Elkins, 1963).

The interview serves many of the same functions. There are, however, additional reasons for using the interview as a learning technique. It brings young people in direct communication with peers, adults, and younger children. To sit down with an adult and hold a conversation, in which he finds out pertinent facts about his life or what he believes, is an experience few of these students have ever had. To them, adults, by and large, are creatures to avoid. In an interview the student functions in a positive relationship and discovers more often than not that adults are flattered by the attention.

Of course, to have interviews function this way requires careful preparation in school. Methods of asking questions need to be practiced in role-playing sessions. "How do you put the adult at ease?" "How do you give him the background and reasons for your questions?" "How do you thank him?" "What do you say to him?" "Do you merely throw question after question at him?" "How do you take notes?" Young people thus prepared usually return to school with glowing reports about the experience. Things that didn't go well need to be subjected to more role-playing and analysis. The results of interviews can also be used in many ways: they can be written up and tallied and the results used again and again for comparison with literature, newspaper items, and historical events.

ORGANIZING THE CLASS FOR STUDY

Any reasonably broad topic can be studied in a variety of ways. Some matters require the participation of the whole class, such as planning the main issues to tackle, converting an aggregate of information into usable ideas, interpreting new facts, and making generalizations. Other matters can be studied more effectively in smaller groups; for example, several committees may undertake to study a number of ethnic groups in order to marshal a wider array of facts and insights for the final comparing and contrasting of similarities and differences between the groups. Other matters are best studied individually.

Combining ways of learning in this fashion extracts the maximum value from the study and uses both the individual powers and the resources of the group to advantage. Such a marshalling of the ways of working also increases the array of skills any one student can acquire in connection with any one learning activity and avoids the necessity of of individuals repeating the same routine over and over again after it has creased to provide new learning for him. This saving of unnecessary routine work is especially important to students whose absorbing powers are slow and whose time, therefore, must be saved for productive activities rather than being spent on routine ones.

CHAPTER V

The Family of Man: Human Hands

A paradox exists in that disadvantaged children need time to study subjects in depth, and yet their short attention span dictates short sequences. To cope with this problem, it is necessary for teachers to discard any attempt at "covering ground," which would probably be meaningless anyway, and to plan on two levels. One is a long-term plan for a theme or a topic and, within it, a series of short sequences that are the ingredients and vital parts of the larger topic, for which they provide the necessary enrichment and a study in depth.

One such topic for sixth- and seventh-graders in the first group was *The Family of Man.* This area was selected because it was important for the pupils' understanding of self as well as for their understanding of society at large. It included a number of concepts that the teachers thought these students needed to examine, such as that human beings all over the world have the same basic needs and emotions and aim for something that is important to them. Through this topic, it is possible to study with some success the basic physical similarities, as well as the more superficial differences, of people everywhere. It is possible, further, to examine the emotional and spiritual needs and aspirations of people, provided that appropriate approaches and materials are used.

The unit consisted of several smaller sequences. Some of these sequences are described in the chapters that follow. Each sequence was closely related to the others, and each contributed to the larger unit. Not all were taught in all classes. Different teachers chose and developed different sequences. It was necessary to break the unit into smaller sequences because at first the students could concentrate on a single topic only a week or two, depending, of course, on what the teacher did with it.

The sequences of these smaller units and the teaching strategies were planned with special regard for the characteristics of these students. For example, it was necessary to begin with concrete topics that were capable of being broken into short-term sequences closely related to previous experiences of the students and, at the same time, honest instances of the concepts planned for the long-term unit. Unless the teacher begins very concretely and moves gradually to the abstract with enriching activities and content all the way along, what looks like a neat package will end up in tatters.

It is the teacher's task, also, to plan in such a way that each topic is explored for its central value, that the first topic is the most appropriate to students' concerns, and that each topic builds upon the learning derived from the preceding one.

For example, a teacher might choose Human Hands for the first sequence, because she knows that the children are concerned with the physical aspects of human beings, because this topic presents ample opportunity for a number of needed learning experiences, because it lends itself to movement from the concrete to the abstract, and because it helps build the concepts delineated for the unit.

To begin with, one teacher asked the students to trace their own hands on a piece of drawing paper. The beauty of human hands and the similarity of everybody's hands was discussed. Then the students wrote on "Important Things My Hands Can Do." Most of them said that hands play, fight, eat, and give people things. Some suggested that hands are used to shake hands with people, pray, change a baby, turn pages, write, touch people, keep clean. Since many students mentioned specifics which could readily be categorized under *work* or *play,* the teacher put these headings on the board and listed the particulars under each as they were offered, thus giving the pupils an informal initial experience with categorizing information. This was quickly done; each student contributed one item, and the teacher promised that all items would be included in a class tally. A small group of students did the tallying, using the categories worked out in the class. A copy of the tally was distributed the next day to be included in each student's notebook, since each would need it immediately to make comparisons.

The fact that whatever is put into a notebook should be used immediately needs to be stressed. In all too many classes, students spend hours copying from the board such items as *aim, summary,* and even *medial summary,* a deadening procedure. When asked what purpose this serves, the teachers answer that it keeps the students quiet for a few minutes, that the supervisor demands it, that it helps them to remember, or that it is a concrete activity. No wonder that children constantly lose pencils and forget notebooks. Of course, there is nothing wrong with the notebook, only with what goes into it.

The next day, the teacher read a chapter from *Big Doc's Girl* (Medearis, 1942). The reading was followed by a brief discussion of what happened—why the one little girl could not accept punishment by an older sister in charge. Referral to the tally of the uses the members of the class made of their hands followed in order to compare these activities with those in the story and to add to the list a new category itemizing what other people do with their hands that "we" don't do. Other teachers used the original tally for a consideration of the relative importance of each category.

Both activities caused sharp emotional reactions. Some pupils claimed that Sis had the right to spank the children. She was taking over the mother's responsibilities in her absence. As might be expected, the line-up of opinion was related to each pupil's experience. It became clear that these students conceived of punishment as a universal method of bringing up children. In the class that attempted to rank the activities of hands in order of importance, an additional task of differentiation, there was disagreement over whether it was more important to work, pray, or play. At one point, the class came very close to a philosophical discussion about the value of play: What *is* play? Does fun for you mean fun for the next fellow? Eventually the class settled on the idea that most people, but not every person, do all of these things.

Because of the short attention span of the students at the beginning of this work, the discussions at first were quite brief, lasting not over five minutes. Teachers need to learn to break up a discussion at a psychologically appropriate moment and to "fire it up again" later in the day or the next day. One way of doing this is to list the names of the students who still want to express a point of view. Because of the need for immediate gratification, the teacher must build faith in the idea that tomorrow will bring new opportunities. Here again we have a paradox. Children who do not converse at home and who need to do so in school cannot sustain a prolonged discussion. The teacher must keep this fact in mind and gradually increase the length of discussions, while moving slowly from issues centered on the students' life to increasingly impersonal issues.

To extend opportunities to talk, teachers need to learn how to arrange for small-group discussions. Often students who hesitate to express themselves in large groups will learn to verbalize about many issues in small groups. (In a later chapter, pp. 154–156, ways of doing this and yet maintaining adequate discipline will be discussed.)

A "new" kind of homework, at least new for most teachers, was then in order. The class had discussed the role of hands, had written about their own, had gained some perspective from the fictional situation, and begun the preliminary steps of tallying. Now they needed to *look*. Their homework assignment was to observe for one-half hour what adults do with hands and to jot down notes on what they saw. In the classes where the attention span was especially short, the group was divided in two, so that half watched babies and the rest watched adults. In some classes, the interest in observing was high enough to continue with this assignment for three nights: one night each to observe adults, babies, and teenagers. If the students were reluctant to take notes because they feared they would not be able to spell correctly, they were asked to do the best they could, and the teacher promised to help them make corrections in class. In every case, a high percentage of students did their homework. This percentage was substantially higher than the percentage who had performed such traditional assignments as: "Do these 10 examples" or "Write a composition" or "Answer these questions after reading pages 69–72 in your social studies book." In fact, teachers who had initially entertained doubts about the observation assignment were pleasantly surprised. Not only did most students complete the assignment, but sharing of their findings created tremendous excitement.

The procedure in handling the information was as follows: First, the reports from notes were shared and tallied, but this time the students decided on one or two categories, and the teacher supplied the rest because the sharing and tallying had to be brief. Each student then summarized his observations in a paragraph. These paragraphs were then rexographed and bound in the booklets entitled "Hands Do," or "Observation of Hands." The fact that their work was represented in a "publication" and that the work of every single student was included provided strong motivation for correcting. To appear in print their work had to be perfection, and students willingly, even eagerly, corrected their papers four, five, or six times. For those who viewed themselves as unable to write, this was a tremendous achievement. Each student carefully wrote his "story" on the master ditto and signed his name as an author.

Even with the greatest of interest in an activity, the teacher dared not let it drag. Generally, the writing, correcting, and copying on a master ditto took a double period. The results had to be seen by the very next day. Therefore, the teacher ran the dittoes off, and the authors collated the papers.

When the students saw their own productions, they *had* to hear and read the creation of each classmate. Since the decision to read all papers was made by the students themselves, interest in this reading and listening was sustained for a whole period. The students literally took over the class. The teacher merely helped them organize themselves and repeatedly had to assure them that all would have a chance. While the excitement continued, discipline problems were nonexistent. Some teachers saw, perhaps for the first time, the relationship between discipline and the nature of learning activities.

After this, the teacher distributed the tallies, made by a student committee, to be used as a summary in the booklet. Then a table of contents had to be made, because books have tables of contents. This was one point at which the textbooks came in handy. Each child had the same edition, so the teacher and students together could examine the format and decide how their table of contents should be set up. For a student to see his name in the table of contents and to have classmates turn to the designated page when they wanted to re-read his story was an unforgettable experience, a cornerstone upon which to begin to build a self-image. When the students took home their productions and saw the adults responding with amazement, they experienced a new feeling about themselves that lasted even into the next day. Unfortunately, some students found no one at home who was interested. Some did not even try to show it to anyone. When this fact was openly stated, the class decided that the book was good enough to place in the Guidance Office so that parents, who had to "sit and sit and sit and wait," could have "something interesting to read while they waited." There was unanimous agreement with one pupil's suggestion that a copy be given to their church.

In classes where separate observations had been made of adults and adolescents, the findings were fascinating. For example, adults shook their index finger at people but teenagers did not! Mothers and teenage girls cuddled babies, but usually fathers did not. Mothers worked in the house after they got home from work; teenagers played when they arrived home from school.

To help the students to interpret their own findings, such as discovering the relationship between emotions and what hands do, and to gain perspective on their findings, the teacher read a chapter from *Caddie Woodlawn* (Brink, 1963) in which Caddie is punished but the younger boys go "scot-free." In this story, the function of hands must be inferred, so the transition has to be made from the concrete to the abstract. Because the story deals with people with whom the students could identify, it was possible to introduce the beginning of inferential thinking. This transition was, in part, helped by a comparison with *Big Doc's Girl* (Medearis, 1942), read earlier, in which the use of hands is more physical and concrete. For example, the students noticed that hands punished and showed anger; that they pleaded for forgiveness when Sis carried the tray to the culprit's room; that they cried out in loneliness when the child drew a picture of her missing mother over one entire wall of her room.

Not all of the foregoing activities can be scheduled for a single week. In some classes the students could and did engage in most of the activities described and went even further. In other classes, the teacher had to limit the choice to the activities most needed by her students. In one class, a seventh grade with several disturbed students, where the teacher had discontinued the topic for fear of lack of interest, the students continued to raise the issue of good and bad things hands do. This went on for the next two or three weeks with students bringing new observations almost daily. The teacher was forced to select a new topic that could be tied in with the subject of hands.

In a number of classes, the topic of hands was extended to include people outside of the students' own immediate world. The teacher brought in rexographed copies of "help wanted" ads from a city newspaper and pasted them on a sheet of paper which was passed around so that students could see that they were "real." This was necessary because these students had no access to newspapers. Care was taken that the ads were for both men and women and sampled a variety of occupations. The students were asked to examine them in order to decide which jobs needed hands most. The teacher also had included some ads for jobs in which the use of hands was obvious, such as "IBM Keypunch Operator" and "Clerk Typist," and for others where the role of hands was much more subtle. At first, the students selected the one or two most obvious ads and rejected all others. In the brief discussion that followed, however, they began to understand that the floorwalker in a large department store also used his hands on the job, as did a manager of a motel, a buyer for a large retail store, or a radio announcer. In classes that were able to read the ads, there was continued interest in exploring this topic. One or two students in each class discussed the matter with their parents, with the result that a new kind of argument began to take place, especially after the class attempted what amounted to rank-ordering the jobs according to the importance of hands in performing them.

The examination of pictures, to see the role of hands, furnished another way of moving the students outside their immediate environment. In general, teachers had to collect pictures from magazines, such as *Life* and *Look,* because they contained photographs large enough to be seen at some distance. These pictures were examined to see how hands were used for "good" and "bad" purposes. Pictures, such as that of an American soldier in Vietnam holding a small child in one arm and a rifle in the other, became the focus of a short but heated discussion of our roles there and elsewhere in the world, an exchange that ended in an uncomfortable stalemate. One child (a disturbed seventh-grader) summarized the issue by stating that our hands do good things and bad things to other people.

Next, the teacher distributed the magazines and asked the students to look for photographs that illustrated other good and bad things we were doing with people in other parts of the world. The children worked together in pairs, and each pair was to find one positive and one negative role, as they defined them, and to prepare to defend their position. Those who could not read the captions were encouraged to ask for help, and the teacher had to reassure them constantly that she was there to help them. The teacher described this as a "great" lesson because she found that students learned much from each other and that there was no need for her to try to "hold" their attention. While each pair reported briefly, the rest of the class noted on a strip of paper whether they agreed or disagreed with the reasons given. Next day the reports were discussed. The pictures were posted around the room and numbered to match the numbers on the students' strips of paper. One class concluded that few things we did with other people were all good or all bad. Each was somewhere in between—not a bad conclusion for children who "can't think" (grade seven, disturbed)! This discussion provided a transition from talk of what people do to their motivation for doing it. In other classes the same purpose was achieved—although to a lesser degree—by a discussion of the reasons why adults used their forefingers more frequently than any other age groups, or by looking at people's actions and facial expressions in order to formulate hypotheses as to their motives.

Once the students were able to develop low-level abstractions from pictures, they were ready to examine articles in newspapers with "human interest" news and to make inferences about the role of hands, even though the word hands never appeared. In some classes, the teacher had to select and reproduce the articles. Other classes were able to read certain newspapers. At first they selected sensational items, such as "Freak Accident: Man Kills Himself with His Own Car," or "Woman Jumps Out of Window with Baby in Arms." If inference-making is an aim, one must use material at a level at which students can function. Such a beginning is a necessary preliminary to handling materials that require a higher level of abstraction and represent more remote events and ideas. For example, materials might be selected which help students to understand the consequences of floods and forest fires, of war and crime, of earthquakes and hurricanes to millions of people, to grasp the idea that people must help each other "pick up the pieces," or to envision the condition of men when power rests in the possession of a few who exploit the others.

Creating a montage of pictures, and writing about what it means, is another activity students enjoy and one that gives them an opportunity to move from the concrete to the abstract, especially for those with severe reading disability. This activity requires an accumulation of a substantial number of magazines with large colorful pictures. With such a supply of magazines, the children can cut out parts of photographs to illustrate certain points. For example, if a student wishes to show the relationship between happiness as shown in facial expression and the movement of position of hands, he can cut out what he needs and mount it on a background of appropriate color and texture. He can then explain what his montage represents and, therefore, why the pictures—or parts of them— were chosen. As artwork the results may be, and usually were, crude. The explanations, however, often reveal the insights into human beings that students have, and offer the teacher a means of evaluating their values, thoughts, and concerns. One sixth-grade class, labeled "emotionally disturbed," was extremely upset by some productions in which parts of people, such as hands, feet, eyes, lips, were cut out. Other classes had no such reaction.

Some classes were able to proceed to a new dimension: going back into history to examine what had happened in certain historical moments, what people did to make them happen, and how the acts of those people now affect us either positively or negatively. For this purpose, the textbooks were useless. Biographical materials such as the "Childhood of Famous Americans" (Indianapolis: Bobbs-Merrill Co.) series, relatively easy to read, were acceptable because they told about real people and because their format did not place them at the "easy" level. Each pupil was encouraged to select his own book. When five or six finished their reading, they reported informally to the class on the three ideas listed above. Some were even able to compare differences and similarities of events in the books they read. Meanwhile, the other members of the class noted what people did and kept score of other related events in the books they had read. These notes served as progress reports, although the bulk of their reporting was much less formal, because not all students reported as panels.

Such a sequence requires much preparation. First, the teams of teachers had to select the appropriate historical events. Often it was necessary to compose brief explanations or even stories of the events when such descriptions were not available from printed sources on a level that students could handle. For example, one team used the theme "Common man gains his rights" and included in it a series of events such as the signing of the Magna Carta, the Mayflower Compact, the Declaration of Independence, the Bill of Rights, and the Supreme Court's decision on civil rights. The human hand and mind had worked together to create these documents.

In other classes, teachers omitted the study of historical events, but provided colorful "skinny" paperbacks such as *Eagle Feather* (Bulla, 1952), *Runner for the King* (Bennett, 1944), *Riding the Pony Express* (Bulla, 1948), *White Sails to China* (Bulla, 1955), *Johnny Appleseed* (Moore, 1964), *Wizard of Menlo Park* (Compere, 1964), *The Superlative Horse* (Merrill, 1961), and *Shan's Lucky Knife* (Merrill, 1960).

Reading time was set aside in the regular class periods until students became interested enough to want to take the books home. Each student signed out his own book on the class roster. He was encouraged to return it if he decided that it didn't interest him. Often students have difficulty accepting this new possibility, because they have heard too often that one should finish what one begins.

With students who have tremendous reading problems, this is a necessary procedure, as is the practice of following the reading with informal discussions instead of requiring written book reports. The format of the informal discussions often is quite simple. The teacher might ask, "Who has read far enough in his book to tell us what people are doing?" "How do their hands help others?" "How do they show they are excited?" etc.

Procedures such as those described above seemed to generate a gradual but steady growth in interest, work habits, and ability to conceptualize. Teachers were often surprised at the number of pupils who finished their books in two days, many of them students who had never done this in all of their previous school years. Consequently, at the end of the year teachers felt rewarded for their work and some even declared that the results had been achieved with remarkable speed.

CHAPTER VI

The Family of Man:
Walls in Our Life

This sequence provided an opportunity to examine, in greater depth and in different ramifications, the idea that people all over the world are alike in many basic ways. In this sequence, the focus was on (1) the ways in which all people build walls—concrete, emotional, and symbolic; (2) the universal reasons for these walls; and (3) their consequences, good and bad.

To begin, the teacher showed four pictures of fences—the school fence, fences around houses like the students', farm fences, and a fence in a zoo. This opener was designed to diagnose what the children did or did not understand and to provide a concrete starting point. The focus was on why these walls were built: which walls were there primarily to keep something or someone in and which to keep something or someone out.

At first, the students were unable to see that most walls or fences are used for both purposes, partly because the meaning of "primarily" escaped them. But the differentiation was difficult for them even after the term was defined and was translated into "main" or "chief" reason. For example, when they argued about reasons for walls in the home, most felt that the chief reason was to keep someone out. Only a few perceived that walls also protected the baby by preventing him from creeping away.

To help the students perceive dual and seemingly contradictory purposes of walls, the teacher made a chart to aid them to differentiate the double function of walls and fences and to focus on the main reasons for building walls.

MAIN REASONS FOR BUILDING WALLS AND FENCES

	Reason for "In"	Reason for "Out"
Home		
School		
Farm		
Zoo		

With this device as an aid, a new level of differentiation emerged. The chart helped make it possible for pupils to perceive the "side" reasons, but they still insisted that the primary one was to *shut someone out*. (Later, compositions on fears led the teachers to see that their arguments were reasonable.) A new column entitled "Other Reasons" was added to protect the feelings of those who advocated this position, as well as to help everyone to see again that most things are not merely black or white, and that reasons for human behavior are more complex. This illustrates how, in planning such sequences, teachers need to consider not only the content of what they are dealing with, but also the processes and the levels of conceptualization involved and the feelings attached to the content. In other words, planning for multiple goals, and therefore along multiple tracks, is indicated.

Analysis of the purposes of the school fence caused a minor upheaval, but created new and intense motivation for the steps that followed. Schools in cities usually have high fences; this one did. The students brought out that the school fences are there to keep people out who don't belong there, which was verified by the fact that over the main entry door was a plaque reading, "All visitors must obtain a pass and explain their mission." They also knew that in several schools, parent aides at the main entrances required visitors to sign in before going to the general office. Their purpose is to protect children and teachers. The fence also keeps students in and prevents them from leaving. Some students were unwilling to recognize this fact, arguing that they could leave by the other door, although they could not enter that way.

Since the argument ended almost in a draw, the students were asked to write a paragraph or two to explain their individual points of view and to give their reasons for holding them. Those who defended the position that school fences were to keep people in described how, on more than one occasion, they had managed to "get out of the prison" or gave details about how and why they thought others accomplished the same thing. In the process they also described their feelings about the school:

> (BOY, GRADE 6, SLOW ACADEMIC): They send letters home
> . . . Mah mother, she got to come to school . . . we get
> letters all the time. Every day he [Assistant Administrator]
> send some kids letters. [This child's mother *wanted* the
> fence to keep her out. She was weary of being called to
> school.]

> (BOY, GRADE 6, AVERAGE): Our science teacher. Every day he
> writes on the board. Every day—take your textbook. He
> don't care how thick it is. We'd have to write the whole
> book down. It would take a month. We write every day.
> Every day. [This child offered this as an explanation of
> why he felt "fenced in."]

> (GIRL, GRADE 6, SLOW): I forgot my book and the teacher
> get mad. I haven't been going to the liberry lately because
> somone stole my liberry card . . . I don't want to join the
> liberry any more because it's too much fuss. And if you lose
> anything you have to pay for it and all that. So I figure
> I stay out of the liberry. But I buy books. I buy Abraham
> Lincoln, books about George Washington, and you know
> dictionaries books I buy 'um. [This child could not write
> and told her "story" on tape.]

Thus, although the analysis of walls began with a tangible object, the school fence, it progressed in the students' papers to reasons why they felt as they did about the school, which revealed the reasons why the school fence was seen primarily as a "prison" device. In this process there was also a transition from considering a tangible object to an analysis of the "intangible" reasons. Next day, by reading some of their papers to the class, the teacher was even able to help them understand that the fence might be only a symbol of how they felt.

A new dimension was introduced by showing several pictures: the Berlin Wall, a dugout in Vietnam, a body of water that serves as a prison wall (Alcatraz) or as a means of isolating lepers (Molokai), and walls that separate one room from another in a home.

The students knew that there was a Berlin Wall and a Vietnam, and that there was trouble connected with both. But they knew nothing else.

Two or three had heard of Alcatraz and knew it was a prison; no one had ever heard of leprosy! A simple explanation of the function of the islands of Alcatraz and Molokai sufficed as answers to, "Where are the walls?" and "Why are they there?" Most students were able to see that a body of water could serve as a wall. This was a new concept and a step in the transition from regarding walls as objects to regarding them as symbols. They had become aware that one thing can stand for another, although the teachers did not use these terms.

It took longer to learn the positive role of walls between rooms of a house. First, the pupils were asked to draw a rough plan of their houses or apartments. They could do this only after the teacher created a model. She drew hers on the chalkboard, labeled each room, assigned a number to each, and told a brief story to describe the functions of, and need for, the walls: Here the baby slept while mother and father entertained in the living room. What might happen if there were no wall separating the two rooms? The students proceeded in like manner, describing what would happen if there were no walls between Rooms No. 1 and No. 2, etc. This assignment helped the students to perceive the positive role walls can play. In this, as well as in other situations, writing and other ways of expressing ideas induced students to examine situations in a manner that prepared them for conceptualization and for generalizing.

In every case there was a purpose for the writing; it was done for reasons the students could accept. Writing was also focused on fairly tangible matters: in this case, on a graphic representation of the layout of their houses or apartments. Such focusing on tangible matters served to hold their attention and provide continuity. It also permitted a continued emphasis on skills. For example, the students were again induced to seek help in spelling and punctuation.

As a homework assignment, the students were asked to find the perimeter of each room in their home. These figures were used to learn how to make drawings to scale. Students also wrote on their drawings what each room was used for: who slept where, who ate where. These explanations were attached to the scale drawings. In one class, this process eventuated in a class booklet entitled, "Why We Need Walls Inside Our Houses." This was placed on the class library table, where it was a favorite book for at least six weeks. When, at the end of that time, the class began to protest that the flimsy cover was not holding up, plans were made for producing a new cover. A committee planned and created a handsomer and sturdier binding. At first, it was suggested that the plans for the binding be submitted to the class as a whole, but, in the end, the committee was given carte blanche to proceed. This decision to delegate responsibility was another "first" in the life of the class—

engaging in group planning, delegating and accepting responsibility, carrying out a commission for the class, the idea that a small group could work as a service to the larger one. Being commissioned to serve the group was exciting to the students and became a status symbol instead of a chore. When the committee presented the newly bound book, there was spontaneous applause in appreciation. This was another milestone in experience, because these students had tended to laugh at each other's efforts, to criticize, and to carp at one another. The teacher had seldom heard one child praise another.

Building an understanding of the Berlin Wall and of the Vietnam dugout was a less successful undertaking. Viewing assigned television programs helped the students learn that far away battles were raging in which our armed forces were fighting "to make people free." But this latter generalization carried no real meaning for these students. Contradictory news announcements confused them hopelessly. Pickets bearing signs saying, "Let's get out of Vietnam," Vietnamese aggression against our "freedom troops," the Presidential decision to send more troops, and the pictures of friendly Vietnamese were beyond the comprehension of these students. The leap to required information and conceptualization was greater than they could span. The teacher decided to abandon the topic and deal solely with the dugout itself and its function as a wall. Since she had had such difficulty with the political issues connected with Vietnam, she decided to turn the process of asking questions about the dugout over to the children. Evidently, this reversal of the usual dominating role of the teacher had a catalyzing effect. The students proceeded to formulate questions far beyond the teacher's expectations. Responses from all groups were of the same general tenor, although the specifics were different. The final conclusion was that dugouts offered only inadequate protection. But the class also began to see that different walls are created for different purposes.

To introduce the Berlin Wall, the teacher brought in back issues of *Life* magazine which showed an attempted escape from East Berlin, a Christmas check-out of persons leaving one side to visit relatives on the other, etc. The students wanted to know, "Who is making it so hard to go through?" "Why?" "Why do 'they' care if people visit relatives?" There was much sensitivity toward, and concern about, separation of family members. The wall now had become a symbol of separation. The students recalled spontaneously a number of incidents of separation and thus came back full circle to applying the newly found insights to their own lives.

To extend the meaning of emotional walls, the teacher read from *The Story of Helen Keller* (Hickock, 1958) the chapter which describes how Helen learns the meaning of "water." This story was so appealing to the students that they sat spellbound throughout the reading. Because interest was high, because identification with the child, Helen, was so apparent, the teacher used this as an occasion to start the development of a sense of sequence. She used the list of events suggested by the students for a task of putting them into chronological order and then as a basis for discussing why the first event *had* to come before the second, etc. Students were asked first what had happened. The teacher listed these events on the chalkboard in the order in which they were mentioned. She then asked the class to help her rearrange the events in the order in which they happened. Then they were given the task of explaining or defending the suggested order. This last step suggested the idea that Helen's inability to communicate was a wall of frustration and tension, an idea which the students sensed at the conclusion of the reading, but which they were unable to grasp or to verbalize adequately. The process of defending the chronological order as they saw it clarified the idea and produced more lucid verbalization.

Of their own accord, the students began relating stories about handicapped siblings, crippled children, retarded children in their neighborhoods, older people who seemed "queer" to them because "they don't talk right." In each case, they found communication difficult and "felt funny about it."

This particular "lesson" took several periods because most teachers not only asked the students to write a chronological order of events but also to write on "What did Helen learn, according to this chapter?" immediately after they heard the story. The reactions showed varied perceptions of what "learning" meant:

(GIRL): She learn how to fold her napkin and ate with a spoon. She went around to everybody plate taking good, good food.

(GIRL): She was learning how to fold her napkin and she was learned how to talk with her hands and she was fighting that lady with her hands.

(BOY): Ann slaped her in the face.

(GIRL): She grab from other people plate. She slap the lady.

(BOY):   hand pinch
hand slap

(BOY):   Hit a girl.
Hit the baby

These six samples, each of which is the complete explanation offered by a student, reveal the struggle involved in individual writing, even with the help offered by the teacher. The samples also suggest that the concern with what hands do continued. Over half of the papers mentioned hands. It was as if this concept was all that the students could be sure of, and therefore had to fall back on, in trying to understand a new situation. These papers also suggested that, when a question was beyond them, they wrote about whatever they were able to write about. Further, the perception of the events in the story was selective. A number of children noted the grabbing of food; almost all recalled that someone hit someone.

These papers suggest the problems involved in teaching children who are emotionally disturbed and whose experience and associations are meager. It is doubly necessary to permit students to build their own bridges from one idea to another, and from one level of cognitive performance to another, by steps which are "bite-size" to them. Whenever the teacher plans without sufficient feedback from the students, she is likely to suggest greater leaps than they are able to master. Inability to answer a question may not always be caused by failure to listen or to follow directions, but rather by an incapacity to understand the concepts or to perform the mental processes required by the question or the task.

At this point one may wonder why the two sequences—the one on hands and this one on walls—are so similar, and whether they are not too repetitive. They are similar insofar as the processes and the structure are concerned. Both start with something very concrete and both ask similar kinds of questions. This structure is repeated partly because teachers without the security of the textbook need the security of a familiar structure for which they can prepare with relative ease. Preparing both new structures and new material is for them a difficult task and one that cannot be faced too frequently.

Another reason is that students, especially educationally deprived students, need much repetition to master new concepts, new ways of handling tasks (especially the cognitive ones that require repetition if they are to be mastered at all), and new ways of thinking about things. If this repetition takes the form of performing the same mental processes and skills in the new context, the learning task is apt to be better motivated and the tasks more adequately mastered.

The development of such sequences is one way of helping teachers begin to see how students function in the absence of textbooks, and of freeing teachers from the bondage of following textbooks which these students never comprehended and which, therefore, frustrated them. (In this situation, the textbooks probably did more to block the students' power to learn than they did to strengthen it.)

This "experience" sequence also helps to develop work habits. These students began to accept the fact that a story would be due soon, that at least one homework assignment would require observation and note-taking, that findings would be tallied. While the assignments were the same, the subject and the objective of their observation were different; they were looking for something new. The experiences in each sequence had to be varied enough to avoid boredom and to assure maximum learning, because these students needed to learn so many things that they had not had a chance to learn.

It must be pointed out that the results described above were not universal. Not all students did all assignments. Most of the students did the observations; fewer took notes. The few who did not complete their observations on the first round were almost certain to do it on the second because they missed out on the excitement of sharing findings and interpretations. Again, not every single student did the required work, but a substantially larger number did than had ever done the more conventional assignments.

In one class, pupils were asked to observe not only how walls between people are built but also how they are broken down. In an "average"[1] seventh-grade class, almost all of the "stories" described the walls as being built by "getting mad" and "hitting":

(GIRL):   Wednesday when I came in from school, I went to the park. When I came in from the park in the night. I was so tired I put my ball on the floor. When I got up Thursday morning my little sister had got my ball off the floor and given it to my big sister. I went and told my mother. She just said, put the ball up. My sister didn't. So I started fighting her over and we kept fighting so my mother said "If I tell you again to put the ball up I'll kill you." So I was mad at my sister all day.

A little bit later my sister came to me with a pack of cookies and said do you want some. I am sorry. I thought that was my ball.

(GIRL):   One day my grandmother came home the house was dirty and she start to yell and telling me to clean up and she got mad and I got mad. So then a little while later she said that she was sorry.

[1] "Average" included a number of disturbed children as well as students with a wide range of abilities.

And my sister she also got mad at me for wearing her blouse. And she was mad for a little while. And then she said that she was sorry for yelling at me so I say sorry to and walked away.

(GIRL):   Last night my mother came home from work, my mother said to my sister why didn't she clean up the house, and to go to the stor. Then my mother and sister was argueing and my mother told my sister to get out of the kitchen. And my sister looked in my mother face and rowed her eyes at her, and my mother turned her face around so fast and slaped her face so hard, her face turn red, and she had turned her face and walked away.

About an hour later at the dinner table my sister had told my mother that she was sorry and she didn't mean what she did. And my mother told my sister that she was sorry too. Now everyone is happy again.

(BOY):   One time my brother kept bothering me and I hit him in his arm then he started crying and my mother heard him crying she asked what's the matter? He said Gerald hit me in the eye and then I said I hit him in the arm not in the eye she believed him and then she hit me and asked me why I hit him I said because he kept brothing me and then she went the room. I hit him and called him a story teller and he [told] my mother and she made me stay in.

(BOY):   When I was in the Basement my sister came inside crying in her nose Bleeding she said a boy name Herb hit her in the nose in Beat her up and he said if I came outside that he Beat it to me to and I came outside in Kick his Butt up in down Kim st. and then I never talked to him from Oct. 1st and to now We made friends yesterday when We Was playing Ball.

(BOY):   When my friend pushed me on the ground.
When I fell and heart my arm and he started laughing.
When I had a fight with my friend and we don't talk to each other.

These papers revealed a great deal about the students. First, almost all of them offered one of two solutions: "Said I'm sorry" or "Gave me something." All involved personal experiences. Only one boy wrote about peer relationships that did not involve himself. No boys described the ways in which walls are torn down. One did give a generalization about how people can do this, but not from his own experience.

This bears out the conclusions reached from an analysis of the papers on "What Makes Me Mad and What I Do about It" from many schools across the country. The solution offered most frequently was to pay back in kind, the second most common was to apologize, the third to withdraw or to reproach oneself, the fourth to talk it over. Very few students in the elementary and junior grades suggested the possibility of analyzing the causes of conflict and projecting ways of eliminating these causes.

These papers also reflected the relationships experienced at home, the kinds of solutions to conflicts and problems that these students had learned, as well as their ability to understand an abtsract "wall."

Data were again tallied, this time by a new committee, and the results were printed on a wall chart for future reference and comparison. During the discussion that followed, the teacher used questions designed to build an awareness of the fact that, just as Helen Keller's problem was one of communication, so was the students'—except that theirs was in a different dimension. To generate this idea, it was necessary to define the ways in which Helen was stymied.

First, Helen couldn't see; people communicate with eyes. How do eyes look when people are sad, mad, or glad? This idea was intriguing. The students suggested that "maybe we can talk about eyes the way we talked about hands." While this was not a new idea to the teacher, she was delighted by the fact that the suggestion came from the students. Her delight, in turn, energized the students into initiating an experiment with moving about while blindfolded.

Second, Helen could not hear. What is communicated through the ears (e.g., Mother's anger through a sharp and high-pitched voice)? What would life be like if we couldn't hear anything at all?

Third, Helen could not speak because she had never heard words. Watch a baby who is just learning to talk and tries to makes sounds such as "wa" for "water," "ba" for "bottle," etc. How does he learn this? Observe the adult who cares for him. What does she do, even unintentionally, in order to teach the baby words? Compare the baby's ability to communicate verbally with that of Helen. How did she learn? Look at the chart on which we tallied types of walls we experienced. How many have to do with speaking: what we say, how we say it?

The study of these questions continued for a considerable period of time. Since teachers were aware that a careful pacing had to be observed if the students were to "stay with it" and learn more or less autonomously, the time devoted to this study varied according to the number of questions tackled at one time as well as the time required to deal with each one. The slower classes focused on only one question at any one time; other classes considered as many as they could handle. In some classes, more elaboration of detail was necessary before generalizing was possible, while other classes proceeded from concrete examples to generalizations more rapidly. A continual examination of what students said and did cued the teachers as to the strategy required.

Through this continuous study of Helen Keller's problems of communication and, later, of the ways in which these problems affected her emotionally, the students began to perceive "walls" as problems of communication. Stories were needed to extend the idea of the universality of human walls and of the needs and emotions that create them. *The Hundred Dresses* (Estes, 1944) met the need for this transition because the main character in the story is a member of an ethnic, rather than a racial, minority. A chapter from *Michael's Victory* (Judson, 1946) showed rejection in a different historical period; "Cemetery Path" (Ross, 1951) dealt with the same problem in the setting of another country. Conflict of interests and a struggle for power were apparent in "Code of the Underworld" (Kielgaard, 1958), the story about a trapper who kills another trapper and is, in turn, killed through his own folly.[2]

In discussing the stories, the procedure described in the sequence on hands was used. The reasons for conflict described in the stories were compared with the reasons for conflicts in the children's own lives as listed earlier on a wall chart.

One first-year teacher's reaction, in an "average" sixth grade, illustrates the enthusiasm with which this work proceeded:

> Their assignment was to observe and write up "Ways People in Our Families Build Walls." I made a play using Albert's composition, and reproduced it so the whole class could have a copy. We discussed how walls are built and broken, and he came up and acted it out. The kids were excited about the idea and asked, "Can I do it? Can I do it?" So I returned all their compositions and they made up plays. Some complained that their compositions "did not make plays." I said it was OK to write another one in that case. When they finished they gave their plays to a neighbor for help with correcting. When they thought there were no more errors, they called on me for a "last inspec

[2] Wherever necessary, teachers changed difficult words and phrases.

tion." Well, it usually wasn't the last. They had to find at least one more neighbor to help again. Well, they still weren't perfect, but they'd corrected their mistakes over and over. So, finally, before they got discouraged, I accepted them and handed them a master ditto on which to re-write their "drama." Then I reproduced these for the next day's work. They made up their own casts and *all* were acted out. There was just no stopping them. They *all* listened to everybody's! I had them for a double period that day and I read them "Double Payment" [Brackett 1958]. They didn't care so much for that, but they always listen when I read. I stopped at an interesting point and they acted out the ending to show what the characters would have to do to break the wall between them. After I read the ending to them, most of them said they liked their own endings better than the real one.

I like this sequence. It's so simple and it took me four days with double periods to get this far. They talk about it. They say, "Oh-oh; they're building walls." It's simple, but they never thought about it before. And it's concrete. It's always with them. They are always aware of fights and tensions, but they don't think in those terms and they don't realize that people can do something about them. When we did the tally about things we do that make walls and what we can do to break them, they really got the idea that walls are temporary, that they *can* be broken. When I yell at them they say, "Oh-oh. Now we are building a wall." It is really very nice. I think it's going very well. The only problem was that they could not find pictures with walls. They found pictures with no walls—people kissing and hugging each other—but not with walls. So they made their own.

An example of one of the plays follows:

Act I, Scene 1

Place: In the living room.

Cast:　RALPH ⎫ brothers
　　　　MARK 　⎭
　　　　TED, RALPH's friend
　　　　MOTHER
　　　　MARIE, sister

MARK:　Ken I play?
RALPH:　No you can't play it's the middle of the game.

MARK: If I don't play nobody going to play. (He picks up the dice.)

RALPH: Better leave us alone, or I'll go tell mom.

TED: Tell him *later*. He can play later.

MARK: Don't fight over *me*.

RALPH: You are nothing to fight over. I'm going across the street. Mom's there. (Leaves and Mark follows.)

Act I, Scene 2

Place: Back in the living room.

RALPH: Mom, Mark keep brothing me.

MOTHER: Mark, you'll stay home.

MARK: He was beating on me all day for nothing.

MOTHER: Ralph, what's all this talk about you hitting Mark?

RALPH: I didn't.

MOTHER: Get to your room and don't come down for the rest of the week.

RALPH: That son of a gun. I am going to Beat his Butt up in down 26 Street. (He goes to his room.)

Act II, Scene 1

Place: In the street.

MARK: What for you hit my sister?

BOY: I got my reasons.

MARK: If you touch my sister again I'll Kick your Butt your Mother's Butt your father's Butt and very Boby else in your family.

Act III, Scene 1

Place: In the kitchen.

MOTHER: Now I mixed some kool aid for tonight so you kids keep away from it.

2 BOYS: O.K.

MARIE: O.K.

Act III, Scene 2

After school.

MARK: Hey, Ralph. You drank up all the kool aid.

RALPH: I was thirsty.

MARK: You heard Momy. If you bother me tonight I will tell
momy you drank it.

Act III, Scene 3

MOTHER: Who drank the kool aid.
MARK: Ralph did.
MOTHER: You did, did you?
RALPH: No I didn't.
MOTHER: Yes you did. No desert for you tonight.

The sequence just described generated many activities in preparation
for the next steps. Students were charged with the responsibility of collect-
ing newspapers and picture magazines. Whenever any one of them found
a few minutes to spare he went to the table and cut out articles and pictures
related to the topic. It is interesting that very few students selected irrelevant or inappropriate pictures or articles. In this sense, the clipping of
magazines was a good evaluation of how much they understood. Those
who could not read well tended to select pictures to put into the collection.
But a few asked classmates to read headlines with them. Pupils signed
their names to each selection they made and were held responsible for
explaining these selections if there was any question about their ap-
propriateness.

Also, in preparation, each student selected a book to read through.
They were allowed to select from among the books used in the Hands
sequence. *Call It Courage* (Sperry, 1964), *Blue Willow* (Gates, 1940),
and *Trolley Car Family* (Clymer, 1947) were among them. These are
attractive paperbacks and sufficiently slim for students to be able to complete them in a reasonable amount of time.

Most of the pictures and articles selected concerned "just people
doing something": war (Vietnam mainly) and riots, racial and otherwise,
here and in other countries. Relatively few cut-outs were found which
illustrated the solutions to the problems that separated people. The few
that were offered included pictures of UN meetings, of a mother comforting
a weeping child, of the President talking on the phone or walking with
diplomats around the White House grounds, two people kissing, and
politicians shaking hands.

Each pupil selected a picture and an article, while the teacher helped
students who had severe reading problems to eliminate over-ambitious
choices they made. Each picture was mounted on a piece of attractive construction paper with space left to attach a piece of writing paper. The
assignment was to write on the following questions: (a) What do you

think is happening in your picture? (b) What makes you think so? (c) How do you think people in the picture feel? (d) Why do you think so?

It is interesting to note that in the classrooms where teachers insisted that stories be written on separate sheets of paper, so that only "polished" copies would be stapled under the picture, the incidence of no writing was high. Evidently, this reflected the rejection of a much repeated and frustrating routine of living up to standards before beginning the task. Where the teacher permitted students to write on paper already attached, all children wrote, even though they knew their creation would have to be detached, re-written, and attached again. The results were so attractive that it was decided to use them for decorations for any one to read when they had time. Within a week almost all children had read all stories! Some were displayed in the room and a few on the bulletin board in the corridor. The latter exhibit was changed every day for a week so that every student's paper could be exhibited. As could be expected, pupils who at first had been satisfied with limited corrections detached their papers and copied them again before permitting them to be displayed in the corridor. In addition, students notified each other of the errors they discovered, which amounted to the "blind leading the blind," as the teachers remarked. Fortunately, not all pupils are blind on precisely the same point. One can spell better than another; a second knows where periods go; a third knows that proper names must be capitalized; and a fourth has discovered a better word for "says." This illustrates the ways in which learning can be extended by initiating an "each one teach one" process.

These articles served also to introduce the world map. Each student was asked to cut out the lead line in an article that illustrated the universality of human walls, to paste the lead line on paper, and to write below why he thought it was important. These papers were then arranged around the map and connected with a string to the appropriate location on the map. These annotated leads, attached to a map, were also exhibited in corridors, which once again prompted voluntary rewriting. This time, the principal commended the students and asked their permission to display the map in his office! The students nodded a beaming and somewhat awestruck consent. When the principal left, there was a flurry of excitement. Was everybody's absolutely correct? Each student chose two people to review his work. Errors which had been previously overlooked were found. In the case of a conflict about who was right, the teacher served as umpire.

This process involves displaying work that contains technical errors. If one assumes that the school is a place where learning goes on, it follows that the pupil, having written and corrected his paper again and again, has learned, even if errors still remain. Short of having the teacher do the final correcting, it is impossible to attain a perfect standard. This standard might destroy the student's willingness to take the initiative in his own learning, and, furthermore, it involves the danger of destroying his self-image. Nor can the student be pushed beyond his endurance. A sample of one student's "first edition" illustrates the point. This child was by no means the poorest writer in the class. In the weeks early in the school year, the poor writers never submitted their few words of writing unless the teacher stood by their desks just before she called for papers to be collected. This child's paper had already landed in the wastepaper basket, crumbled into a ball. The teacher had helped him with the spelling of several words at his request:

> My firend and I was walking in a chaurch hall when he hate [hit] me in my hade we were the only one's there. He sad that he dided hate me in my hade. I new he was lieying to me the time was 1105 when he hit me in my hade around 25 miniutes he tell me the truth.

The important thing is to help students to continue to try to write and, eventually, to *want* to write. By the time they enter junior high school, they have already learned that the more they write, the greater the number of red marks likely on the paper, which involves more work in correcting, even if one does not understand what errors have been made and why they are errors.

The idea of universality of conflict was now extended to include ways in which people elsewhere, outside of their own lives, try to, and often succeed in, tearing down the walls, so that positive communication can be resumed. The comparison of solutions to conflicts in communication was now in order. As they examined the varieties of solutions, the students discovered that those in *Crow Boy* (Yashima, 1955) were different from those in *Bronko* (Eichelberger, 1955), which in turn were different from those in *Quarterback's Aim* (Lord, 1960). If the solutions were not the same, how would they all "work"? A few pupils began to get the idea that no two situations were exactly alike and that, therefore, each required a unique solution.

Some classes were ready to consider walls in history, how they have been dealt with, and what the price has been for unsolved conflict. This sequence again required creation of new materials. Teams of teachers composed stories on the French Revolution and the Russian Revolution of 1917. Books were available on the Civil War, though only a few students could read them without the teacher's help. Each conflict was studied in terms of the following questions: "What happened?" "Why did it happen?" "Between whom were walls built?" "How was the conflict resolved?" "In which cases are people still paying the penalty for an improper solution?"

In one class, illustrated time lines were made to show that conflict and the fight by, and for, the disenfranchised have occurred over a long span of time. This was a revelation to the children who knew only of their own plight, and that imperfectly.

CHAPTER VII

The Family of Man: Aspirations

This third sequence in "The Family of Man" is the longest and consists of several sub-sequences. It illustrates: (1) the ways in which abstractions can be developed from concrete items that do not represent tangible objects or events, and how different types of concreteness are required for groups with different learning gaps; (2) how multiple objectives can be developed simultaneously, e.g., how concepts, skills, and emotional changes can be fostered at the same time; (3) that a given universal need can be studied in a way that simultaneously cultivates objectivity and an insight into the students' own behavior.

These emphases, of course, were also present in the sequences described earlier, but not in the same measure. Furthermore, since teaching is a complex activity, descriptions of teaching strategies are inadequate and apt to cause confusion when illustrated only by single sequence.

Aspirations is a concept which is only partly understood by adolescents. Culturally deprived adolescents in large cities are especially baffled about what they want to or can be. They may want a job and at the same time college training that conflicts with aspiration toward such a job. Their parents may want to have their children "amount to something" without knowing what that "something" might be. Only a few parents who were interviewed could mention a specific goal for their children. Still fewer knew what steps were necessary to achieve a specific occupational goal.

Thus the study of aspirations was important in several ways. These students needed to understand the universality of aspirations, that is, that all people strive for something, but do it in different ways. The study of this topic also provided the teacher a greater opportunity to determine the student's own level of aspiration than had the preceding sequences. Naturally, the ways in which concreteness was used had to differ. Some students could grasp the idea through the simple device of relating aspirations to something in their own experience. For the students in the groups described here, this was not enough. They needed, in addition, something tangible to hold onto while developing their ideas. For this reason the study of aspirations began with examination of advertisements of three common items—a rather elemental way of achieving concreteness.

The teacher brought in three pictorial advertisements which described such items as cars, refrigerators, types of food, pieces of clothing, radios, or television sets. When she asked the students to tell what was similar about them, they had no difficulty identifying the similarities. When she asked which of the three they would buy, they did not all make the same choice. The reasons students gave for their choices furnished the teacher with information about their values, as well as an opportunity to begin to develop the concept that advertisements appeal to certain desires and needs. When the teacher held up three advertisements for automobiles, one captured the majority vote for the following reasons: "They show you the inside." "They put a lady in it to show it's easy to drive." "Rich people have it . . . they house is big, like a palace." "The lady be dressed beautiful." "It says 'jet,' so it go fast." "Pretty color." The explanations for the second choice included more negative remarks, such as: "Looks too cheap." "Not so perty." "Take a small space to park." "Use not so much gas."

These initial exercises helped cultivate discriminating observation. The written responses served to continue the training in writing skills in which the students were so defective. Writing individually first and then pooling the ideas also introduced the notion of learning from listening to each other. Stressing that all of them together knew more than any single one of them, the teacher called on two or three students to add illustrations to her point. This was the beginning of cultivating the awareness of the group as a source of information and of noting the contributions of individuals in it.

After this, the students collected their own ads and selected the item they would most like to own. Each picture was mounted, and each student was asked to write what he would do with that object. It was easier for them to answer this question than "Why do you want it?" The answer to this question provided material to help evolve the idea that all people want something. This task involved several skills, such as evaluating objects and selecting materials appropriate to the task. At this stage, all wanted something of a material nature, ranging from pretty houses to a nurse's uniform selected as a symbol of the profession to which the student aspired. Cars were chosen by the greatest number of students, but bicycles, television sets, sports items, clothes, and food were also favored.

The reasons for these choices covered a wide range too. "If you have a home, you can keep your whole family in it." "I would drive all over the country in my car and go anywhere I want." "With a suit like that anybody can get a girl." "Food is the most important thing of all . . . down South we didn't have to worry because food was not so expensive and there was more." These statements were offered during an ensuing discussion.

The reasons were reproduced in order to provide the material for translating "what we'd do" into generalizations about human needs, while keeping the reasons themselves specific. The teacher helped the class to turn their reasons for wanting the things in advertisements into labels, such as "Wanting the family together," "Seeing the world," and "Wanting to be healthy," because this task was as yet difficult for them to complete alone. This list of labels became the table of contents for a booklet that contained the students' pictures and compositions. A committee completed the table of contents after all had helped to group the pictures under appropriate categories. The "book" was placed on the library table for all to read in their spare time. This activity was the first to consciously emphasize generalizing as a process, and it repeated the opportunity for a small group to work on behalf of the whole class.

Such "introductory" activities give diagnostic information to help the teacher plan more intelligently. They also create motivation. The reaction of a student teacher describes how enthusiasm was generated in a class from which usually little was expected, and how a focus for planning was established for the teacher.

We talked about places where they see advertisements and listed these on the board. They mentioned things like trains, buses and magazines. Then they were asked to note other places where ads can be seen or heard. Next day they had about 20 of them and got very excited because of the difference in the amount of information they now had. It was funny, because I didn't motivate anything very special. I guess it was because it was something they knew. Also, they knew that what they said was acceptable, because I was writing on the board. Everybody's hand was up, even Jim's. Everybody was involved, and you have to remember that Jim is usually out of it. If you begin with something very familiar to them, you CAN involve them relatively easily. And it did something for me. The other day when you asked me where I wanted to go from here, I really wasn't sure.

But once I saw what they knew and the direction in which their minds were working, it gave me a focus for planning. For example, right away I thought of using a tally because they were just enumerating many things. We just looked for similarities in them and because there were rather definite ones, the process went fast and held their interest.

Classes that needed more introductory experiences drew a picture of something they owned and regarded as so precious that they thought others might like to own it, too, and then wrote captions for these pictures. Because they had been asked to be persuasive in these captions, they wrote first about why *they* selected it as their most cherished possession. This composition was used as thinking material for creating a "persuasive advertisement." These pictures were put up around the room, unsigned but numbered. Next day the students were given a strip of paper which they numbered from 1 to 25. On this they voted *yes* or *no* for each item. The "yes's" were counted, indicating the numbers in favor of ownership, and the pictures rearranged in the order of votes they received.

The connection had been made with human needs and wants, and the teacher was ready to let it go at that. But not the class. They wanted to know why individuals had voted either *yes* and *no*. The teacher told them that no more class time was available for this purpose, and, therefore, that they were on their own. There was a burst of anger from the class, but the teacher held her ground. Apparently this "injustice" was discussed in the cafeteria, for Reginald was commissioned to ask the teacher for ten minutes of class time, which was granted. Rolf, "the verbal one," as the teacher once labeled him, walked up to the front of the room and asked, "What do ya wanna do?" That was all. No introduction. No explanation. Not a sound from the class, which was usually quite disorderly. Rolf asked the teacher whether she would take down the suggestions, because "people don't write so fast in this class." She said later that for one split second she was about to suggest a girl who could do it, in order to give her a chance to serve the group. "Luckily, I decided against that, got a piece of paper, and sat down in the capacity of class secretary, awaiting their orders." Within ten minutes the final decision came:

1. Each pupil was to write his reactions to the caption he felt was most persuasive and give it to the composer.

2. If any student received no written reaction, he could ask one or two classmates to react in writing to his choices, giving his reasons for choosing.

3. These reasons, rewritten, were to become the contents of a book

for leisure reading at the library table *if* the author chose to include his picture and the classmates' comments. The teacher said later, "I'd never have dreamed of suggesting another book so soon."

This demonstrates that involvement in a project can advance a number of learnings. It can bring leadership to light and stimulate academic learning. The "abdication" of the teacher at the right psychological moment set the stage for evolving indigenous group leadership and organized action.

The same content can be approached in a manner that retards both involvement and group leadership as well as learning. The following account by a student teacher illustrates how a promising learning experience can fall apart, because the teacher did for students what they should have done themselves.

Well, the whole thing held their interest for about seven minutes and then they began to get restless, so I cut it short.

The preparation I did for the advertisements sequence was much too time-consuming, but maybe it was worth it. I don't know. But they like to see somebody else's preparation. It makes them feel like something's being done. Teachers don't usually do that. The kids say certain teachers don't even want to teach them, don't even try, and don't care whether they learn or not. The preparation makes them feel like something's being done FOR THEM. And they get a good feeling from just seeing that work is in the making.

I tried to get three pictures for each child, so they could put them in rank order. So I cut out about 66 pictures. The day before I had asked them to bring in magazines. And they did bring some. About thirty.

How can this be done with less stress? I don't know. We did talk about committees to bring in magazines and cut out pictures and get them ready for the kids to select and to paste on paper. The children *could* have done the pasting, but I'm not sure about the selecting. They surely could have done the cutting out. They did some of the pasting because I could not finish all of them myself. They just couldn't get three similar products; because they could not get the idea of similarity. And I could have asked them, "What is the same about these three?" I did one set of three. They knew the products and how they are similar. But maybe one set was not enough. And I taught them the meaning of "persuasion," which some already knew. I was surprised. They surprise me. Some days you'd think they were absolutely know-nothings and the next day they'll come back with something that they know. I told them about the three I had cut out, reviewed why they were similar and said that I wanted them to do the same and to decide which of their three they liked the best; that is, which one persuaded them to buy it, which one they would go out and buy. Then, if they could not find the first in a store, which would be second choice, and which they would probably not buy at all. I know now that I should have gone over those steps with them when I discussed my three with them.

This account makes it quite clear that the teacher did not know at which points to give initiative to the students. She failed to create initiative by depriving the students of an opportunity to make their own selections. Nor did she see what constituted the bite-size steps for her group when she assumed that her demonstration of similarity created a concept of similarity. She expected perfect responses to demonstration of similarity by sheer imitation of her.

After the class had received the extra time it requested, the teacher wanted to give them a chance to look at the universal nature of aspirations and to understand how people feel when they cannot fulfill them. To introduce this, the story "The Happiest Man On Earth" (Maltz, 1942) was used. It tells of the desperation of a man who cannot support his family during the great depression; his one aspiration is to find a job.

The teacher read to the climax and then asked the students to write about what they thought would happen and what made them think so. The hypotheses students offered were quite stereotyped, such as: "He's going to get a new pair of shoes and make some money for new clothes and for his family to have some new clothes." "He's gonna take that dangerous job and he's blown up."

When the teacher read the ending of the story, a few students squealed with delight because they had guessed right, and others complained that the author had not told everything. What shocked the teacher most was the number of students who did not understand the language, despite the fact that she had done some careful editing. Therefore she followed up immediately with a story "I Like It Here" (Zuckmayer, 1958) using the same procedure. The students were able to handle this story and to make the transition from what they knew about the wants of people, namely, wanting only material things to more intangible aspirations. To reinforce the idea of intangible aspirations, she read in *Mama's Bank Account* (Forbes, 1943) the chapter about the boarder who moved without paying his rent, but left his books and the knowledge that books can offer. Most students rejected Mama's feeling that he had paid them well. They thought that the boarder had been dishonest and that the police should go after him. They did not, however, reject Mama's ambition for her children.

These two stories set the stage for writing about something non-material that the students wanted more than anything else.

(GIRL):   I want to do better and get my marks higher. That's the thing I want and to be the smartest one. I want to be better in my work and let my teacher, Miss ——————, be very pleased.

(BOY):   I want to go to a new school and I will tear down this school to get (?) it.

(GIRL):   I would like a baby brother. Sisters like to boss you around too much and they think they are big. . . .

(GIRL [a foster child]):   I want to help my sister because she had a baby and she is rooming with a girl from her church. I want to go to work and make enough money. Then I want to give it to her and I want her to get a house of her own. Then I want to make enough money to give to my brother. He did not get anything for his birthday and I felt so mad. . . .

Because many of these papers were marked "private," the teacher merely summarized the contents of all the student's desires so that the group would know "what is important to the people in our class." This was also their first experience with the concept of anonymity.

To extend the idea of aspiration, but also to teach the class to interview, the teacher next asked them to hypothesize about whether or not adults would want pretty much the same things as teenagers do. Then she helped the class to work out an interview questionnaire. Two or three interviews were practiced in a role-playing session. In these the students learned that interview questions can be threatening and that, therefore, they needed to give a full explanation of the purpose of the interview and of what they were learning in school. Meantime, the "audience" took notes which were examined briefly to make sure they included the following three questions:

1. "What do you want that you were never able to have?"
2. "Why do you want this?"
3. "How would things be different if you had this?"

In class, each student wrote up the notes of his interview, which were then summarized and tallied. Both the students and the teacher were surprised that the majority of adults had *not* mentioned material things as the class had assumed. The most common wishes were for "peace and happiness" because "I am tired of the old, unrestful world"; "an education" because "it would be a better life"; "to be a nurse because I would be useful and helpful to people."

At this point it should be noted that the introduction of each new skill—for example, that of interviewing—must be preceded by careful preparation and that other skills such as note-taking require continual practice to be mastered. The same is true of sequences in concept formation. The transition from material wants to nonmaterial wants was worked out step by step so that students could master the distinction.

There was a solemn air about this class session. The group wanted to hear everyone's report. When the teacher questioned whether they should listen to all stories, they assured her that they should because "It's interesting," and "Hearing the stories won't spoil it." (Four students who did not do their assignment interviewed each other about what they thought the adults would say. They were told that they could check their hypotheses later. And they did!)

The students described whom they interviewed, even though they were told that they did not have to identify the person. Most of them wrote about how they initiated the interview. The idea of the human relations involved in such an assignment seemed to intrigue them enough to make them bear the drudgery of the extra writing this involved. It had never occurred to them that the way one approached people made a difference.

> "I interviewed my cousin. First, I went up to him and asked very politely can I ask him a few questions and explained why I was asking him and why I needed the answers. . . ."

A comparatively high level of thinking was apparent when they examined the differences and similarities between the aspirations of adults and their own. "If you look at the adults, they have many more who want education. We didn't think of it too much." "Maybe we didn't say because we have it." "Teenagers and adults both want good jobs, but we say 'lots of money' more times." "Adults want a trip to go back home and see old friends. We want trips just to go away."

One teacher who wanted to carry on the study of aspirations by asking students to select pictures that showed certain social problems, and then by using both the pictures and the captions to write about what those people wanted, was disappointed. The interpretations were far from being profound. As an example, one girl selected a picture of an artist with a caption that included the words, "strikes a contemplative pose beside one of her paintings," regarding which she wrote:

"This ladey she is on a book strike because she didn't do one of her own paintings so she wants her job back."

A boy selected a picture of a national golf champion and said, "He wants to win the gold tuornament."

Another boy used a feature article which was accompanied by a picture of "Uganda's official court strangler" which explained that he has been jobless for 40 years. His comment was: "The picture . . . . is about a man 40 years old who needs a job. This is what most people want me you everybody. But he is 40 without a job."

This was the second time that the students told the same teacher that they "didn't understand the words too good." (The first time was when they heard her read "The Happiest Man.") This induced the teacher to build up more experience with less symbolic content. She planned more work with advertisements. This time she reproduced some "situations wanted" ads to reintroduce the tangible material, this time at a higher level.

By now the students were able to search the newspapers themselves to discover how ads were written. They did this to prepare to write their own advertisements in which they would tell about themselves and why they would be well qualified for the job they wanted. They were asked to select a job that they might genuinely want, and to insure their being serious about it, were promised an opportunity to do "funny stuff" later in the study (folk tales and tall tales).

The work on "situations wanted" was most revealing. There was none of the balking that teachers had experienced earlier when they asked the class to write about "Things I Like About Myself." However, many students could not decide what specific job they wanted, and, when they finally did, they were unable to see anything in themselves that anyone else would want or appreciate. The teacher had to help them individually. She also read a chapter from *Old Con and Patrick* (Sawyer, 1946), a story of a crippled boy, and from *A Tree for Peter* (Seredy, 1941), a story of a desperately poor and lonely boy. She paired the students sociometrically to talk about the jobs and to help each other discover something about himself that others *would* want. This last attempt bore fruit, though it was impossible to determine whether this technique would have succeeded without the preceding two attempts. At any rate, a new appreciation of peer help developed, so much so that the teacher felt that work in pairs could be started for many other activities.

As the teacher moved from desk to desk, she noted some of the attempts at specific support. "You'll be a good nurse because you are patient, very patient, and little children like you." "I'll come to you to do my hair when you're a beautician. You like to fuss with hair and you like to talk so they won't be bored. You'll get good tips 'cause you'll talk nice."

She was delighted with the way students worked together and supported each other and rated this experience in the top 10 per cent of the ego-building activities. At last the students were getting help and support from each other instead of depending exclusively on her.

That the writing of advertisements had a psychological significance to students was illustrated by one boy who had no father and whose mother bore a different name. He wanted a job making nameplates for desks such as he had seen in administrators' offices. Asked why, he replied that he had to think about it. He did, partly on paper:

"You are a person and you have a name it is important.
You have a name. For a person must have a name it is not important what it is. For it is you that is import. . . ."

A brochure including every student's "Situation Wanted" advertisement was made, and copies posted in all administrative offices "in case they can use anyone now." One student's advertisement stood out:

Woman wants to be a baby's mother. Likes babies. Will clean up the baby. Will be sure to.

Next, each student selected a classmate—other than the one who had helped him—to be an employer and to answer his "ad." This required writing a business letter and role-playing the business interview. The teacher secured envelopes, most of the students brought stamps, and the letters were actually mailed to home addresses of the "prospective employers." No addressee was permitted to see his letter before he received it in the mail. Since most of these students had never posted or received a letter, the arrival of a letter created much excitement and wonderment at home. There was something about receiving a real letter addressed to "Miss" or "Mr." that added a grain of respect for a growing son, daughter, granddaughter, or brother.

The "employer" and "employee" pairs were given two minutes to "plot" their role-playing scene and then the show was on. As usual, the class wanted to hear all interviews. This was possible if no discussions followed the playing of the scenes. Where time was short, the interviews were taped so that others could listen to them in the library section of the room during their spare time. In one class the children took it upon themselves to reproduce all skits so that all could read them before discussing them. Whichever procedure was used, most classes and teachers felt the need to discuss the scenes. The discussions were brief and concentrated on the evaluation of the behavior and knowledge of the employee, as well as of the employer. The boys especially had no intentions of working for a boss that gave *you* "lip."

Other classes planned and executed a "TV commercial-type" advertisement. These skits were produced after watching and carefully analyzing both their favorite television commercials and their own "talents." "What was in the ad?" "What is in me?" Almost always they selected an advertisement to which they themselves had responded. Ads ranged from cigarettes to washing soda to food. Because of the "What's in me?" element which could hit sensitive spots, simple puppets were made to enact the commercials so that the students did not need to identify themselves.

Meantime, in all classes the reading routines described in the sequences on Hands and Walls were continued. Each child read a book on his level of interest and ability. *The Big Wave* (Buck, 1947), *Runner for the King* (Bennett, 1944), *Secret of the Andes* (Clark, 1952), *Crow Boy* (Yashima, 1955), *Sensible Kate* (Gates, 1943), and some biographies were the favorites. Because by this time several students had read each book, the informal book-reporting sessions became more critical. For example, the third student to read *The Big Wave* (Buck, 1947) did not believe that aspirations were central to the story. The ensuing altercation led the teacher to ask two more students to read the book and to join the other three in a panel to enlighten the class on the pros and cons of this issue. The discussions also became more abstract, because the books selected for this sequence were set in another country or era and selected for value in extending the perspective on the universality of the problem of aspirations.

The questions for analysis were also more numerous, complex, and abstract. "What aspirations [the students knew the word by now] does each character have?" "How do you know?" "What is said or done that gives you this idea?" "How do people feel when their ambitions can't be achieved?" "What do they do to try to achieve them?" A good portion of the class was able to respond to them. Because the books were written on a level that coincided with the class's ability and interest, the students were free to do some serious thinking about what they read. The findings from books also were continuously compared with the list of their aspirations they had made earlier.

In most cases, a study of newspapers followed. Headlines were examined to determine whether or not they implied aspirations, and the articles bearing them classified and piled under a large label. For example, upheavals in Africa were classified as "People Want to Be Free." So were the riots in the South, although some students argued that the aspirations in the South were focused on being "equal." An article about a blind man was "catalogued" under "Wants to Make a Living"; a UN decision under "Want Peace"; the President's foreign aid speech under "Help Others Have a Good Life."

The historical aspect of aspirations was not neglected. The discussions covered the aspirations of the Russian serfs in the Revolution of 1917; of the people who made their way west during the Gold Rush in our country; of the peoples who came to America in the periods of great immigration waves; of the workers who flooded the cities in the era of industrialization; and of men like Roger Williams, Simón Bolívar, Gandhi, and Socrates.

The teachers agreed that this was a fruitful way to help the class learn to categorize: the procedure was concrete and all the students "caught" the idea. Searching for the articles and piling and labeling them all worked together to sustain the process and to make categorizing meaningful. Since each student wrote his name on his article, it was possible to question him regarding his reasons for choosing it. This provided fuel for some of the most exciting discussions, many of which were concluded with "It would go in both piles" (multiple grouping).

The discussions of the reasons for classifying an article in a certain way were also more sharply focused because discussions were permitted only if the article chosen for class analysis had a bearing on the subject of aspirations. The way one approached a classmate in questioning him was crucial. Role-playing of this approach was again necessary. In groups where children tend to flare up and to take offense easily, it is necessary to learn the controlling skills before using the technique.

For the first time a "textbook" suitable to the children's needs became available: *Squanto and the Pilgrims* (Anderson, 1949). This story was read and re-read for many purposes. It is a story of a young Indian boy and of his difficulties in becoming a "brave" in his tribe. It was thoroughly enjoyed by girls as well as boys because it moves quickly. This description by a first-year teacher of the reaction in her class conveys the impact of this book on students who had never read a book through and who generally detested reading.

> In the better class, I let them draw any scene from *Squanto* they wanted. The potential for role playing is there, beautiful role-playing . . . Holbrook *steals* the book out of my closet; he's *got* to read it. He's finishing it; he reads ahead. Even reads ahead when we read together. He *runs* in and *steals* it all day long. He doesn't have good reading skills. He goes to special reading class, but he stole that book! He gets into all sorts of trouble to read *Squanto.* . . . I think they all love it, completely, every one, even the two who called it phoney in the other class.

Holbrook was enchanted with *Squanto*. This boy, who had never before opened a book voluntarily, finished it in two days, reading at odd moments during school hours. He carried it with him to all of his classes and, because he was usually "kicked out of class" for "doing another subject" during mathematics, science, or physical education, he was able to read for extended periods while waiting to see the administrator in charge of punishment for such misdeeds. (The students were not permitted to take these books home because loss of even one copy would create too much trouble.) Holbrook was even seen walking down the halls reading *Squanto,* not noticing anyone or anything else, unaware of a push or a shove from pupils passing him. On other occasions, even the possibility of a push enraged Holbrook. Later, when the books to be used as comparisons with *Squanto* were being selected, Holbrook found another book about *Squanto* (Stevenson, 1953) and read it from cover to cover in one night. The teacher brought in more materials, and Holbrook became an official expert on the personage Squanto.

This book merited its unusual reception for several reasons. First, it was written on a second-grade reading level, yet could be used for fairly mature interpretation, as is described later. Second, since the action was fast-moving, there was rapid involvement in the story, and there were many points these students wanted to discuss. In fact, they suggested many of the questions discussed in class such as, "Is it real?" "Is it really real?" "Why did he get so excited about the snow? Was he down South?" (They had missed the sentence that implied that snow meant the onset of the season for testing braves.) Third, the chief character was Indian, not Negro or white. This permitted a freer discussion of aspirations in classes in which students were Negroes and the teacher white. Furthermore, the implications of the story for aspirations are clear enough to be understood even by the few who still had trouble with the meaning of aspirations. Fourth, the action in the book is varied and rich. Consequently the book could be used for developing a variety of skills, such as constructing sequences of events and giving reasons for these sequences, exploring inferential reading, and hypothesizing from clues. For example, the class was asked to identify the cues which suggested that Squanto's friend intended to steal the wolfskin robe. Finally, because the students were so interested in the book, it was possible to use it repeatedly to practice such skills as re-reading for different points and writing on a variety of questions.

To systematize some aspects of the work, guide sheets on at least two levels of difficulty were prepared by teachers working in teams. The content and the format of these guide sheets were changed every two or three days to teach new skills and to prevent boredom. Instructions for filling in the guide sheet were also taped for the simple reason that children who could not read *Squanto* could not read instructions. A sample of a Level I guide sheet follows:

SQUANTO AND THE PILGRIMS

"The War Chief Speaks," pages 1–7

A. Write the names of the people you meet in this chapter. You may use your book to help you find them.
B. Here are four things that happened in the story. Copy them on this sheet in the order in which they happened. [*Four events are listed.*]

These guide sheets were used to develop a variety of analyses. One was that of understanding the sequence of events. Some chapters provided opportunities to test the students' ability to read clues and to support their explanations, such as asking how they knew that Squanto's arrival in the test area of the forest had to come after his father blindfolded him.

Other questions provoked hypothesizing in the form of picking up clues and predicting what would follow. For example, students picked up the clues that indicated that Squanto's friend was going to steal the robe made of the skin of the white wolf that Squanto had shot to become a brave. They could not understand how a "smart boy like Squanto" could be stupid enough not to know it too. For these students it was gratifying to realize that a bright boy—though a character in a book—can be "stupider than you." The teacher pursued similar inferential veins by asking, "How did you detect the fact that Squanto *is* bright?" Because pupils were excited about this issue, they eagerly reviewed several preceding chapters to "prove it," and together discovered nine reasons. Thus, the work on the guide sheets provided motivation for rereading the same material for new purposes, which is a way of generating new learning on the part of students with meager reading skills and poor motivation for reading practice (see Elkins, 1963).

At a later point, the guide sheets included items such as, "Make a list of questions you would like us to discuss," and "What questions might other students enjoy discussing?" Some classes were asked to give opinions on whether *Squanto* should be used with the next year's class and if so, why, and how these classes could work with it.

Another common procedure was to make up plays and dramatize special incidents. This was a favorite activity, and the students recommended that the teacher continue it with the next class. The students did not tire of making up plays and enacting them, no matter how many times they repeated the activity. This was a boon, for rereading for fuller comprehension and analysis was necessary.

Beyond these common routines, different teachers used different strategies, depending on their judgment of what their groups needed. One teacher proceeded systematically from Level I guide sheet to the Level II guide sheet and was surprised and delighted when all not only took the second sheet but finished it.

> I read the first chapter and they just sat there, you know, with their mouths open and, of course, when I said we're going to do some writing, there were groans. Once they began it was easy and *everyone* took and finished the second sheet!. . . . I said the second sheet was extra credit.

In another very poor class the guide sheets were filled in collaboratively. The teacher described her procedure as follows: ·

> There is such a range. Some write as well as my first class, but on the other end there are those six kids. . . . They collaborated on the work sheets for *Squanto*. . . . Beautiful! I let them. . . . They help each other because one has a bit more ability to read the question, another has the answer, and the third one knows how to write it. And all sign their names to the sheet. . . . As we planned, only the first two days all had the same type of worksheet. Then we changed the type for the

third day. They did four. They didn't want to stop. But we planned to cut it off while they're still hot, so I won't do it tomorrow. . . . Or maybe it *will* go another two days; hot.

In the disturbed class, where the six most difficult ones were collaborating, when I asked them to write in one sentence how they like *Squanto,* two children with most reading difficulty called it "phoney." Jeffrey didn't even ask me to spell phoney, but Lenny did. And Lucifer writes, "I love."

They answered the worksheet questions right from the book as we planned, so they had to reread. Sometimes I read to them while they looked on. In fact, every day I did that. They are so interested that I read them two chapters one day.

In some classes this book provided a sustained experience for almost two weeks. The entire book was used to teach students to anticipate events, to hypothesize, and to reread to test their hypotheses. A running account was made daily; students dated their entries in notebooks, wrote their hypotheses, described the clues they used to make them, and then wrote on "What a Good Guesser I Am." When they finished reading the book, they reviewed their notebook entries, reread sections of *Squanto* to determine where they missed clues, and then summarized in a paragraph on "What a Detective I'd Make"!

In still other classes, teachers read portions or chapters of the story ending on a highly interesting point and then left the students to finish the chapter. For the few who could scarcely read, the tape-recorded version was used virtually as a second teacher. The chapters were pre-recorded, sometimes to music. Students were given earphones and books so that they could both listen and look, and they were allowed to do this as many times as they felt it necessary to be able to answer questions on guide sheets, or to pursue whatever activity had been planned.

This was a very useful device because students who have no functional reading power by the time they reach junior high school are usually easily distracted. The book and the earphones, the pencil and paper compel complete attention to the task at hand, for eyes, ears, and hands are occupied. Furthermore, for children who grow up in a noisy environment, this was a rare experience in privacy and freedom from distraction. This type of activity, when continued over a period of time, is almost the quickest way to increase reading power. It is also a way to immobilize defeatist attitudes which, after years of unsuccessful experience with reading, have become a deterrent to attempting to read at all.

Excerpts from a discussion of two chapters in *Squanto* will serve to illustrate the progress in conceptualization and abstraction of students who began with little or no ability in these processes:

TEACHER: Why did Squanto want to trap the white wolf?

WALTER: So he could have honor.

JEAN: It would give him meat to eat.

ALICE: That wasn't the main reason. He wanted to be a brave—that was the main thing.

JOHN: I think he didn't want to be hungry too.

BEATRICE: The white robe would prove he was a brave.

LEON: Whoever trapped the white robe believed in God.

TEACHER: Why didn't the second Indian boy go hunting with Squanto?

GERRY: He was planning to steal my robe. [*The word* my *is not an error.*]

REED: He wanted the honor of his tribe and was planning to steal that robe all the time.

TEACHER: Do you think Squanto will keep his promise to the rich merchant?

BERTHA: Yes, because he is a worthy brave.

PATTY: Anyway, Squanto never told a lie before.

RONALD: I think he will keep the promise. I believe in words of someone like Squanto.

TIM: People go back on their words sometime even if they are good. But Squanto will keep his promise because the man was kind to him and feed him and treat him nice.

ALBERT: And he got him clothes too.

LARRY: He'll keep his promise because he likes the merchant.

LINDA: He'll keep it because deep down in his heart he mean it.

GEORGE: He said he'll never forget him, and he won't.

ALBERT: He'll tell his people that those white men were good and to forget the bad white men.

LEONARD: He said he would like white men.

CARL: And he would forget the bad white men.

LILLIAN: He gave his promise when he passed the test to be a brave. He told the war chief he would always keep his promise.

JOAN: Patty said he never told a lie before and he didn't, but once he didn't tell anything when he should.

PEARL: You mean he should squeal on that boy that stole his robe?

(Cries of "Yes," "Yes," everyone talking at once.)

HOLBROOK: Ain't no squealer—Squanto. People gonna know someday thout [without] his squealin!

The capstone of the Squanto sequence was the comparative analysis of the aspirations of Squanto and of the characters in the book each student had read by himself. "What do the people in your book want most?" "How do you know that?" "Did anyone fail to get what he wanted?" "How did he feel?" "How do you know?" Excerpts from average sixth-grade papers follow:

(GIRL): In my book, Maria [Curie] wants to be a scientist and study about the moon and stars and the body. Squanto wants to be a brave. Mine is know where near Squanto. Maria has a hard time because she can't be what she wants, but she never give up even if she be feeling crying.

(GIRL): . . . . They both wanted to be grown up . . . . and Squanto wanted to go home and Francis Scott Key wanted go hom. But they had to wait. Squanto felt bad becauxe he don't have food and maybe die. Francis have food and a rich house but he don't like wait 3 days. . . .

(BOY): . . . . Both of them wanted to be something but Kit Carson wanted to show he could do what other people can't do. . . . Squanto wanted to be a brave and kit wanted to be a frontcer boy. . . . I read about him in a different book too—In the American history. He git what he want but he almost git killed. And Squanto almost die. Kit get mad but Squanto be quiet when he think he can't be a brave.

The general feeling of teacher and pupils about the experiences in this sequence on Squanto can best be summarized by excerpts from a young teacher's account of what she did and how she felt:

I hate having them for one period only. It's really frustrating. A period always seemed long to me before, but all of a sudden, doing things this way and having a variety of connected activities, it seems like I barely get started, and I barely understand what's happening, and it's over. And you know, it's very funny, I had to bring them to their other class late, because the bell rang, and no one got out of his seat. And the second bell rang and no one got out of his seat. That was the day Rodney ran out of the room. Even Jeffrey was doing the ads. Everybody was doing it. [*Squanto "advertised" for his lost wolfskin, the students' idea.*]

Evidently *Squanto* provided several ways of making certain concepts and sequences of events concrete. This concreteness was of a different order from the concreteness provided by the study of Hands and Walls. It did not represent tangible objects, as was the case in previous sequences. The tangibility was supplied by the learning activities that the students carried on, such as tracing the sequences of events and looking for specific clues in order to explain what happened. It was these activities that furnished the material from which to form abstractions. The students could "hold on" to these while struggling with thinking. The activities also supplied an alternative something that helped them to carry on when the required thinking became too much of a task. It seems then that this provision of tangible learning experiences in elaborating the abstract concepts that have no concrete referents provides another method for rendering these concepts concrete and thereby making them accessible to learning.

This second alternative enlarges the scope of the problems to which the method can be applied. For example, a long sequence on the study of fears was carried on, in which each sequence was tied to producing a newspaper on exploration of fears. The class used this concrete task to explore a variety of topics. They observed fears in younger children, using as a guide a set of questions such as the following: "What happened?" "What frightened him?" "What did he do that made you think he was frightened?" Similar questions were used in analyzing stories read in class or individually.

The activities described above were used to examine the fears of the small colonies at the time the United States became a nation, as expressed in the Bill of Rights; the fears of Great Britain in the Suez Canal episode, of Russia in the Black Sea area, and of the United States in the Panama Canal area. In these latter pursuits, the questions were more than a means of focusing on the essentials while plowing through unknown "territory." They also served as common threads for comparison and for sharing information by groups who had used different sources to seek information on the same questions.

Without the concrete objective of producing a newspaper, these students could not have carried on such a long-term project on one topic. Yet a project of length afforded several types of experiences these students needed, but had not had. First, it permitted examination of several types of content and materials by the same criteria: did they, or did they not, illustrate a particular kind of a fear, how fear worked, how fears could be detected? The necessity of applying such criteria to the selection as well as interpretation of materials caused the students to become more thoughtful about what they read, extended the range of the hypotheses they proposed, and helped them to empathize with others whose feelings they had rarely, if ever, considered.

These long-term projects also created opportunities for establishing habits of disciplined work continued over a greater period of time. Because the students had some opportunity to make decisions, they were introduced to planning and working for distant goals—a new experience for a group so bound by a need for immediate gratification and success.

There is an infinite range of possibilities for such efforts. However, it must be realized that in order to build intellectual power, it is necessary to strengthen, gradually and almost painfully, many abilities at the same time: the ability to think abstractly, to project consequences, to acquire and use skills intelligently, to control one's emotions and to channel them into socially useful activities, to achieve a sense of belonging to the world of wanted people, to set one's goals and know how to attain them, to communicate with peers, adults, and younger children, and to work with and for others as a team. These goals can be attained only when consistent effort is made over a long period of time and when curriculum at each grade level represents a definite step toward them.

CHAPTER VIII

Industrial Development:
The Triangle Fire

The curriculum for most junior high schools usually includes a study of the Industrial Revolution and its effects on the lives of the people. This curriculum is often inaccessible to learning by culturally deprived students for reasons that have already been described: unintelligible textbooks, incomprehensible concepts and generalizations, and lack of meaning. What follows is an illustration of the way in which meaning emerges from consideration of events that have an emotional impact.

Teachers began the study of industrial development with an aspect of the students' lives, in this case the work of their parents. Often the students knew what their parents or other adults in the household did for a living—housework for most mothers, janitorial work or work in garages for the fathers. They were, however, unaware of the specific nature of this work. Interviews with adults in the household about their work was then the first step. These interviews were handled in much the same way as in other sequences described earlier.

The next step was the reading of stories to help them identify with people at work, to extend their insight into the joys, the problems, and the human consequences of earning a living in particular instances. They were helped to compare situations they found in stories with their own, especially with respect to things that bothered them about what adults did upon arrival home from work.

A whole set of new avenues to motivation, involvement, and cognitive development suddenly opened up when a teacher read to her class a chapter from *East River* (Asch, 1946) which described the Triangle Fire in the sweatshops of the garment district of New York City in the first decade of the twentieth century. The reaction to this story, as described by one experienced observer, was quite unexpected:

134

Children who appeared not to be listening as the teacher read actually were deeply involved. Some pretended not to listen, stared out of the window with a far-away look. Yet these very children were following the story, as were most of them who could comprehend. Others covered their ears and ostensibly refused to listen, but heard nonetheless. Two boys broke the silence with cries of "No! No!" Two more asked questions aloud with almost every new paragraph: "Is she gonna die?" etc. A boy and a girl, both 14, sucked their thumbs like crazy. Still others pretended to think it was a joke but displayed evidences of being extremely upset two seconds later. The talking out, the shuffling of feet by two boys were attempts to cover up feelings and even to force the teacher to stop reading. When the teacher read the words "Jesus Christ" there was a low, soft chorus of "Amen". . . .

In the light of these responses it seemed wise to the teacher to disregard the lesson plans she had made in order to capitalize on the rapt attention and emotional reaction of the class, which heretofore had usually been rather disorderly and inattentive. She had planned to ask the usual set of questions: "What happened?" "Why?" "Whose fault was it?" She asked instead, "What part bothered you most?" recognizing from their behavior that the students needed to talk about this first. The remarks below show that the students had listened and did identify with the characters, even though some facts were twisted.

JOHN: . . . . when the girl was falling out the window and the glass kept going into her leg.

CAROL: When Sara broke the window with her hand and the fire fell on her.

* * *

GEORGE: When the fire got on the girls' pocket and the girl was hangin' from the window and she fainted. When she was hanging.

PEARL: When Mary knocked open the window and she's tryin' to get to the balcony and couldn't. And when Sara fell down.

GEORGE: She have to take that job 'cause her family was poor.

BETTY: They couldn't go down stairs. They have no stairs down there. The elevator was stuck, and door was stuck too.

* * *

JEAN: When Sara was hangin' out the window and was cut in her side. The glass was cuttin' her stomach.

REED: When the fire was gittin' close to dem, and when Sara fainted. And the fire was gittin' closer.

*   *   *

JOHN: When the ladies tried to open the door and they couldn't get out.

FRANCIS: When that girl get cut and smashed and crushed on the ground when she fell.

*   *   *

RUPERT: When the fire first started and it was comin' up from the floor and they started banging the chairs and trying to get out and threw the sewing machine at the door.

LARRY: . . . . Before they got pretty near the end of the story, I thought the floor was going to cave in. And everybody die.

LIONEL: . . . . If I had to see a girl fall out of the window, I'd scream. It would startle me and I'd let go.

ALEX: . . . . the girl leanin' against the window and gettin' cut. The glass was goin' into her and fire was lickin' at her stockings.

LARRY: If I thought a part of my family was in the building, I would try to break through the cops and firemen to try to save them. I might die and they might live. I don't know.

"What do you wish didn't happen in the story?" was the next question, and the responses were as follows:

LIONEL: I wish the factory didn't catch a fire in the first place and that Sara didn't get killed.

FRANCIS: I wish Sara didn't get her side cut and get smashed to the ground when she fell out of the window.

*   *   *

JOHN: I wish that if the fire had started the door wouldn't be locked so they could's gotten out to safety.

*   *   *

LARRY: The story wasn't real, was it?"

TEACHER: Yes, it was. The fire did happen. [*She had explained at least four times earlier, when she introduced the story and when she was reading it, that there* was *such a real fire, that people* like *Sara and Mary were in the fire, etc., etc.*]

FRANK: I wish they didn't went to the other factory and that the door had been open so that they can get out and the girl didn't catch on fire and fall out the window.

FRANCIS: And I wish the door wouldna got jammed and the fire didn't come and the crowd didn't stay by the door.

TEACHER: Larry asked if the story was real.

EUGENE: I knew it was real right from the beginning.

TEACHER: What made you think so?

*   *   *

FRANCIS: I know because the story said East River. Then I knew it was true.

JOHN: Because the firemen came and had nets and things.

RICHARD: In factories they do have boxes in front of doors.

LARRY: I thought it was real because the teacher used expression she never used before. She did this in another story.

These two questions seem and are repetitive. Yet they have a function. It was necessary to release their general feelings as well as to probe into their concerns. But mainly the repetition was necessary to establish a disciplined method of discussion: to help them listen to each other, to respond to the remarks of other students, to focus on a particular target, and to wait for their turn to speak. This is extremely hard for students who lack such training, and who are used to an immediate expression of their feelings. The conventional classroom dialogue, in which teacher questions are interspersed between each student response, establishes a habit of listening only to teachers' remarks. This habit is difficult to break, as is the practice of directing questions and remarks only to the teacher and not also to other students.

The quotations above show that students did continue responding without waiting for new questions from the teacher. They still had difficulty in listening to each other, but at least they waited for their turn, and did not all speak at once. To initiate the habit of responding to each other's remarks, the teacher picked up remarks made by one student and redirected them to the class.

The next discussion was designed to establish the time the fire occurred. These students' concepts of time are often distorted. To teach the growth of the Industrial Revolution requires some relative ideas of when things happened. Time lines help, but it equally important to help students to read the context clues to establish the period of the event.

> TEACHER: When do you think the fire started—last year or a long time ago?
>
> JOHN: Last year maybe because they didn't have a Union in that place and anything could happen and some of the people could have started a fire.
>
> RONALD: Last year, because someone started a fire because the machine was all broken up.
>
> CAROL: This year because the old machine was no good.
>
> LIONEL: This year because they were probably using new machines too much.
>
> REED: It happened a long time ago because they was only gettin' $12 a week and long ago they didn't get much.
>
> CALHOUN: It was two years ago because they had big buildings.
>
> RICHARD: I think it was long ago because now in these days you don't have children working in factories.
>
> ANDREW: I think it was last year because they have elevators and they didn't have elevators long ago.
>
> ALICE: Long ago they didn't have glass windows.
>
> PEARL: It started long ago because they had stools and they had to make these blouses different from they do today.
>
> BETTY: It was long ago because the building was old-fashioned. This year they have elevators and stairs too.
>
> FRANCIS: How old was she when she started to work?

At a later point—

> JOHN: It happened long ago. The factories were very old. [*Since the issue of time was left dangling, and since the students apparently were disturbed by the lack of closure, it was bound to come up again no matter what the context. This happens only when children feel free to do it.*]
>
> FRANCIS: It was 1929 or something like that. Long ago. They had no hook and ladders. [*There had been a long discussion about hook and ladders previously.*]
>
> HARVEY: It was long ago. Now they make a lot of money in a factory. Then they was makin' $12 a week.

RICHARD: And they had the doors locked so you couldn't get out. It was 1709. *(Shouts of "What?")*

The seemingly illogical rationale contained clues to further work that was needed. There were students who could help once they learned to question classmates who evolved such reasons as ". . . . they were probably using new machines too much." Reed was able to pick up a reasonable clue of wage difference. Richard knew that today children don't work in factories, though the two girls in the story were adolescents, not children. Francis picked this up. There was much yet to be done by the teacher, but there was also something for her to build upon and to develop.

While the teacher was reading the story, there was a gasp at the mention of $12 per week as total salary. Later the teacher picked up this point in an attempt to discover what he class knew about reasonable wages. The discussion that follows demonstrates an unrealistic idea of the wages it takes to support a family.

TEACHER: You thought $12 a week was very little money for Mary and Sara to earn. How much money do people you know earn these days? What jobs do they have?

CAROL: My father he work in a cleaning job and he make $200 a week and a lady next door works in a hospital and make $300 a week.

NEOAUDREY: My mother works for———————Company and make from $25 to $30 a week and when she sell a lot of things she make a lot of money.

FRANCIS: $12 or $14 today is a little money according how young you are, how old you are.

WILLIAM: If you are an adult you supposed to get around $50 or $40 sumpin' dollars.

PEARL: You should get more money now because these days youngsters don't work as much as older persons does. [*Up to this point there are beginnings of a conversation centered around wages relative to age.*]

BETTY: You need a lot of money because you need a lot of clothes and everything.

ALICE: You need more money these days and work harder because things are so expensive and food is so high and clothes is too and you need home to sleep in.

AGNES: I think you git a lot of money because you need some food, clothes, and socks and everything, and feed the family.

BETTY: $14 can't buy you a whole lot of food and clothes. [*Again there are the rudiments of a conversation about money and its relation to needs.*]

LARRY: People today earn $3000, like the Sanitation. They work hard; yes, they do. [*Defensively because of protest of peer.*] And those are very good jobs today, and I think the jobs we have today is better than the jobs they had like in the book.

RICHARD: People earn about $59 a week in factories. Sometimes if they work *very* hard all the time they earn about $150 a year. [*Whispers of "a week."*] Yes, a week. If they work in Sanitation Departments or stores or things, they'll earn about $69.00 or something. But in Sanitation Department they earn $150. That's why they earn more than $12 in the old days. The good old days. *(Laughter.)*

* * *

TEACHER: If I told you they were making $14 a day, would you think that was a good wage?

RICHARD: That's good money because in a week it would add up.

TEACHER: What if it's $14 a week?

ANDREW: That wouldn't be so good because everybody don't get paid that much.

JEAN: You couldn't live on $14 a week. No! You couldn't.

SAUNDERS: It's good because you don't have to buy no house or nuthin! You live in an apartment.

A similar misconception prevailed about religion, as shown in reactions to questions about the religion of the two girls in *East River*.

TEACHER: One of the girls in the story was Jewish and the other was Catholic. Which girl was Jewish and which was Catholic? Please tell why you think so. You'll *all* have a chance to talk. Don't worry.

SAUNDERS: Sara was Catholic and Mary was Jewish, because their family came from a Catholic . . . . I don't know.

NEOAUDREY: I think Mary was Jewish because Jewish, they pray a lot. She was praying when she was getting ready to jump.

VALERIE: Mary was Jewish and Sara was Catholic because when . . . . I don't know. I just think that—

ELIZABETH: I think Mary was Jewish and Sara was Catholic because that day when Mary went to go home she had to go to church.

ARLENE: Jewish people are not rich and most people Catholics are rich and she had to work hard. So, I think Sara was Jewish.

* * *

JOHN: When Sara was out on the ledge and Mary was holding her she started praying and she said a Catholic prayer.

CAROL: Mary was Jewish I think because they were saying prayers. *Mary* was. Sara was listening.

TEACHER: What did she say when she prayed?

STUDENTS: Jesus Maria, Jesus Maria.

Such findings of necessity compelled the teachers to change the sequence originally planned. First, however, they had to analyze why this particular story had such an impact on the students. One reason was undoubtedly their fear of fire. Many lived in wooden houses or in apartments heated by kerosene stoves. Every winter the local newspapers carried stories of fires caused by the highly inflammable fuel or defective heating units. Fear of physical injury may have been another reason. Many students live in an emotionally volatile environment where physical threats and beatings are not infrequent.

Because of the high interest in reality of the story—"Was this true?" "Did it really happen?"—the teachers prepared a three-page historical account of the Triangle Fire. Before the children read it, the teachers showed their classes the books they had read in order to prepare the material and explained the differences between history and fiction through the display of the books themselves. The pupils then read the historical account to familiarize themselves with facts about the fire not described in the story.[1]

The first thing that struck the students was the fact that the stairway by which hundreds of panic-stricken people had to escape was only 22 inches wide. "Twenty-two inches!" "How wide is that?" "Measure me." The teacher called two boys to the front of the room and had each measure the other across the shoulders. Since everybody wanted to be measured, one student was set to work cutting string into lengths of 22 inches so that pairs of students could measure each other to see which could have escaped had they been involved.

[1] For other ways in which this sequence can be used, see Elkins and Seifman (1965), pp. 245–250.

The measuring brought a flood of questions. "How could that be?" "Why didn't someone do something before it happened?" "My mother says there are laws now, and inspectors come." With each new point in the history of the case came other questions. From this point on, the questions of students rather than what the teacher had originally planned focused the activities.

For example, the direction in which doors open became a topic for debate. The historical account referred to the fact that the doors were locked and that they opened inward. A committee was dispatched to check the doors at the exits in the school building. They returned with a report that they all opened outward. But then it was discovered that the classroom door opened *in*. "How come?" Further group discussion resulted in a reason acceptable to all: If the classroom door opened out, anyone coming by in the corridor could be injured if the door flew open.

Reading about the Triangle Fire also provoked a study sequence on labor unions. By a happy coincidence, one teacher possessed a large picture book, a commemorative edition, with historical accounts of the fire and of the activities of the International Ladies' Garment Workers Union (ILGWU) before and after the fire. This book stimulated another series of sustained discussions and activities.

These excerpts from a teacher's account describe some reactions:

Wesley sat down and read article after article from that commemorative issue. The other kids stood around him and read along with him or just looked at the pictures. They couldn't stop talking about them. It went on for two whole periods. Unbelievable. What they liked best was the group of pictures and the accompanying text which showed sanitation facilities in a factory and how filthy it was. And another article was about *bundles* in the days when they carried bundles home. They *loved* the pictures in that book. They liked the reprints of the old newspaper articles that were in the book. They read every single one. They talked about them, over and over, for days and days. . . . The readings on Industrial Revolution showed how the immigrant first took work home and got paid by the piece, and then the factory system when they got paid per hour. And they said, "That's a good salary?" And they realized it wasn't *now*. They found out that the factory doors were locked and wanted to know *why*. They made a long solid list of things that made the fire as bad as it was. They *worked*. . . . The thing is, they are interested in the *truth*. It's not make believe. That's important to them.

The interest in labor unions kindled by the book was fanned by the teachers, who had collected full-page ads and historical accounts that appeared occasionally in the newspapers to which they subscribed. Among these was a full-page picture of the Triangle Fire in an advertisement financed by the ILGWU.

TEACHER: "Why do you suppose the labor unions paid about $12,000 to put this ad in the paper?" [*This had been preceded by discussion about names they knew in the labor unions, how unions functioned, and what they did for workers.*]

FRANCINE: They are celebrating 50 years later because they improved things.

JERRY: You don't celebrate a fire! You don't celebrate people dying. . . .

JASMINE: They spent the money to remind people how important it is to have a fire escape and all that.

* * *

BEATRICE: They'd get laws to do protect people so people wouldn't die like that.

CAROL: They said you should work shorter hours.

JOHN: And more money for their work.

* * *

TEACHER: [*Showing picture of union members marching in protest against conditions in the Triangle Fire era.*] Why were they marching? Why were they protesting? They were marching even in the rain. To whom did they want to talk about the tragedy?

LISA: The head of the law. They wanted the head of the law to know

MARIA: If they have more fires, they'll lose more people. So they have to show the head of the law.

TEACHER: Who would that be?

LISA: The mayor?

The students ended their work in this sequence with a study of newspaper articles to learn about labor union activities today and to compare them with those of the early 1900's. They "tested" their hypotheses about what would happen if a factory fire broke out today. "The union would call a strike." "How did they know?" "There were articles about strikes for other reasons." "And fires are worse reasons." "Would they *have* to strike for this reason?" "Was no one else concerned?" "Yes, there are laws. There are rules. The factories are inspected." "What right has anyone to come in and inspect private property?" "There's a law." "The mayor said."

Students also examined a social studies text to see what *other* things unions did for people. For example, did business people do anything? Thus, while the Triangle Fire was only one episode in the study of the Industrial Revolution, it gave impetus to the entire study.

CHAPTER IX

Peer Relationships

This sequence and those that follow in Chapters X and XI were developed for the eighth-grade group. They were originally published in *With Focus on Human Relations* (Taba & Elkins, 1950), which is now out of print.

The diagnosis at the beginning of the year (see Chapter III) had suggested that above all things these students wanted the companionship of peers. All the papers they had written at the beginning of the year spoke of this desire. It was the cause of many a conflict with parents; it was the root of their distaste for homework and chores. Classroom discussions had revealed the tremendous impact of peer opinion. Behavior toward parents, their feelings about their home, and seemingly their whole moral code were influenced by what their peers thought.

To learn to what extent the life of these adolescents permitted peer association and what they learned from that association, the teacher asked them to keep diaries. From them they hoped to learn in what type of social context these students lived, what social experiences they had outside the school, and what their views and feelings were about their environment. The students were asked to record what they did, with whom they did it, and how they felt about these experiences.

DIAGNOSIS

Four diaries, two covering a weekday and two a weekend, were assigned, the first pair in October and the second in May. The activities recorded in the diaries were classified into eight categories: work, active and passive recreation, socializing, loafing, routines, religion, grooming, and health. They were also grouped according to whether they had occurred in the company of peers or of family, or had been carried on alone.[1]

[1] See Taba (1955), Ch. 2; and Taba, *et al.* (1951), Ch. 1, for further details on administering diaries and findings from them.

Diary records of this sort are designed to describe the social and psychological reality of the individual's environment as *he* sees and feels it. When events are described in brief time intervals, such as for each half hour, they provide information that is useful for many purposes: to describe the life space, how broad or how limited the experiences, associations, and contacts with other people are and what opportunities for communication exist. Diaries also can describe the work load and the roles young people and children play in their families and, to some extent, the nature of relationships within the family. Some may subordinate themselves to routines established by their elders, while others may carry nearly adult responsibilities for housekeeping and for taking care of siblings. In some families children may live as unwelcome strangers, and in others they may be the centers of attention and care. Some experience only cleavage and authority demands, and others receive a good deal of affection and support.

These patterns of life in home and in the neighborhood set the background for behavior and learning in school. Students with limited experience with peers need opportunity in school to learn the elementary human relations skills. The lone wolf is apt to be a problem in school because controlled group behavior and self controls are foreign to him. A student whose home life continually explodes cannot simply forget it when he enters the classroom. Diary material, properly analyzed, provides explanation for many problems in school, such as inability to get along with other students, disinterest in learning, difficulty in accepting authority. The main contribution of diaries, however, is their disclosure of the gaps in social learning which the school program needs to fill, such as defective development of values and standards.

Below are excerpts from the diaries of several students with contrasting patterns of social life, with additional data from their writing, sociometric tests, and parent interviews to complete the picture.[2]

Bob, the Disinherited

Bob's diary shows him to be the class member with the greatest proportion of solitary activities and the least experiences with peers. The content of his life is limited. His diary entries contain many routine movements. Sports are important. He seems to spend all his free time outside of school in earning money, chiefly from his newspaper route, and seems nonplused by difficulties connected with it. This makes him a poor student, even though everyone seems to recognize that he has a reasonably acute mind.

[2] These case studies were taken from Taba (1955), pp. 31–39.

His intelligence seems buried under fatigue, and his work suffers from lack of preparation.

His days seem to be spent in endless frustration over trying to get some affection from his stepmother and his little sister, as the following diary excerpt illustrates:

Wednesday—I got up at 5:00. Got dressed and had a snack to eat. Went down to the cellar and found my bike had a flat tire. So I had to do my papers walking. I received a complaint from a lady because I didn't have the paper there early enough. (I didn't enjoy that.) Then I came home, had my breakfast and played with my sister and talked with my mother (enjoyed it). Got my books together, gave my mother a kiss good-by, then went over to give my sister a kiss. She gave me a sock in the eye. I came out from the house and met George. We talked about school and the kids and we went into Mike's store and got a candy bar. We split it up with Harry. I played football with the boys. We won (our side). Enjoyed it all, but it was the daily routine.

I came home and ate my dinner and talked all the time while I ate. After dinner I started to make my sister a little gingerbread boy out of that red celluloid I brought from school. Then I fussed with my sister and then helped my mother with the dishes. Gave my mother a kiss and when I came to my sister, got another sock, this time a couple of kicks to go with it. I went to school with George again and we talked about things all the way to school. (It was just a so-so conversation.)

I came home and fussed around. I had an argument with my mother as to when I was to do my homework. She won, of course. So I did my homework then, right after school. Then I went next door, got a ladder and asked gramp if I could pick some crab apples for my mother. I got up in the tree and shook some down, then came down a picked them up. A friend of mine was with me and he was picking apples from my or rather his mother. So I went up, shook, came down, and that went on from four to six o'clock, and then I came in. (It was hard work but I enjoyed it.)

I had supper (I enjoyed it) and then fussed with the apples I had picked. I finished my diary, then read and fussed with my sister. I also read to her. I went to bed at 7:30.

Thursday—I got up at 5:00 and had a snack to eat by myself. I went downstairs and found my bike still had a flat. My father was supposed to have fixed it, but it was flat. So I thought my father didn't bring it down to the gas station. So I brought it down, filled it up, put my papers on it and rode a little way and it was flat again. I brought it home and that night I learned that there was two flats; my father just fixed one. So I had to do my route on foot again. I got another complaint, but not from the same lady. I didn't enjoy that. I came home and had my breakfast and made some more of the Gingerbread Boy and fussed with my sister and gathered my books. All went well with the kisses. None of my friends were at hand so I went to school by myself.

I came home, had my breakfast, or dinner, rather, and finished making my sister a boat. Did the dishes and went to school. No one was around, so I went to school by myself.

I came home and had to collect. I collected $11.40 and my bookkeeping came out right.

Bob seems to be disinherited at home. As a young child he was sent from institution to institution. His stepmother took him in at the insistence of his father and decidedly against her own wishes. She cannot bear him and is especially disgusted by his advances for affection. She hates him for "slopping up" the house and for still wetting the bed. She says frankly that he is just a boarder in the house and that that is all he means to her.

He apparently makes a big fuss over his sister and his stepmother, trying in his clumsy ways to be affectionate to them, and is repulsed by both. Evidently, being kicked and repulsed is commonplace in his life, and he reports it as such. His father is very strict with him and does not allow any children from the school or neighborhood in the house. His father confesses that he refrains from siding with Bob for fear his wife will leave him. Thus Bob has really no one to turn to and no way to learn social skills.

This is reflected in his behavior in school. Even to the boys who accepted their classmates most readily and uncritically, Bob seems "sort of off the track, sort of crazy." He teases the girls continually and acts up in front of the class.

Ginger, the Sociable, Religious Girl

Ginger is predominantly a sociable soul. To her, contacts with people around her, her gang and her friends, are the center of life. In her diary the social and religious activities stand high. But her total life pattern includes a few solitary activities and contacts with her family and peer associates in a balanced fashion.

Ginger strives consciously for association and uses her social environment aggressively to achieve her goals, which, however, are not self-centered. She likes to help people, worries over their problems and continually mediates other people's conflicts. She runs breathlessly from one activity to another and is always with people. She gathers a group around her for walking to and from school, going skating, or having lunch. The "gang" has a great importance to her, and she carries on a variety of activities with different members of it. Her relations with people are filled with small chatter and gaiety; she enjoys conversation and self-dramatization.

She is also a devout Catholic, and her diary is filled with accounts of prayers and rosaries. She seems to go to Mass or confession practically every morning—at least, on the days that she reports in diaries—and very carefully mentions her evening prayers. Her diary is a chatty, voluble description of her many activities. "The gang" figures heavily, as the following excerpt shows:

Although I awoke at six, I did not get up till 7:30. I dressed and woke Yvonne. She rested while I read my book. Then we did a little housework and had our orange juice and toast. Alice called us and she saved us a place in the bus line. After two buses left, we boarded the third, not seeing Alice.

This afternoon I ate with the usual gang. Amy came to school early, seven minutes late. She usually arrives at 9:30. First I walked Carol to S's shop to get a guinea grinder. After lunch I went with Yvonne to shop for the teacher. We went to the Kay. We got her beans, but had trouble finding them without pork. Then we couldn't find Lipton's vegetable soup. We got in school late, but were excused.

I rode home on the bus. When we got home, a boy broke the bus window. I went over to Alice's and did my homework. Picking up my clothes and books I left for home. I had 10 minutes to pick up my room and go to catechism.

In class we answered our questions. Sister read to us part of the story "Our Lady of Fatima." I walked home with Yvonne. I went to Carol's house, told her what she had to do for homework. Went to church, and spoke to Father S. about attendance. I saw Alice trading cards. She walked me home and gave me some cards. I ate supper, did dishes and played monopoly with

Barbara P. and Pat P. I came home and finished my diary, got the kids to bed and crawled in myself. I considered yesterday to be a more interesting day, as much had happened.

Ginger is fairly bright (IQ 107) and is above the grade average in her studies. Her work habits are good. She enjoys school thoroughly, her studies as well as the social contacts. She is active in after-school sports and loves to skate. She revels in "gang" fun and parties and loves to delve into discussions of teenage problems and activities. Wherever she goes, there is laughter and chatter. Though new in the school, she had become friendly with many of the pupils within a few days. She is a great reader of teenage books.

Her family life is healthy. She lives with both parents, two brothers —one nineteen and the other twelve—and an eight-year-old sister. Both parents work. The mother gets a great deal of pleasure from her daughter. Having been shy herself, she is proud of Ginger's ability to make friends, to help other people, to patch up feuds, and to organize fun.

The major cleavage in the home concerns her younger brother. The mother worries about him, and if one is to believe Ginger's diary, Ginger spends her time bickering with him. The mother is concerned about Ginger's future but does not expect her to go to college. (She wanted to become a nun.) According to the home culture, college education is reserved for boys. Since there is not enough money to send several children to college, Ginger, the oldest girl, will not go. Ginger is somewhat angry at the men in the family for requiring too much service of her.

In school, Ginger is much concerned with the progress, problems, and behavior of others in the classroom. If she finds someone she thinks "is not going to pass," she spends much time helping and encouraging him. It was she who took Ralph under her wing when he was practically ostracized because of his behavior in school and his difficulties outside of school. She realized that he was an unwanted child, that he needed a close friend, and, upon the suggestion of the teacher, she fell wholeheartedly into the plan of helping Ralph. She became his champion when he was verbally attacked by others, invited him to her house to help him with his work. The teacher says she is the one who must receive credit for any good that was done for this boy that year.

Her self-expectations are centered in her social role, around making people like her and being popular. She is deeply concerned lest she say or do something that will displease others. She admires people who are "good" and wants to "learn to be like them."

Evidently, Ginger has all the qualifications for a successful social career. She is not burdened by cleavages either in herself or with her family. She has an active, outgoing temperament, the "gift of gab," and a disposition to please. The content of her life, however, is somewhat shallow and immature. Having no problems, she has few occasions to meditate on life, her role in it, or on the ways of people.

Ralph, the Aimless Wanderer

Ralph, the boy that Ginger "helped," recorded in his diary the smallest number of social activities and the most loafing and routine of anyone in the class, and the fewest peer and family contacts. He spends his time delivering papers, playing chess in the game room at school, and playing with his dog. He is shunned by the class because he robbed a candy store and has a reputation for getting other people in trouble. His contacts seem to be casual and limited to a few "hellos." In his diary he displays a complete lack of self-consciousness about the store robbery and the court order. He describes the robbery almost as an ordinary event, as the following excerpt illustrates:

I got up at 5:30, got dressed and did my papers. I did them alone. I like to do my papers because when I do, my customers crack jokes and make me happy. I got home about 6:30. I slept until 8:00. I then got to school on my bike.

At lunch hour, I came home and ate with my mother. I read a funny book and came to school. I didn't enjoy it at home today, because my father was fixing the radio and got mad.

At three I stayed after school with a few children and my teacher. I am writing my report now. It is exactly 4:00 on the dot when I started "it." I like to stay after because I get an earful of the teacher's problems. I went home and did my dishes, cooked supper and ate with my mother, father, sister, and brothers. I sat down, read a while, and then went to George's [a candy store] on the corner of 18th and Jefferson. I met a kid I knew there, and he gave me an idea to stay in the store when he, George, locked the door to go home, and open the back door for him (the kid). I did that and took $58.00 from him [George]. I then went down town to different stores and cashed the change into bills. We did that for about two hours. I came home about 10:00.

6:30—10:00. I got up by myself, read a funny book, entitled "Crime", and fooled with my dog for a while, and then got dressed to go to do the papers. I started my papers about

7:30. I met no one that I knew and talked to no one during papers. I did, delivered to the houses, two streets, and then felt thirsty, so I went to a candy store, where I met two friends, Bill and Harry, and had a soda. I talked to them about papers and asked if any of them wanted to help me finish my route. I played the pin ball machine, and read funny books, told jokes, and had another grape soda. I saw that it was beginning to snow a little harder and thought of my papers on the corner getting wet with snow. I started to do the other two streets at about 9:30. I finished at about 10:00.

I came home, played with my dog, washed up, ate, and hunted for my Sunday clothes. My mother helped me find them, and I was soon ready to go to church, at 11:00.

I came home, said hello to my mother, father, grandmother, sister, and brother. I ate a good dinner with my family and then played with my dog. I made him roll over, stand up, and retrieve the ball I shot away. At 1:30 Tom D. called. We went to the show to see the picture, "The Yearling." This picture showed how an early American family lived. It showed how a boy about 11 years old found a baby deer, and brought it up. The deer then began to eat, at night, small corn. The deer ruined the fields about three times. They finally had to shoot it, and the boy was so heartbroken that he ran away. I left the show at the beginning of the next picture. I had to go to rehearsals at O.D.S. minstrel. I went there, and heard some beautiful song solos.

I went to the drug store at 5:30 and had a sundae. I read a few funny books and then went home. I felt so tired that I went to bed right away.

Ralph's home life is marred by many difficulties. His sister continually belittles him, and his father rages every time Ralph does not do his part of the home chores while the mother is working.

His mother does not have much time for Ralph, nor does she know what he is doing. Her feelings toward him are tinged with a good deal of displeasure over his reading so many "funny books." She also worries about the kind of friends he has and often asks him to bring them home, but he never does. She was the only one among the parents of the class who felt that her child *has* to get through school.

Ralph is on probation from the Juvenile Court, and as a result he has to be home at eight o'clock by court order. The mother's relief over this fact is greater than is her concern over the trouble that landed him in Juvenile Court.

From all that one can see, Ralph has not much to draw on from his home atmosphere. It cannot contribute much to his moral, intellectual, or personal development. Since the home itself does not have any routine, and since he spends a good deal of time on his own, Ralph has acquired a habit of aimless wandering. In school he is shunned, and the teacher has to take special steps to secure help for him from other students.

Generally these diaries showed a drab and barren life. The days seem to pass in a monotonous succession of commonplace routines and chores: people going to work, coming home late, preparing meals, washing floors, and distributing newspapers. The family as a unit enjoys few activities together: an occasional ride in a car, a visit to a ball park, or a shopping trip downtown.

These diaries also bespoke a distance between generations, perhaps for lack of time and opportunity, as well as for lack of skills, to maintain contact with children. There was relatively little evidence that parents influenced their children's manners, morals, or sense of values. Such controls as existed took a negative form, such as forbidding girls to stay out late and warnings about "going bad."

Several of these students were almost strangers at home, for they came and went unnoticed and seemed to have no vital connection with their parents. Home life was further complicated by the presence of extended family, each of whom set up different expectations.

The opportunities for peer association were meager and rather disorganized. Home chores or jobs were heavy. Many lived far away from people they knew, or else parents did not permit them to be out. Much of their time was spent on such solitary pastimes as listening to the radio and sitting in movie theaters. Some students took advantage of organized groups in the community, such as Scouts and church clubs; they joined in the sports and went to the game rooms sponsored by the city park department. Attempts to discover why so few of these students participated in such activities revealed that some lived too far away; some had little time; others were not aware of what these organizations offered; still others were not interested.

Spontaneous peer group activities were limited to street games of football and baseball for boys and walking on the streets, chatting, and joking for girls. Yet in the minds of these students peer contacts assumed a tremendous importance. The desire for peer contact, for belonging to a "gang," was great, and, seemingly, peers were expected to provide everything: excitement, communication, counseling, a sense of belonging.

Most diaries had two refrains. One was the perennial search for "someone to be with." Many seemed to be continually waiting for someone to turn up. The second was parental restrictions that children refused to obey. They devised ways of getting out and seeing friends even if it spelled rebellion. The boys seemed to spend their days planning how to get together to play or sulking because they could not. There were endless accounts of plots of how to get to walk with someone to and from school.

Other sources—sociograms, papers on their worries and what they did about them—indicated that some of the students had poor status in peer groups and many more did not know how to gain or keep the recognition of their group (Elkins, 1958).

This gap in out-of-school experiences created needs that the school could fill. What the teacher did about individual cases was illustrated in the case studies earlier in this chapter. But it was evident also that it was necessary to build an atmosphere in the classroom to fill the gap left by home and the neighborhood, as well as to develop a program around understandings and values to give new direction and meaning to peer life.

The class needed some awareness of what it means to be "left out" and of the group's responsibility in making a place for all sorts of people. The class could study some of these problems together, but more important than the study itself were the opportunities in school to work out some of these problems and to practice the skills needed in peer relationships. This became the main task of the peer relations unit.

GROUP ACTIVITIES

Planning opportunities for small-group activities was the first step, and it shortly became an occasion for social and business get-togethers. Students began to meet in one another's homes to plan the panel presentations. Parents were satisfied that this was an acceptable reason for boys and girls to be together. Sometimes they obtained a record player, and when work was done they danced and sang together. Sometimes parents furnished refreshments to top off the evening.

The teacher tried to design the activities and to group students for them in such a way that each student would have an opportunity to develop and display some skill. She hoped to help students learn that many skills besides sports are important. One boy, whose status with others was very precarious, gained prestige when the students organized noon-hour dancing classes. They found him a good dancer and a willing teacher. The dancing remained a small-group activity because of limited space in the classroom, and because the gymnasium was in use at that time. By trial and error, the students determined how many could be on the floor comfortably at one time and then scheduled who should come on what days.

Other students found a place in other activities. For example, one boy, whose academic work was especially poor, had "all the ideas" when it came to planning and playing sociodrama. He was an actor, and the students clamored for him whenever they "got stuck." One girl could "make a dull report have a little life," and even groups in which she had no part at a particular moment would come to her for the final touches. Others had a chance to display their skill in art or in costume-making. There was opportunity for academic prestige too; committees offered some a chance to show their skill in "putting everybody's reports together," in "taking notes on hard books," or in serving as chairmen during the final reporting to the class.

Still others found a role through their service to kindergartens. The teacher had arranged to have the eighth-graders help out in the kindergarten. The little ones became attached to some of the helpers; whenever these kindergarteners came up to deliver a message, they would single out their favorite for a fond "hello." When the groups that were helping in the kindergarten reported, some member was often singled out for praise because of his skill in handling a difficult problem.

As the year progressed, students became better acquainted with each other, especially as the membership in committees was shifted from time to time to extend contact and the leadership roles. Several clubs were formed. One girl whose mother had a sewing machine offered to let the girls come to her house once a week to sew. Evidently, when parents understand the importance of what they can do, they are more than willing to help. Parents need to understand the aims of the school before they can help. The interviews with parents earlier in the year had prepared them so that many of them were eager to do what they could to assist. Girls who were interested in baseball and skating pooled their equipment and organized a team called "Toughies." However, this was a "good weather" team; they could meet only when the weather permitted the use of a public park.

The boys also organized a team, but they had better luck with equipment and seemed to know how to avoid being "kicked off" vacant lots. One boy had some choice woodworking equipment in his cellar and offered its use to a maximum of three other boys at a time because "they had to be very quiet, or the landlord would raise the roof." One corner blackboard became a bulletin board on which any group could announce the time and place it was meeting for any activity, and this alone seemed to do much to help the students organize. At least, anyone with time on a certain afternoon or evening could find out where several others would be "hanging out," and since the notice was posted on the board with an "Everybody Welcome" sign, no student felt he was not wanted. Sometimes several things were going on at once:

Come for a game of catch on the lot behind ——— Company.

We're off to the movies tonight. Meet you in front of the Hippodrome at 7:00.

Rest up for a long hike tomorrow. Time 10:00 a.m. Place, Ye Olde Drugee Store.

One club activity was planned for the whole group during school time. Its purposes were to make equipment for the kindergartens and to service them in general. The club made a playhouse for the "babies" out of orange crates, painted it, and papered the four rooms. They made trains out of cheese boxes, painted wooden blocks in attractive colors, made picture books, and washed and ironed soiled dolls' dresses and doll-carriage covers. Although the entire class planned time, space, assembly and use of equipment, the actual work was done in small, flexible groups. This is a very good activity for teenagers. It helps their own social relationships and teaches them to provide for younger children's needs. But the teacher needs a strong constitution.

GROWING UP WITH FRIENDS

In addition to participating in activities for the development of group skills, the class studied the problems of peer relationships that concerned them. Together the pupils and teacher planned what should be studied in the unit. They developed an extensive list of things they wanted to know, including the following:

How to get into a gang

How to make others like you and to make new friends

How to take criticism and teasing

How to conduct yourself at a dance, to make introductions, and to ask someone to a dance

What can be done about name-calling

How to help others be comfortable at a party

How to plan parties that are fun for everybody, even those who like different things.

Together the class found the common points in the long list and decided to study "Growing Up with Friends" and "Boy-Girl Relationships." If there was time they planned to go on to "Friends and the Family" and "Getting a Job." The last two topics had already been touched on, but apparently not to the satisfaction of the group. They felt that many problems had not been considered fully enough.

The class had at its disposal such books as *Trudy Terrill: Eighth Grader* (Bryant, 1946), *Going on Sixteen* (Cavanna, 1946), *A Girl Can Dream* (Cavanna, 1948), *Linda Marsh* (De Leeuw, 1943), *Tradition* (Emery, 1946), *Bertie Comes Through* (Felsen, 1948a), *Bertie Takes Care* (Felsen, 1948b), *Us and the Duchess* (Fenton, 1947), *Johnny Tremain* (Forbes, 1943), *Rebel Halfback* (Archibald, 1947), *Granite Harbor* (Bird, 1944), *Blue Willow* (Gates, 1940), *Sensible Kate* (Gates, 1943), *North Fork* (Gates, 1945), *Anchor Man* (Jackson, 1947), *Call Me Charley* (Jackson, 1945), *Michael's Victory* (Judson, 1946), *Betsy Was a Junior* (Lovelace, 1947), *Somebody Else's Shoes* (Lowe, 1948), *The Moved-Outers* (Means, 1945), *Giant Mountain* (Neilson, 1946), *Call It Courage* (Sperry, 1964), *All-American* (Tunis, 1942), *Keystone Kids* (Tunis, 1943), *The Kid from Tomkinsville* (Tunis, 1940), *Yea! Wildcats!* (Tunis, 1944), *Willow Hill* (Whitney, 1947). Many of these books had been used earlier in the family unit and in the social studies, but, considered in a new light, they provided further selections of incidents suitable for the study of peer relationships.

In the unit "Growing Up with Friends," several problems were studied. The first topic was acceptance in a group, the great concern for most of these teenagers. The procedure used in the family unit was followed, with the difference that now there was a laboratory—the students' own classroom groups —from which to select the problems of relationships that needed to be examined. First, students described their own experiences; then they analyzed the way that people, including themselves, feel and why they behave as they do. Short stories were read to create an awareness of the problems of acceptance. Situations involving acceptance were analyzed at first by the entire class. Subsequently, "book panels" were set up in which the students did the same thing independently. Group discussion to develop and pool new ideas followed. Often sociodrama was employed to create insight into how people feel and to learn new ways of handling acceptance and rejection situations. There was written work and class discussion for diagnosis and evaluation.

The class first considered the question, "Why do you want friends?" This produced such answers as the following:

No one likes to be lonely.
I need someone to understand me.
Having friends makes you feel wanted.
I need someone to confide in.
They make me laugh and feel gay and happy.

To put the class in a frame of mind to accept ideas that were to come later, a discussion of what they looked for in their friends and why, and of what one can do with friends that one cannot do alone was conducted. It appeared that they wanted someone to listen to their troubles and their jokes.

Being left out was discussed next: why people are or feel left out, and what can be done about it. "The Horse" [McNeely, 1947] was a good story with which to open this discussion. "The Horse" tells about a naive farm girl who wanted an education so much that she walked miles to get to high school. In a faded and outlandish outfit she recited an original poem and found herself ridiculed so cruelly that school life became intolerable; after a series of incidents she was forced to pack her books and go home, never to return. Discussion of this story gave the teacher a chance to see how limited was the students' understanding of what caused acceptance and rejection. They seemed to think that when an individual was left out, it was his own fault. Their remarks did not show any awareness that the reasons may also lie in the group and that the group may have some responsibility.

If people aren't in a gang it's their own fault.
Nobody else should mix in.
If you stick up for someone your friends do not like, you
will lose your friends.
Name-calling is just for fun, and no one has the right to be
hurt by it.   '

Since name-calling became a great issue in this discussion, consideration of this topic seemed to offer an opportunity to begin to look at the feelings of people who are left out. At first, students made no distinction between "names that hurt" and names that are a sign of affection. One boy said he called his best friend "wop" and knew "he didn't mind." Another student challenged this. "How do you know it didn't hurt him?" "Because I asked him and he said it didn't hurt as long as I didn't call his parents that," was the answer. A third student felt that the very fact that "something made you ask him if he was hurt shows he probably was," to which the first boy replied, "Well, I'm proud of my nationality and he should be proud of his." This led the class to consider why people of some nationalities are hurt by slurs and others are not. They recalled all the occasions in which they were hurt by name-calling and then looked at similar situations in books like *Tradition* (Emery, 1946) and *Michael's Victory* (Judson, 1946) to see how other people felt and to compare what they found with their own feelings.

Apparently, at some time or other, most students had been called a hurtful name and remembered that the feeling was distinctly unpleasant. Some insisted, however, that they "didn't mind."

Other stories, such as "That's What Happened to Me" (Fessier, 1961), *Linda Marsh* (De Leeuw, 1943), and *Trudy Terrill: Eighth Grader* (Bryant, 1946), helped the class to comprehend how security and acceptance are related to being able to take name-calling. The boy in "That's What Happened to Me" (Fessier, 1961) is not accepted in his peer group. Deeply hurt by their name-calling, he turns to fantasy. Comparison with other stories that described similar incidents with both common and contrasting factors began to bring out conclusions such as these:

He wasn't sure of himself, so he couldn't take it.

If they showed him they liked him, then such names would be OK.

You have to feel secure. I thought I had no friends when the kids called me "Barnyard Bess." Now I can laugh at names because I know I have friends.

If you know people feel warm toward you, almost anything goes, but if you think they don't like you, you take everything for a hurt.

After examining the fact and feeling in name-calling, the class explored the cases of people who are left out for one reason or another. They wrote compositions on "When I Felt Left Out." One student felt left out when she listened to her mother and father talking together after she had gone to bed. A few papers had to do with "duty" visits, when children were forced to accompany parents on social calls and had to "just sit and listen to dull conversation and act polite." Some dealt with the more serious problem of nonacceptance by peers both in school and out.

In class, the students enumerated the things that people did that made them feel left out and explored possible reasons. Although at first most students said they could cite no experience of being left out, they came to see that practically everyone had had such an experience at some time or other. When they were affected themselves, they felt it was "plain unjust" to leave people out. The class then tried to speculate on how people feel who are left out often and what happens to them.

One local event served as a focus for considering how a group can help to develop a sense of belonging in newcomers and what the "old-timers" can gain from this experience. The city zoning lines were changed, and as a result one-third of the enrollment in the class consisted of new students from a housing project. The students were aware that the housing project was not in good standing in the community. The old-timers organized to show the new students around the building and through the neighborhood and gave each new student a hearty welcome. Each took at least one new person under his wing. The teacher arranged for messages to be taken in pairs that included new and old students. Committees were organized for room management, and students from the housing project were included on each. On the sociogram made two weeks after school opened, new students were chosen. Apparently this procedure impressed the newcomers also. They mentioned it often throughout the whole year—in sociometric interviews, in written work, and in discussions.

While the class was studying the responsibility of the group in making a place for people, the teacher discovered that gang leadership was an important issue in the neighborhood. She noted that the whole class accepted the leadership of the "Ruffians." When one of their leaders said, "Break into the school or else," they broke in. If he ordered them "to beat up a kid," they did it. Moreover, each individual was so cowed by the gang leaders that it did not occur to any of them to refuse collectively to obey. During the reading of "Reprisal," which deals with the gang situation, one boy said, "I wouldn't go with them when they do damage, but I'd stay in the gang." The others assured him that "the leader will kill him if he did that." The girls had a comparable problem in learning to deal with "the big mouth."

What concerned the teacher most, however, was that toughness seemed to be the sole criterion for leadership. Only after examining several kinds of leadership in several different stories would the students even question this standard of leadership. Now the class was ready to reconsider what they liked in a leader and listed the following qualities:

> Someone who uses good judgment in settling an argument.
> Who likes the same kind of fun as I do.
> Who is not chummy with just one kid but is with all the kids.
> Who doesn't try to boss everybody or smack 'em if he disagrees.
> Who gives everyone a fair chance to prove himself.

Who isn't a dictator.

Whom you can trust to keep your secrets.

Who doesn't lead the gang into trouble.

Who asks the kids for advice, not just do what he wants all the time.

Who's cheerful and not always sad.

Who can take a joke if the joke is on him.

Who knows how to plan fun.

When the teacher asked the class to compare this list with their former criterion, "You have to be tough," there was a long silence.

To enlarge their understanding of bullying "leadership," the teacher read "The New Kid" (Heyert, 1941). In this story Marty is anxious to be a part of the neighborhood gang and to join in their games. He is unwanted because of his lack of skill in sports. Whenever he fumbles the ball, much abuse is heaped on him. When a new boy arrives on the scene and Marty realizes that he is equally unskilled, Marty heaps on the new boy the abuse to which he himself had so often been subjected.

The class analyzed the factors in Marty's life that caused him to want to abuse others. The children saw the connection between the way others had treated Marty and the way he treated the new boy. They considered his feelings of inferiority and saw how he needed the feeling of power over another person.

When he gets into power, he will try to hurt others. Those people are the ones who hate others because someone makes more money than they do.

They later hate people they don't even know and people who didn't ever do anything to them. They get their little mobs together and go around hurting others.

Next the class examined the various reasons why people gain the status of leader, as the teacher sought to correct the notion that a leader must have physical strength, be a "big mouth," or excel in sports. The idea that there is room for many kinds of leaders, in many different endeavors, and for a variety of reasons, was apparently new to them.

The class also looked at the consequences of being left out:

They become anti-social and close up into a shell.

They worry so much that they can't do their work well and their marks go down.

They stop brooding and begin to be real mean and beat up everybody.

They cannot grow out of their baby ways because they were treated that way.

They soon refuse to trust others because they are laughed at so much.

They become discouraged and hate the whole world.

They try to hurt others as they were hurt.

They go off and start with the wrong gangs because no one will let them into good gangs.

It was now possible to reopen the discussion of what one can do to extend acceptance to other people. The previous work on group acceptance softened the notion that "I'll lose my friends if I'm nice to someone that the others don't like." However, not all students were convinced. Therefore, the class read "The Clodhopper" (Addington, 1932), to see whether friendships were lost because of kindness to a rejected person. The conclusions in this story were compared with those in "The Horse" (McNealy, 1947), in which no peer makes any solid attempt to help Martha stay in school despite her academic achievements, except Ruth, who makes only a fainthearted effort. What would have happened if Ruth had taken a stronger stand?

The class then examined a group of books—*Tradition* (Emery, 1946), *Sensible Kate* (Gates, 1943), *All-American* (Tunis, 1942)—to see what happened to the rebel who befriended an outcast. Then they pooled their findings and drew the following conclusions:

You may lose friends at first but eventually you may gain more.

If you start it, others will follow you.

You have to make others see that the gang will be bigger and more fun that way.

If you are so worried about losing those friends, maybe they aren't friends at all, and the new one will be better.

There were several chances to try out these new ideas. One girl in the class was losing status because she befriended a girl outside her group whose character the others questioned. It was a difficult time for April, who had previously enjoyed a short period of high status, but ultimately two other girls rallied to her to help her regain her place in the group.

There were several other similar experiments. Ella was too bossy, and the class told her so. She disagreed. She lost ground, was miserable for a short time, made a sincere effort to be more pleasant, and in time was accepted by a new group. Several students took others under their wing, all with good results. This was the case with Ginger, who befriended Ralph, as described above (p. 150).

The class also considered how people need to change themselves to become more acceptable to others and how others can help them change. Some objected to changing solely to win acceptance. They protested, not because change is difficult but because "it's copying someone else." It was necessary to differentiate between mimicking people's ways and adopting behaviors that win acceptability without losing individuality. "Reflection of Luanne" (Holmes, 1949) helped to clarify this distinction. Next the class analyzed situations in books that told why people felt the need for change, how they brought about the change, how hard it was, and how others helped them. "That's What Happened to Me" (Fessier, 1961) helped to contrast wishful thinking with doing something about a problem. This led to a consideration of the ways to criticize others and the effects of honest praise. Situations in books were analyzed to see how to criticize others constructively, and the class played several sociodramas to develop the skills in handling such situations. They considered how one could defend the unjustly criticized and the victims of gossip. The class asked a girl to play a "real-life" situation in which she had taken an important role. When a group was "ripping someone up the back," the girl asked, "What's so terrible about that? My face would stop a train going ninety miles an hour." The class decided that her technique was best. She stopped the unjust criticism but avoided bringing wrath down on her head. One boy said, "Lots of times we're cruel too—everyone is—and we don't realize we're hurting anyone, but we do."

The final sequence included many practical discussions of what people can do to help others to know and to accept them and to create opportunities for others to be accepted. Since these discussions came just before graduation, students were especially concerned about "being accepted in high school." They wanted to know "if everybody has a handle that makes it easier for others to know and like him." Introductions to adults were practiced as preparation for graduation ceremonies when the students would be expected to introduce their parents to teachers. Time was taken to talk about the positive qualities of each person in the class.

High school clubs and what to do about joining them were also thoroughly evaluated. The students analyzed these clubs with the help of several magazine articles and two stories. They concluded:

Some are the right kind, but some the wrong kind.
They won't give the new guy a chance.
They do a lot of damage when they leave people out.
Some people are left out on account of their religion or on account of not having enough money.

These conclusions were not formulated without a battle. Some students reminded the class that if you're not in the clubs, "you miss so much fun." Besides, they said, "You can go away to camp for two weeks if you belong." They made up rules for the kind of club that they would like to join in high school. These rules evidently made an impression, for when some students returned for a visit the next year, they reported that they had refused to join the sororities and had formed clubs that permitted anyone to join who would "pitch in and help" with whatever activities the club had set itself.

This attempt to lead students to accept differences in people, to understand their own behavior and the behavior of others, to learn to organize their own social and work groups so that they might find a place for themselves and for others, to learn to anticipate how their own behavior will affect other people, brought individual and collective satisfactions. These were expressed in the papers students wrote at the end of the year on how they had grown.

I understand people's actions more. I stop to think why they are doing it.

I realize that knowing how to get more friends means I'm growing up and I should let my friends get others, too.

My faults are being corrected. I study them and try to change them. I'm holding my temper, for one thing.

Now when somebody tells me a rumor about someone else I say, "That's just a rumor," and try not to believe it until I can check it.

You start to think of your future and you plan for it.

Now I think much more of how I can make other people happy instead of just myself.

You begin to recognize prejudice in yourself and in your friends, and you figure what it does to you and to the other person.

I don't just ask for things at home any more and rave if I don't get 'em. Instead I talk about it to my mother, and we plan how we can save for it and how long it will take to get it.

When I have a success like in *North Fork* (Gates, 1945) I figure it wasn't just what I did. My parents did a lot too, or I couldn't get there.

It seemed that the program provided in school did have a significant effect. These students gratefully responded to the invitation to read and discuss, to express their feelings and concerns. The content of this topic furnished them with a welcome emotional and intellectual excitement. By combining the psychologically oriented organization of peer activities with the intellectual understanding of human relations, the school program filled a gap in the lives of these students and contributed to their academic as well as social and spiritual development. They learned to marshal the emotional reserves needed for genuine tolerance and mutual ego support. They developed a rather surprising degree of sensitivity to human problems and a reasonable understanding of the whys and wherefores of human motivation and feelings. They began to be able to evolve elaborate group goals in school and to maintain a high morale, in spite of an almost complete lack of support for either of these efforts from the home.

It seems that by combining a fair understanding of the group one guides, with an effort to create a psychologically favorable climate, and by creating a reasonably effective learning sequence, the school can succeed in modifying the socially conditioned aspects of personality and in controlling or counteracting rather potent social learnings.

CHAPTER X

Family

This chapter describes an experimental sequence in the study of family life in an eighth-grade class which, up to that time, had been trying unsuccessfully to study *Evangeline*. The diagnostic evidence had shown that family and peer relations were the two concerns that could be profitably studied in the time available for both literature and guidance periods, a total of seven class periods a week. Since there was no model for such a sequence, the teacher used the diagnostic evidence she already had to develop clues about what to teach and how to go about it. In the new model, literature, social studies, and guidance periods were combined into one sequence that gave twelve periods per week for this study.

This chapter describes how the teacher proceeded from the discussion of individual episodes to a more systematic analysis of certain aspects of family relations.

The first step was to have the class write on such themes as "Changes I Would Like to Make in My Home," "Things That Make Me Happy," "Things I Like to Do," and "Things I Hate to Do," "My Worries," and "My Wishes." The teacher examined these papers to see what they revealed of students' problems and concerns. She also looked for gaps in the students' learning and awareness: what skills should be mastered to handle the situations they faced, what new experiences they needed to increase their ability to make judgments, and what insights were required to understand more clearly the problems they encountered in daily living.

FAMILY PROBLEMS

These papers revealed an array of problems. Some of the students were disturbed by the physical condition of their homes. They wanted grass in the backyard, new stove pipes, or fresh paint. They were ashamed to invite their friends to their homes.

I would like to have the hallway painted and more lights put into it. Most of my friends don't like to come up to my house because the hallway is always so dark.

Crowded homes caused distress, and almost all children without a room of their own wanted one. One girl wanted an extra living room for her father, so

. . . he could sleep there and not where the people and friends come to sit. It embarrasses us and him. A warm house and full stomach always makes him fall asleep. There he stays till he goes to bed.

There were tensions between children and parents or other adult relatives:

I wish my father would listen to me when I do something wrong. He thinks he can read my mind and he tells me why I did it.

I would like to have a father that I could reason with. When I get in trouble my father never listens to my side of the story.

I would try to make my father more understanding toward us kids.

My father does not want me to get anything I do not need, but he seems to think I do not need anything.

He nags at any little thing he can find, but not all the time—just when he is in a bad mood. Other times you can have an awful lot of fun with him. I want him to change so that he won't have his moods and it'll be a more happy home.[1]

---

[1] This group complained that their fathers did not understand them, whereas the first group accepted the disinterest of their fathers. Both groups, however, worried about their mothers.

I would like my mother and father to stop always yelling at me. I wish they would stop always saying, "You're not going out because you did this or that." I would like this to be changed because it doesn't seem fair to me that they should always be punishing me for such little things.

In my house we have three chefs, my grandmother, step-father, and mother, and it's terrible! Yes! They're all excellent cooks but gosh all they do is fight over the food. They all want to cook something different. Now what I would do is make them get together and agree who would cook a certain meal at a certain time instead of arguing and ending up mad at each other.

There were also worries about parent's problems:

I'd like to make my brother understand that my mother isn't rich. My brother gets an allowance of one dollar a week. This my father gives to him on Sunday. He goes skating in the afternoon and to the show at night, and before the day is over his allowance is spent. Then, during the week he has nothing to spend, so he always asks my mother for money. Although I don't like this, I can't say anything because he's hot-tempered and he'll hit me.

I'd like to change my sister. My mother goes out very seldom because when she does my kid sister complains and threatens my mother by telling her all the bad things she'll do when she goes. My mother is very nervous and gives in easily to her. And, when she goes, my sister carries out her threats by teasing me. I wish my sister would let my mother go out when she wishes and be reasonable with my mother.

I worry that my mother is lonely when I go out, so I stay home with her most of the time. She works too hard, and that worries me.

I always worry whenever there's an argument between my mother and father. I'm afraid they'll separate.

Two girls recognized that some of the difficulty lay with themselves:

> I want to learn to understand people in my family more.
> I'm afraid I don't understand them too much.

> I always lose my temper very fast. I would like very much
> to overcome this because I find it gets me into a lot of trouble.

Much was said about the chores. Most of the students, especially
the girls, had many duties. Apparently, these families required a good
deal of help from their children, and these requirements seemed to stir
up conflict and confusion. (This was not true of the first group.)

> I hate to do dishes. Every time I do them, I break one.
> My father gets mad and soon I won't be able to do them any
> more. (I'll be dead.)

> I hate to go to the store just before supper. Sometimes
> mother forgets to tell me to get a loaf of bread or something
> and just as I'm ready to sit down and eat I have to go to the
> store. Then when I get back, everyone has started eating already.

Only two individuals mentioned anything that they liked to do at
home. A few things made them happy, among them being trusted and seeing mothers relieved of extra work and of financial worry.

In summary, a great many felt rejected and insecure, or thought
they did, and only a few received sufficient attention and affection. Many
were harassed by shouting parents, by arguments and tension between
parents and between older and younger children. Even though their ideas
about their troubles may have been exaggerated, the descriptions of
harsh punishments, misunderstandings, and lack of communication were
too vivid to be overlooked. In general, there seemed to be a sense of
puzzlement and of concern about the home situation, a feeling of conflict
between what they wanted to be and to do, and what the home situation
or the parents seemed to require. Obviously there was much for the
teacher and the students to study, to discuss, and to learn.

The teacher told the class how helpful their papers had been and
summarized them in a general way. Next, the class planned what to
study about families, listing what they would like to know. Care was
taken to have each student make suggestions and thereby become in-

volved in what was about to be done. The list included the following items:

Dividing responsibilities
Talking things over
Owning pets
Drinking
Who makes decisions
Quarrels
Permission to "go out"
Who disciplines
Making a living
Understanding the parents
"Picking on each other"
Family fun
Growing up in the family
What we learn from families
Ways of working together

Illness
Different religions in the family
Family ambitions
Care of younger children
Allowances
Hobbies
Earning money
Dividing attention among children
Teasing
Being understood by parents
Divided opinion among parents
Housing space
Sizes of families
Stepchildren

The class realized that each item could not be considered separately, and proceeded to combine them. Three main topics emerged: "Family Problems," "Growing Up in the Family," and "Patterns of Family Life." The class wanted to start with "Family Problems."

Since the papers had shown that the children were disturbed over the appearance of their homes, they needed to know that others had similar experiences. They needed also to look at aspects of their homes that might compensate for crowded rooms, shabby furniture, and cracked ceilings. For the opening on this topic, "I Hated the House I Lived In" (Ferris, 1929) was read to the class—a story about a middle-class girl who hesitates to invite an upper-class friend to her home. Later the girl realizes how unhappy her wealthy friend is in the cold atmosphere that her father creates. The discussion was opened with a broad question that would permit spontaneous talk: What do you think the story is trying to show? An excerpt from this discussion follows:

JENNY: It is very natural. I think that most girls are afraid their schoolmates won't like them if there's something wrong about their homes or their parents. They're afraid to bring their friends home because they're afraid they'll lose their friends.

FAITH: We live in a brick building, too, and instead of grass there's stones. But in some ways the inside of our house is like that story. The story proves that it's not what your house is made of, but what it's like inside.

IDA: Our house has no grass in the back and when the machines in the nearby factory go, it shakes the foundation of our house. I wouldn't want a girl friend of mine to come the back way.

JUDY: Ours is just the opposite. We have a nice back but not a nice front. And my grandmother is so old-fashioned, and she has old-fashioned furniture. I go to other places, and they have nice furniture. I don't like people to see ours.

IRENE: I feel funny because we live at Webster Housing Project, and people make fun of it, and I feel funny about it, and don't like to tell people where I live.

LOUIS: But why? It depends on what's inside it.

IRENE: The trouble is, that's not everyone's thoughts, Louis. People don't say what you say about it.

LOUIS: There's one house we pass by. It's terrible outside, but you can eat off the floor inside, it's so clean.

TOM: I don't agree with Jenny. I don't think you lose friends that way. What difference does that make, anyway?

POLLY: I got a nice house, but I live upstairs in the attic. I felt very funny when I had my surprise party last year. Our ceilings are so low, you know, and I imagined everybody noticed it.

TOM: So what?

JENNY: I suppose a real good friend won't feel that way

RITA: When I go to a friend's home, and the dishes are not done, and the beds not made, they always make it worse by trying to cover it up.

HELEN: If my house is messy when a friend comes, I'm afraid they'll think it's always that way. They won't think it's just once. But I don't think that way if I go to another's house and her room is messy.

TIM: When someone comes to our house, my mother is very particular. She cleans up so thoroughly, and she won't even let us sit on the chairs.

EVELYN: My mother's the same way. Everything's got to be fixed up. Our halls are not nice, and the girls must

think I live in a terrible place when they see them. I told
my mother I wish we could move and I do, but maybe
it is the inside that counts.

MARK: My mother's fussy, too. If we have company at night,
we have to get the dishes done before going to bed, no
matter what. She won't leave them.

HARRIET: It's not the house. It's the people that make the
house laugh and cry.

LOUIS: I don't think boys are that way so much. Women are
more sensitive about things like that. They're more easily
hurt. I go to my boy friend's house, and I wouldn't even
notice about dishes. But if it's a girl friend, she'd feel
funny.

The teacher asked the class which home in the story they would
pick, Anne's (the poor home) or Isabel's (the wealthy home). Most
decided they'd pick Anne's.

> I'd rather be happy than rich.
> Her father was fun.
> You could at least eat and talk with him.
> I'd want a father that would talk to me.
> I wouldn't want to be afraid of my father.

This story proved to be a good opener. It permitted the students
to air their fears and grievances, to see that their problems were common
rather than unique, and to look at factors other than the physical condition of the house.

Next, the class reviewed the list of family problems they had outlined and added new points. It was decided to start by examining the
family problems and to concentrate on the relationships between parents
and children, and especially on the barriers to understanding between
them. The class listed some obstacles. The general nature of their replies
showed that these students had never really analyzed the problems they
had and perhaps did not know how to. It seemed clear, also, that to
learn to analyze, they needed to start on something more concrete than
obstacles to understanding. Family tasks seemed to meet this requirement—what needs to be done in the family, who does these things, how
people feel about having these tasks, and what problems they create.
The topic was tangible enough; it illustrated many kinds of family problems about which the students had shown concern and interest.

To start off, the teacher asked the class to list what has to be done to run a family. They listed in some detail such duties as earning money, making decisions, cleaning house, shopping, cooking, washing dishes, taking care of small children, teaching children to behave, disciplining them, taking care of sick family members. The class then discussed who did these things in their families. This introduced the concept of family roles by using the experiences known by the students and prepared them to understand and accept variations in the roles of family members in general. When, for example, the class listed the breadwinners in their families, they could see many variations. In some families the father was the breadwinner, but just as often both mother and father helped support the family. In a number of cases there was no father, and the mother had to take on this task. In a few families older siblings contributed a fairly large share of the family upkeep. In several families, aunts, uncles, and grandparents added to the family income or were the sole breadwinners. Thus, the class found that the person or persons who took on the role of the family supporter varied from family to family and that variation was due to many different circumstances: the size of the family, health and age of former breadwinners, absence of father or mother, amount that could be earned. The emphasis on *why* the role of breadwinner differed in each family gave the students an awareness of factors that cause differences.

In a similar manner the class talked about decisions—who in each family cleans the house, takes care of the children, manages money, and does the disciplining. Again, wide variations from family to family were observed. The reasons for these differences were somewhat similar to the reasons for the differences in the breadwinner's role, but they were more numerous, especially with regard to managing the money, making decisions, and disciplining the children.

The class was then ready to discuss roles of family members found in books they had been reading. The preceding discussions of their own families prepared them to look at similarities and differences in roles in other families. Some students were ready to assist the class with the listing of helpful books, and to tell what these books had to say about the roles of family members and the circumstances that dictated who should carry these roles. The idea in *Gid Granger* (Davis, 1945) of a whole family, including children, earning the living cooperatively on a farm was new to the class. *Dot for Short* (Friedman, 1948), in which a child plays the role of comforter and confidante, appealed to them.

Then the class was ready to study how and why family tasks create problems. At that point, the students were most concerned about two roles: making decisions, especially those that directly affected them, and disciplining. These two roles, therefore, were studied first. Actually, the problem of making decisions became all-inclusive later on, since all other problems from punishing to managing money at some time or other involved making decisions.

The conflict that caused most unhappiness was that of discipline connected with "going out" and "staying out late." The teacher was aware that she would have no success in dealing directly with a problem so charged with emotion. For that reason, she decided to use a story with a background very much like that of the students', yet sufficiently removed so that they could discuss the problem more objectively. She chose two short sections from *A Bend in the Road* (Raymond, 1934), which has several elements that made it strike close to home. The story deals with a first-generation father who had to bring up his children alone after their mother died. The teenage daughter insisted on her right to go out without telling him where she went or when she would return.

TEACHER: What do you think was responsible for the situation which occurred?

JENNY: When the father went out after he whipped her. He was sorry he did it. . . .

HOWARD: She was mad. She planned on running away before. If my aunt hit me, I'd get mad, too, even if I did know that they were sorry. I don't blame her for going.

JUDY: If I were hit, I'd walk out. . . .

LOUIS: . . . The father shouldn't be so stubborn, and she should not do what she did. They should reason with each other

GWEN: She was wrong first. She walked out without telling him where she was going when he asked her.

TIM: I think the father was wrong when he said she was hurting his name by staying out late. . . .

TOM: If I were the father, I'd ask other fathers what they'd do in a case like that.

HARRIET: I think it was a fifty-fifty proposition. She was too hasty, and he shouldn't have hit her.

FAITH: Yes, I agree. It's not altogether the father's fault. He did come from a different land and was brought up different, and he didn't see things the same way.

VERA: The father jumped to conclusions too much. He thinks the boys won't walk her to the door because they're afraid.

JACK: The father cared so much for her. If he didn't he wouldn't try to find out where she lived.

EDITH: If he talked it over instead of giving her a beating . . . she wouldn't have to run away.

RITA: It wasn't the father's fault entirely. She should explain where she's going. She should even ask if she can bring the gang home. Then he'd know everything was all right.

TEACHER: How would you act in that situation?

MARK: In the first place, I would not have slammed the door. She shouldn't have run away. But I guess I'd run away, too.

BARRY: I'd go to my room and let him cool off . . .

IDA: If I were the father I'd let her tell me what happened.

GWEN: I'd tell him where I was going in the first place. He's entitled to know.

HOWARD: If I were the father, I'd have gone looking for her when she ran away. She felt bad that he didn't come to see her.

LOUIS: The father thought she should have a chance to see how hard life is out in the world. That's why he didn't get her.

HOWARD: That's right too, Louis. He did want to have her see hardships. I guess he just didn't know what to do.

LOUIS: I think the father is right. Fathers *are* worried about daughters. He thinks she's a baby yet.

TOM: Fathers think boys can take care of themselves better than girls.

BONNIE: I don't think a girl should be beaten when she's sixteen or seventeen years old.

HELEN: A lot of times it was her fault. . . .

TIM: And she ran out . . . like she had something to hide.

EVELYN: She was almost seventeen and thought she could take care of herself. My sister is sixteen and my father worries when she's out. But he doesn't yell when she comes home. He's so glad to see her home and see her OK.

TEACHER: Does this situation sound real to you?

EVELYN: Yes, foreign parents had to be in at a certain time and couldn't talk back, and [the father] doesn't understand a daughter who walks out.

HARRIET: . . . my father gives me the first degree when I go out . . . I'm an only child and he's strict with me.

JENNY: Parents do worry. Not my father, because he's never around to know what to worry about, but my mother tells me just what time to be in, and, boy, I have to!

EDITH: Last Saturday night . . . my mother was mad because a boy walked me home. Then I was mad at *her*. The next day I thought it over, and I realized neighbors would wonder what kind of girl I was.

GINGER: At Webster there's no place to hang around, so we go by the telephone pole. But my parents don't like it. Once I got mad and stamped my feet, but I thought it over and realized how my parents figured.

The class then summarized the problems of discipline, what decisions were made, why they caused conflict, why each person behaved as he did, and how the situation could have been handled more satisfactorily. This was possible because the students related what they read to their experiences. Otherwise more stories might have been needed to produce the required insight.

This discussion impressed on the teacher how strongly the opinions of the peer group and its leaders influenced the feelings and viewpoints of many students. Running away from home was a fairly common problem in the community. When Judy announced that she had "walked out" and Louis countered with, "Yeah, but you had to come back," he gave Judy a bit to digest. At first Howard and Judy, and no doubt many others who had not yet talked, were in sympathy with the daughter. Then Gwen, a leader in the group, pointed out that the girl "was wrong first." Louis's position was that "fathers worried about daughters." Helen, another leader, declared that "the daughter gave snappy answers." The others then saw it as a "fifty-fifty proposition." Some attempted to explain; others merely stated their opinion as a fact. Opinions of leaders counted a great deal, and while they might not have swayed the entire group immediately, they certainly had more effect during the weeks that followed than a teacher's preaching ever could have had. Not all leaders were clear thinkers, but the teacher soon learned which of them could sway opinion with such force as to be a valuable aid to her in clarifying issues or formulating opinions.

By this time, a shelf of family stories had been accumulated. Class time was used to let each student select a story and read it. Of course, there was now a great demand for *A Bend in the Road* (Raymond, 1943). Since only two copies were available, the committee in charge of library books posted a sheet for reservations.

To continue creating interest in reading, ten minutes of class time was allowed for each student who had finished a book to tell the others what it was about, to read interesting portions of it, or to indicate what they liked about it. This resulted in more reading than this class had ever done before. Most students read at least one book a week and many read two or three a week throughout the year and clamored for more. Many books were used both in the social studies and the literature classes, but for different purposes. In the latter the focus was on family problems: the kinds of conflicts that arose between parents and children as a result of decisions, the ways in which these conflicts were handled, and the elements that fostered good relationships.

Favorites among the books were *Dynamo Farm* (Allen, 1942), *The Hidden Valley* (Benet, 1938), *Mama's Bank Account* (Forbes, 1943), *Caddie Woodlawn* (Brink, 1963), *Trudy Terrill: Eighth Grader* (Bryant, 1946), *Going on Sixteen* (Cavanna, 1946), *The People Upstairs* (Coté, 1946), *Gid Granger* (Davis, 1945), *Linda Marsh* (De Leeuw, 1943), *Dot for Short* (Friedman, 1947), *Joan and Michael* (Gale, 1941), *Blue Willow* (Gates, 1940), *Sensible Kate* (Gates, 1943), *The Lost Violin* (Judson, 1946), *Petar's Treasure* (Judson, 1945), *The Divided Heart* (Lewiton, 1947), *Somebody Else's Shoes* (Lowe, 1948), *Jonica's Island* (Malvern, 1945), *The Moved-Outers* (Means, 1945), *Big Doc's Girl* (Medearis, 1942), *Giant Mountain* (Neilson, 1946), *Old Con and Patrick* (Sawyer, 1946), *Call It Courage* (Sperry, 1964), *The Railroad to Freedom* (Swift, 1932), *Willow Hill* (Whitney, 1947).[2]

Caddie Woodlawn (Brink, 1963), was discussed next to provide a contrast with *A Bend in the Road* (Raymond, 1934). Caddie lived with her family in the Midwest when it was still a frontier. Her city-bred cousin from the East visits them, and the children, not understanding her behavior, make life miserable for their visitor. The mother blames Caddie for the tricks played upon the visitor and punishes her. The father gently tries to make her see that growing up involves something more than playing the role of a tomboy and keeps her from running away. The class compared these two stories in an effort to find the elements that make for good or bad relationships.

TEACHER: How were the two incidents different?
EDITH: In *Bend,* the father didn't go to the girl and make her understand. In *Caddie,* he talked to her. He said, "All things in life aren't hard things. There are some pleasures."

[2] See Staff of Intergroup Education in Cooperating Schools (1949).

VICTORIA: In both stories the parents cared more about their sons than their daughters.

HELEN: Caddie's parents explained that they cared even if they whipped her. She did plan to run away but didn't do it.

LOUIS: In *Caddie,* the father knew her feeling but not in the other story.

HOWARD: He came up, and talked to her without asking her to look at him.

JENNY: In *Bend,* the father didn't show his affection, though he had it. Here he did show his affection, though the mother didn't.

VICTORIA: The father didn't understand her in *Bend in the Road.* Here he does.

TIM: In *Bend,* they were both too stubborn. In this, the father wanted to make up for the mother's doing the wrong thing.

BONNIE: When he let her run around he told the mother she'd still be a lady. The mother would blame him if she ran away.

MARK: The father in *Bend* was never close. He was kinda queer. But this father was close.

LOUIS: This father believed in a just treatment. He hit the boys, too. In the other story the father hit the girl, and the boy ran around.

HARRIET: He was going to hit the boy, too, but Martha said not to, so he didn't.

JERRY: One father tried to learn how his daughter felt. The other didn't.

FAITH: Caddie had only one unhappy night that she had to face. In the other book years went by before things were straightened out.

A discussion followed on the uselessness of running away. The students remarked on how "it helped Caddie face everybody the next day, when he made her feel better."

The comparison of these two books ended with a discussion of the differences in ways of showing affection. This discussion and an attempt to enact a sociodrama on good family relations showed inability to visualize affectionate relations. The scenes were played several times without ever getting a good portrayal. None of the scenes showed any cooperative decision-making; always someone issued an order to others or carried out the action.

Since there seemed so little understanding of how family members can solve conflicts or promote affectionate relationships, five titles were selected which the students felt best described how to maintain warm relations, how conflicts arise and are solved, and what creates walls between parents and children. They chose *Mama's Bank Account* (Forbes, 1943), *Going on Sixteen* (Cavanna, 1946), *Dynamo Farm* (Allen, 1942), *The Divided Heart* (Lewiton, 1947), and *Willow Hill* (Whitney, 1947). The students formed groups according to books they had read and then discussed how to prepare for a panel discussion. For this, their first experience in conducting a panel, they worked out a procedure for presenting the material, lifting out issues, and giving a brief resumé. They also talked about ways to create interest so that the class would want to participate.

All panel groups used a common question sequence to prepare their reports. These questions were designed to permit comparing and contrasting various stories and to lead to generalized insights. Most of these questions had already been used in analyzing stories read to them:

1. What did people do or say that caused conflict?
2. Why did they do or say it?
3. How did they feel?
4. How was the situation finally handled?
5. How could the situation have been handled in a more satisfying way?

Some panels presented their story by acting out scenes; others, by telling parts and reading; still others, by discussing the issues. In discussing *Going on Sixteen,* they cited the death of the mother and the loneliness of the father as factors that helped bring the father and daughter together and told how companionship grew when they worked together to save the puppies' lives and how, for the first time, Julie took her father to a school performance. In *Dynamo Farm* they talked about the preoccupation of the mother with making a new farm pay, about the sense of not belonging that caused the boy to behave as he did, about his unreasonable anger when she suggested a project for him. The students doubted that things "turn out so nice in real life," or that the mother would simply say, "We all make mistakes," when the chickens died because Terry failed to put in the water pipes. In *Willow Hill* the mother's prejudice against Negroes conflicts with her daughter's growing sense of democracy. In *The Divided Heart,* the daughter is persuaded by the mother to accept a gift from the father, from whom she is separated.

Separation was familiar to these students; they agreed that a mother should not encourage her child to be friendly with the father only "to get something out of him."

Mama's Bank Account raises the issue of family and peer loyalties among first-generation children. Discussion of this book gave the class a wonderful opportunity to bring into the open some of their feelings about the conflicts in their own families.

The incident in which the foreign-born mother brings meat balls to a school tea launched a frank session.

EVELYN: What would you have done if you saw your mother come to the tea in the same situation—bringing meat balls?

LOUIS: I'd meet her half way down the hall and tell her to go home, or I'd just leave myself to save myself from disgrace.

MARK: I'd meet my mother and say, "Get out fast."

POLLY: Mama would have felt terribly hurt, and Katrin knew it. Besides, she trusted Mama not to disgrace her. I'd let her come. I'd rather be disgraced if it was my mother than hurt her.

LOUIS: Your mother would forgive you even if she was hurt, but the school kids wouldn't forgive you. I'd rather take a chance on my mother. The kids would laugh at you all year long.

HARRIET: Louis, would you rather have your mother hurt or rather have the kids laugh if you realized that if they do laugh they are not your true friends? Why should you care what they say if you know they are not your friends—and they certainly are not if they laugh.

LOUIS: But you can't explain to children. You can explain to your mother.

JERRY: If my mother was where the kids saw her, I'd take her outside and I'd say, "Meat balls are not right for this occasion."

VINCENT: If your mother is an understanding woman and she knew it was cold outside and inside the building, she'd still go in with the coffee to warm the people, because she'd know they'd be glad.

VERA: I don't agree with Louis that kids would tease you all year. They might for a little while but not all year.

GINGER: It's true that your mother would understand more than the kids would, but I'd feel bad if I hurt her. If kids are too snobbish, I wouldn't associate with them anyway.

FAITH: I wouldn't want friends who didn't like my mom because of her old country habits.

LOUIS: That girl would be the laughingstock all year. When I was younger, I was in the room with a boy whose mother came to school and said funny things, and he felt like dying.

GINGER: I wouldn't even call it disgrace or think it was disgrace.

LOUIS: If you don't call it disgrace, what would you call it?

GINGER: I wouldn't have a word for it. I wouldn't care.

HOWARD: I know if someone laughed at my aunt, I'd poke him.

LOUIS: But they'd laugh at the child, not at her. I know, I was once disgraced like that.

HOWARD: I wouldn't care. I wouldn't feel disgraced one bit. I'd know it's just their dumb ignorance.

LOUIS: But humans don't realize it's just dumb ignorance.

HOWARD: If she came to open house here in school, I wouldn't care. I'd not be disgraced.

LOUIS: Even with meat balls?

HOWARD: No!

LOUIS: I think you kids are just saying that, but you don't really think that's right. *(A gasp goes around the room at such an idea.)*

HELEN: Louis, just put yourself in Mama's place. Just tell me how you'd feel if your child said a thing like that to you.

LOUIS: Just tell me how you'd feel if you put yourself in that child's place. Just how would you feel when your mother starts passing meat balls!

HELEN: But in the book, everybody liked them!

LOUIS: That's in the book. That's not in life.

IRENE: A tea party and open house are two different things. You don't eat at open house, so of course it would be funny to pass meat balls.

HARRIET: I still can't see being nice to your friends and telling your mother to get off.

MARK: But you're forgetting we said Mama was the kind of woman who would understand.

HARRIET: But Mama was also the kind of woman who'd be easily hurt.

MARK: Well, of course, it's not a disgrace to be different. The world would sure be screwy if we were all the same.

LOUIS: American children don't realize about foreign countries. It *would* be a disgrace. I still think so.

MARK: Do you know what a disgrace is? I don't think you do if you call that a disgrace.

LOUIS: Hey, whose side are you on anyway?

VINCENT: If my mother walked in to a tea, I'd not feel disgraced. I'd be used to having meat balls, and why should I think anything was funny?

POLLY: Most of us are proud of our parents. I'd be proud if my mother came in with such delicious food.

GINGER: Louis said something about American kids. We're American kids, and we wouldn't laugh if it happened to this gang.

HARRIET: I disagree with you there, Ginger. This class or any class would laugh.

LOUIS: Yes, boys and girls don't realize sometimes that they hurt others. Miss ———— admitted that herself one time. I think any human being would laugh at that.

IRENE: *Did* the kids in the story laugh?

EVELYN: Yes, they did—they sort of giggled.

BONNIE: I think it would be worse for the kid if she told her mother to go home. They would think she didn't think much of *her*.

JENNY: If my friends didn't accept my mother as she is, I'd not want them to accept me.

LOUIS: She wasn't accepted anyway in the book. Not by the kids in that school.

JENNY: Then it would hurt me less.

HOWARD: Louis, you can have lots of friends, but you can only have one real mother.

EVELYN: My mother makes scones, and my sister's girl friend loves them. If my mother walked into this room, I'd feel funny when the kids turned around to look at me, but I'd not feel ashamed.

TIM: If my mother came in and the kids laughed, I'd feel embarrassed.

EDITH: Once my mother did come, and I felt so worried because I was afraid she'd say something wrong.

FAITH: My mother visited the teacher in the sixth grade, and she passed a joke to the kids when the teacher went out and I thought it was all right.

This discussion shows the ability to project into people other than adolescents. Further, the issue of power of peer group to influence an individual's behavior is clearly raised. The discussion is interesting from still another angle. It brings out heretofore unsuspected qualities in some students. Louis, who was so concerned about peer opinion, was sociometrically unchosen for a good part of the year. He usually did not dare to deviate from the class opinion, but did so on this occasion. Many others who sided with Mama could well afford it, being well chosen sociometrically and secure with their peers.

The same panel also discussed another scene from this book to show how love and trust helped tide a child over a crucial moment in her life, namely, the incident in which Katrin eats the candy bars she took while working in the drug store.

EDITH: What would you do if you were the mother? She really did steal but she didn't mean to.

JACK: I'd tell her to go back and tell the man she is sorry and she will do something to make it up.

HOWARD: I'd tell her she is not bad, and I'd pay the man, and then I'd make Katrin do extra work for me until she paid me back.

GINGER: I'd not say she is good, but I'd tell her she is not a thief. I'd explain she just made a mistake, and she must never do it again.

JENNY: That's a childish thing that Katrin did anyway. Children just do that sort of thing. It starts out by just tasting the candy, and then you keep it up. I wouldn't tell her she is good, but she must understand she is not bad either.

BARRY: She is right to say she is a good girl deep down. She just has to learn not to do those things.

POLLY: If she said she is a good girl, she'd do it over.

FAITH: But she is still good. She had all the right in the world to tell her that.

BARRY: I disagree with Howard. How could she pay him back? They didn't have any money to spare.

BONNIE: The kid was punished enough. She wasn't used to the kind of treatment that she got from the storekeeper's wife.

IDA: She wasn't exactly good, but I'd do the same if I was with all those candy bars all the time.

JACK: I'd talk to the man, but I'd not pay. I'd have her work for him until she paid it off.

EVELYN: When I read it I said to myself, "It must be Almond Joy bars, and I would do it, too." My mother would make me go back and pull myself out of my own mess.

EDITH: If Carmelita were not there, do you think Katrin would still do it?

IRENE: Carmelita helped her eat it, but she'd take it even if Carmelita were not there. I don't see why she didn't explain. I'd say I would work to make up for it. Or I'd ask to take me away from the candy counter and work until I repaid for all the candy I ate.

GINGER: But I'd be sure not to tell that my friend had a part of it.

JENNY: If I were the mother I'd comfort her. She thinks she's a thief, and she's not. Those ideas are not good for children to have.

HOWARD: If her mother thought her a thief, too, the kid would hate her afterward.

JACK: And if the mother said she was bad, she'd mix in with the wrong crowd and get into real trouble.

LOUIS: I'd make her return it if it was something that can be returned. A couple of kids I know took some balls and stuff from Bryant's and they were caught and taken up to the office. The man talked to them and said why did they steal? They said they wanted it real bad. He said they could keep it, but if they ever want anything in the store so much, they should come and tell him, not take it.

GINGER: It's a good thing her mother didn't scold her, because she would run away.

JUDY: When I was two, my mother took me to a store. They had a little knicknack there and I took one and put it in her bag. She sent me back with it when she discovered it, and she told the man I had taken it. I kept it but mother paid for it.

VERA: My nephew is three years old, and he thinks that everything he sees is his. He picks up everything and brings it to his father and says, "That's mine."

After all panels had discussed their books, the class analyzed the many things that create walls, or warm feelings, between parents and children and the many ways people use to solve their problems. This was done by applying the five study questions described earlier to each book, comparing findings, and selecting common points and differences. For example, the class saw that in each case conflict arose from some misunderstanding of the other person's feelings or motives and that solutions were reached more easily when people did things together and were, therefore, ready to understand each other's feelings. Finally, a comparison was made of the types of conflicts described in the books and those in the students' own lives: how people felt in these situations, why they behaved as they did, and how these situations might be handled.

In conducting discussions of this type the teacher often finds herself in a ticklish position. Almost invariably, when students discuss personal difficulties, they want the teacher to advise them on what they should do about them. It takes them a long time to see that the purpose of the analysis is not to solve a specific conflict, but to help them understand why conflicts occur, how the other person feels, why they, as well as the next fellow, act as they do, so that, from a deeper understanding, they will work out for themselves a better way of coping with the many problems in human relations they will meet through life. Unless students understand this purpose they are apt to regard the teacher as a kind of "Ann Landers," and some may even feel temporarily that the teacher is "letting them down" when the answer they are seeking is not forthcoming. However, the two discussions of episodes from *Mama's Bank Account* show that these students no longer depended on the teacher. They were wrestling with the problems on their own and were responding to each other rather than to the teacher.

After these discussions, the class wrote compositions on an incident between them and one of their parents. They told briefly what caused the situation, what prompted the parent and the child to behave as they did, how each felt, and why. Then they told how they could best handle the situation. The analyses of the causes and effects of conflicts were fairly sharp, but the suggestions for solving them were weak. Only one or two mentioned preventive measures or cooperative effort.

WORRIES OF PARENTS

The teacher, however, decided to postpone the discussion of methods of solving family problems until after they had discussed parents' worries, because she felt that understanding these worries, and their effect on parental behavior, was a necessary prerequisite to discussing problem-solving.

The teacher then read "Like Son" (Summers, 1948), for this story deals directly with parents' worries, and she felt that it would lead easily into a discussion of the ways in which worries breed misunderstandings. In analyzing the story the children picked out the factors that caused conflict between father and son: stubbornness of both; the father pushing his boy too hard "because he wanted him to have a better life"; the failure of the father to explain why he was anxious. "He was looking out for his son's benefit but the son didn't realize it"; "it's hard for a father to be both a father and a mother." The class recognized the son's failure to give the satisfactions that the father craved. "The boy wanted to show he could do good without studying." "He wanted to show his father he couldn't run his life for him." "The father was trying to plan his future too much for him." The class felt that the situation was realistic. "I won't study either, when my mother tells me." "Fathers do keep nagging about school work."

However, most students failed to see that the problem grew out of the father's concern for his boy; at least, they talked around that point, not to it. Neither did they see that the son's actions stemmed from his concern over not being able to live up to his father's expectations. The discussion was confined to the father's or the son's overt behavior as the factor contributing to the rift between the two.

To help deepen the understanding of the behavior of worried people, and what that behavior contributes to conflict, the teacher assigned a composition on "What My Parents Worry About and How I Know That." These papers showed that the students knew some of their parents' worries. They mentioned bills, poor health, "too little time to do all her work," "we just got an eviction notice." But they seldom connected parents' worries with their behavior. So the teacher read the story, "Aw, Go Chase Yourself" (Fisher, 1943), which describes the behavior of a boy who is worried because he neglected to bring a toy in out of the rain. He does not want his mother to know it is ruined. The story led the children to discuss how they behaved when they were worried. One girl said:

JENNY: When I'm worried, I close up tight and get mad. I
          don't want to speak to anyone. Like I read in my mother's
          room because it's warm in there. My brother likes to come,
          and pretty soon everyone is settled there. They turn on the
          radio and make a lot of noise, and I can't read. I get
          cranky. I don't want them to do anything, and after all it's

her room and not mine, and that means it's theirs, too, and I know I have no right to get mad, but I do.

GINGER: Recently, I've been worried about my marks and I'm trying to shove all I can into my bean. My sister comes in and disturbs me, and I hit her, and I get all crabby. Harriet was over to my house, and I kicked my sister out of my room, and I'm usually not like that.

The class then discussed how the people in the books behaved when they were worried.

LOUIS: Well, in *The Owen Boys* [Wilson, 1947] the mother deep down is worried, so she acts mad at everyone because she wants the kids to be careful when they go through the woods alone.

JERRY: Sometimes I'm downstairs, and nobody seems to care what is going on; they're all so absent-minded because they are worried about something. In *New Broome Experiment* [Allen, 1944] they all make fun of this guy, and he didn't talk to anybody because he was worried. Sometimes when people are worried, they are very still instead of crabby.

TIM: In *River Treasure* [Burgwyn, 1947] the lady beat the boy, and then another lady adopts him, and he keeps worrying if he is doing right. He keeps talking to himself about how he can please her. He says to himself "I don't want to make you mad at me." He keeps talking to himself.

From this point on, it seemed easier for the students to discuss the behavior of adults in the family:

HOWARD: My brother just shut up and wouldn't pay any attention to anyone and wouldn't talk to anyone. That's how we knew he was worried when he was laid off.

JERRY: I live with my grandmother and grandfather and they are sick, and my mother worries about them. Once I went in and turned on the radio, and boy did I get clipped!

The class then talked about the ways in which the behavior of worried persons builds barriers when the other members of a family do not understand, and how such parental behavior is sometimes interpreted by the children as a sign of lack of affection.

The discussion took an interesting turn as the students realized that when parents were worried they might not understand their children, and that, therefore, it was necessary to lie to them; the lies worried the children and piled more bricks on the wall.

EVELYN: Something like that happened to us. My mother bought a dresser set and said, "Don't you girls use it." My sister washed her hair, and it was all in snarls. She broke that comb, and I said, "You're always doing something like that. Now you're gonna get Ma good and mad. We decided to just put it in the drawer and not say anything. One day she noticed it and asked who did it. "I don't know," we said—both of us. We didn't tell. My sister was scared, though, and my mother was blazing, so I told her that Dorothy used the comb when it happened to break, but I was just as much at fault because I had used it plenty of times, too.

IRENE: My sister got some new jewelry, and I used it. It broke, and I was scared, so I put it in the box as if nothing had happened. She found it and asked if I knew anything about it. I said, "No." But in the end she made me admit it because no-one else shares our bedroom. She said it made her madder that I put it in the box and made it look new instead of telling her right off.

HARRIET: I don't think you *would* admit it right off.

HOWARD: Yes, I think I would now, because once I left some guns outside and my aunt said, "How did they get out there?" I said I didn't know and later when she found out I was the one who left them she said, "Why didn't you tell me in the first place?"

GINGER: I take three or four chocolate bars from the refrigerator, and it's not fair of me to do that, but when my mother asks me, I don't lie about it.

POLLY: Howard is brave. I got a watch for Christmas, and wound it too tight. I put it in the jewel box, and I said mother did it because she was the last one who did wind it, but it was already broken when she did it.

TOM: I'd tell a fib if I was scared to tell the truth, but if I wasn't scared to tell the truth, I'd just as soon.

IRENE: I just don't have the courage to tell the truth.

GINGER: Everybody is afraid of the consequence. That's why they tell lies.

All students admitted that they worried after they lied, but they differed on whether or not the lie was worth the worry it caused. Some insisted that the lie was worth while, because by the time their parents learned the truth they were no longer angry. But most felt that the worry was too much to endure.

After this digression, the class returned to the books to find out what else parents worry about, why they are concerned about those things, how they behave when they are worried, and what other people can do to help. Here they had the help of such books as *Old Con and Patrick* (Sawyer, 1946), which portrays the irritability of a mother worried about her crippled child, and *Trudy Terrill: Eighth Grader* (Bryant, 1946), which shows a mother concerned over household duties and the care of a sick youngster.

By now, the ideas were well enough in hand for the class to be divided into sociometric groups to discuss the kinds of life situations caused by parents' worries and ways of handling them. Next, they were to select the situation most common in their group and use it as the basis for sociodrama about the ways of handling the situation. They had scenes about parents worrying "when children sneak behind their back," "when I don't get home in time," "when we play near the railroad tracks," "when the bills come due and I want a new dress," "when my father is sick and everything I do gets on my mother's nerves."

Role-playing and discussing the solutions offered in these incidents helped in many ways. First, many common complaints were aired, and the misunderstandings that caused the difficulties were clarified. For example, many families put aside the earnings of their children to buy them clothing. Since the money was not spent weekly, and since the very dollar bills the children had earned were not spent, the young workers failed to see that the money was spent on them.

The students also began to offer more considered judgments about parents and more adequate solutions. They began to see that "sometimes when parents 'yell' they are not mad, but worried." They realized that they were powerless to relieve some of the major concerns, especially those having to do with finances, but that they could refrain from aggravating the situation. They began to see that if they could not remove the cause for concern, they could at least help to relieve other pressures.

After the series of sociodramas, some ideas gleaned from books and from each other were summarized:

> If children prove they are trustworthy, parents won't have
> to worry when they are out.
> Show your parents you know how to judge friends.

Show them you are a man of your word; set the time you will be in, and stick to it.

Let them know you understand they are worried.

Encourage them to bring their worries out in the open for everybody to talk over.

Talk over things you plan to do to prepare for your future so they'll know you are thinking about it too.

GROWING UP IN THE FAMILY

"My family doesn't realize that I'm growing up." This complaint appeared often in the first papers, and it cropped up again in discussions of parents' worries. Papers written later in the year showed signs of rebellion against parental controls. The teacher already knew that dating boys and staying out late gave continual cause for arguments. She realized that it was important to help the students see that each maturity level has its own range of accepted behavior and that people grow up at different rates.

To find out how the students handled their problems, the teacher asked them to write on what they did when something troubled them. The replies were surprisingly meager and immature in comparison with the descriptions of their difficulties: they sulked, slammed doors, refused to wear the dresses their mothers bought for them, or left home—for a few hours. The students admitted the futility of this conduct but felt that "going out and slamming the door made you feel better."

It was time to begin to study the problems adolescents had in growing up and ways in which these problems could be solved. For a start, the teacher read a section from *The Middle Button* (Worth, 1941), which told how one girl succeeded in making her family recognize that she was growing up. The class discussed the methods used by the heroine in winning respect, which were in contrast to sulking in one's room, and analyzed the effect of her behavior on the attitudes and behavior of the other members of the family.

Since the class had been reading throughout the unit, selecting a few books for another panel discussion was not so great a problem as it had been at first. *The Trolley Car Family* (Clymer, 1947), *Jonica's Island* (Malvern, 1945), *Big Doc's Girl* (Medearis, 1942), *The Hidden Valley* (Benét, 1938), and *Mama's Bank Account* (Forbes, 1943), were chosen. In most of these books, solutions to problems are somewhat unrealistic. The students recognized this shortcoming, and one said, "We don't often have a chance to do one big thing like that to prove ourselves. It's the little everyday things that really count, and it's harder to do them every day." However, the discussion ended in describing more reality-oriented solutions than were offered in books.

The students who reported on the incident from *Mama's Bank Account*, in which Mama pawned her treasured brooch to buy her daughter a coveted graduation gift, raised the question of whether or not it is selfish to want a gift that the family cannot afford. Since these students were about to graduate from the eighth grade, the problem was close to them and discussion became heated. They could come to no conclusions; some were even willing to be stamped as utterly selfish, but a gift they must have.

JUDY: I don't think she was selfish. It's everyone's heart's desire to get a graduation gift.

TOM: If I knew my father couldn't afford what I wanted, I'd not ask for it.

HOWARD: I think she was selfish because Mama wouldn't say it hurt her feelings for her daughter to refuse that brooch.

LOUIS: I think it's selfish, too. When Nels called her and explained the situation she said, "I don't care. I want that gift."

JUDY: Can't you realize she wanted a gift? If it was her birthday, she'd be selfish. Birthdays come every year. But this is graduation. That doesn't come very often. If my mother couldn't afford a present for me, I'd not want a graduation at all. I wouldn't want to come that day.

LOUIS: Would you want your mother's love or a gift?

JENNY: I'd like to get something as good as the other girls do.

LOUIS: Her mother was expressing her love to her daughter that way—by giving her a pin she valued so much.

IDA: I agree with Louis. My sister wants something for graduation, but I don't care if I get it or not. It is true it takes long to graduate, but I'd even take a picture of my mother.

VERA: I agree with both sides. You knew everyone else was getting it, so you'd want it. You'd feel low if you had to say you were not getting anything. But I suppose it is selfish in a way. But I'd want it just the same.

FAITH: Then you'd have to call me selfish. I want a dress for *this* graduation. I don't want someone else's. I want my own even if I have to make it myself. Every five minutes at home, Ida takes me aside and tells me I'm selfish. I know things are bad at home, but *I want that dress.*

LOUIS: Would you rather have the love of your mother or that dress?

FAITH: I'll have her love anyway. But I want that dress. She knows how I feel and respects me for it.

HELEN: It's not really selfish to want it, but if you knew she can't afford it at that time, but if you knew you'll have it later, I'd take it when the bills are paid. Judy, I think your social life is more important to you than your mother's feelings. You're saying really that it hurts not to get it when the others do. It's the fact that the others are getting it that bothers you.

JUDY: You'd never get it if you didn't get it right then and there. It's only once in eight years!

FAITH: I don't want a dress because others get it. I want one just because I've always wanted one for graduation. I've thought about it ever since I was a little girl.

HELEN: If my parents give me a gift, OK. But if not, I'll get over it.

JUDY: I would never forget it if I don't get it.

This discussion could not possibly settle an issue filled with so much emotion, but the students had a chance to see the question in relation to their parents. The discussion also helped them to look at the problem in the light of considering feelings other than their own.

FAITH: I think Helen is grown-up more than Judy. Helen had a happy home life, but Judy always had it tougher, always had difficulty. It is hard for her to take slaps. She has to learn how. It's hard to learn how. I know.

JERRY: Judy already had too many disappointments. That's why she doesn't want another. Helen hasn't had so many, and she can take more.

MARK: Helen—well, if you hit her on the head, she'll forgive you and forget it.

Taking the other side, the class discussed how parents feel when they cannot afford to buy the things they would like for their children. This opened up a completely new idea even to those who had earlier sided with the parents.

The class then discussed what could be done when parents' concern about money clashed with children's wishes. The problem of young people not being permitted to select their own clothing was used as a focus. The class decided that the first step in these conflicts is to look at reasons, because, as Mark said, "It's like a doctor. If he doesn't know the cause he can't give you the cure." So the class and teacher together listed the reasons for parents being reluctant to let their children do their own shopping.

Money is scarce in many families, and prices are so high that parents cannot afford to waste it on poor choices.

Children might not know the value of clothing and might overpay.

Shopping with children is a chance for parents to be with their children if they work.

Children might select something that does not fit.

They might buy something that is a luxury, not a necessity.

Regarding what could be done about this problem besides "slamming doors" and "sulking," the class had several suggestions:

Study what color combinations are best for you, and let your parents know you know.

Tell your mother what color you intend to buy and get her approval.

Discuss with her what size you should buy.

Discuss what stores you should shop in.

Talk over the kinds of material you will look at.

Decide on how much you will pay.

Tell her you will make sure the purchase can be returned if she does not approve.

Ask your father or mother to take you with them on a few shopping trips so you can learn how to shop economically first. On these trips, show that you have good judgment in how money should be spent and in what kind of things to buy.

The merits of this method of demonstrating to parents that teenagers are growing up were then considered. This session, coming as it did after building a concept of barriers and worries, had an almost immediate effect. Students told one another how it worked with such problems as selecting clothing, choosing friends to whom their parents had objections, or "always having to go to the store." One student constructed a bulletin board in his kitchen so that his mother could jot down grocery items she needed. After school he picked up the list and completed the shopping in one trip.

To extend insight into the ways in which children can show parents that they are growing up, the class returned to the incidents in *Mama's Bank Account* that they had not been able to consider earlier because of the concern about the graduation gifts. They could now talk coolly about the fact that Katrin "really did grow up when she traded the dresser set for the brooch," that "always expecting Mother to find some way to get things was a little childish and really asking too much of her."

They then considered the reactions of the family when Katrin proved that she understood her mother's feeling about the brooch, reactions such as the father offering Katrin coffee in recognition that she was no longer "a baby." Because young adolescents are so restless about "not being recognized" and because it helps their feelings if they can see that parents are aware that time is passing, a long discussion was devoted to how their parents might show this. Some children thought parents simply did not see that their children were growing up; they changed their minds when others told of their experiences:

> They let me stay up later than the others when company is there.

> They give me more spending money than the younger ones because I have to pay more to get into the show.

> They let me plan the whole supper for the kids when they are away.

> They tell me things they don't tell the others.

> When we have a lot of company my mother lets me sit with the grown-ups instead of at the kids' table.

This session was an eye opener to those who had been receiving these advantages, but had never recognized them as such.

The class was then divided into groups, to discuss parents' attitudes toward growing up as shown in books. *The Trolley Car Family* (Clymer, 1947), *Caddie Woodlawn* (Brink, 1963), *Big Doc's Girl* (Medearis, 1942), *Dot for Short* (Friedman, 1947), and *Gid Granger* (Davis, 1945) were chosen. In order to extend the skills for panel discussions, this discussion was conducted differently from previous ones. Each group talked over the issue while the chairman took notes and prepared to report findings. The panel that finally reported consisted of the five chairmen, who discussed five books instead of each panel discussing one book. This was a step up in group skills. The discussion was not as confused as it might have been, because all books were discussed with only two points in mind, and each idea offered was listed under one of these two points. Then the class discussed the reality of the signs of growing up, and of parents' reactions to these incidents cited in books: the trust and confidence a parent puts in a child when he tells her a secret; the effect of an effort one makes to be less prejudiced and to respect differences in people. The books themselves also offered help: *Big Doc's Girl* gave them a chance to discuss how choosing a career, "planning for your future," is a factor in becoming an adult. *The Trolley Car Family* considered the relationship between taking responsibility and the way families regard their adolescents, a point which only a few could see.

Next the students were asked to write on "How I Help at Home" and to tell how they felt about their duties. The stories showed that some youngsters managed a surprising number of jobs while others had practically no duties at all. Those who had many tasks seemed to take them in their stride; those who had few either complained that they interfered with time for peer relationships or talked about their skill in "getting out of them."

These papers furnished a basis for the next discussion. A few samples were read to the class. After each, the teacher asked the students to put themselves in the place of the parents of that particular student and to discuss what privileges they would give him and why. They pointed out:

If I could trust her to take such good care of the baby, I could trust her in other ways, too.

He was so good at straightening the house and getting supper started before the parents came home. That means both parents can work and not worry about things getting done, so I'd give him a good allowance.

If my child did all the shopping and knew how to manage money I could let her shop for herself, too.

He goes to the store and forgets to come back. They'll think he's not trustworthy.

He makes a promise and then doesn't keep it, and his mother has to do the work herself. Then if he wants to go out and promises to be back at a certain time, they won't believe him.

Because of the perennial cry, "Why should I have to do this? My friends don't," the teacher wanted the class to see that circumstances often dictate how much responsibility is given to young people and that these circumstances and responsibilities differ from family to family. The story "Judge" (Edmonds, 1955) furnished an example of the heavy load some children have to shoulder. It is the story of a boy who has to become the breadwinner for the family. The situation was extreme; the setting was far removed from these children's experiences, but the story gave them a chance to see, step by step, how a boy won an adult's confidence though all odds were against him. The students were also able to see the change in people's attitudes toward him, the change in the community's attitude toward his family, and the change in his concept of self.

A completely different picture unfolded in "A Mother in Manville" (Rawlings, 1947), the story of a boy in an orphanage who pretends to have a loving mother and who tells the woman for whom he works about all his mother does for him. In this story it was possible to study the feelings of a boy who took responsibility because of his yearning to feel needed, to have a sense of belonging to someone. One boy said, "I can feel just how that kid felt. I was in a place like that. It's like a concentration camp. Let me tell you, being away from home is no fun." The class then talked about the ways in which their families made them feel needed, such as caring for younger children, or doing household tasks while the parents worked.

After this, the tenor of remarks about family relations changed. The students began to think of their own role in the family, and to realize that they had the power to change some things. They therefore began to talk over, among themselves, the matters that bothered them concerning their parents. This change is reflected in the following discussion excerpt:

BRIDGET: Having children gives them a certain responsibility in life. Without you, they'd wander around maybe. But children give them something to take care of.

CLAIRE: Well, at home Frank and I are awfully silly. We make my mother and father laugh. He does, anyway. But all I'm good for is talking.

MARJORIE: They love you so much. They have someone to love. I didn't understand that before, but now I do.

EMMA: It's easy to think you're not needed, especially when you put up a fuss when they ask you to do something. But when I take care of my sister for my mother, she really gets a thrill out of it. And when I go away, I know she misses me.

ROGER: I don't think it's so much the things you do that makes the difference. It's that you miss each other so. Last summer I went to my grandmother's and my mother wrote to me every day, she missed me so much.

ESTELLE: Yes, and children give them something to work for, not just themselves. They give them a sort of sense of accomplishment.

CLAIRE: They feel so good if something nice is happening to you, like getting you a dress for your first graduation. You'd think they were graduating instead of you, they're so proud.

MARJORIE: And parents need you just because you talk to them. They remember things you say, and they know you love them. And they love to have you around. Now my mother tells me to come home early so I can talk to her.

Several students who had read *Sensible Kate* (Gates, 1943) thought that this book showed especially well how parents made a child feel needed and how that child felt when she realized this. They listed the various ways Nora and Chris made Kate feel wanted:

They plainly told her they appreciated her help.

They made a party for her as if she was their own daughter.

When she helped them clean they didn't offer her money as if she was paid help.

Nora told her a secret, and Kate felt that she really trusted her.

They talked about the change that came over Kate when Chris explained to her that "you didn't have to be pretty outside. It was inside that counted. It was feelings toward other people."

To help the class realize that parents too are not free, students wrote on "Are My Parents Free To Do What They Want?" The clarity of thinking in some papers surprised the teacher. They spoke of their parents not having time for fun because of housework, care of children, and work outside the home; of family illnesses that "bust up plans"; of lack of money that prevented them from having a vacation; of differences of opinion between parents when "one always has to give in." A few, of course, continued to stress that their parents could "stay up late" and "go out with anyone they wanted." Compositions at each extreme were read aloud and the students helped one another to see the fallacies in their thinking. Then the class reread the section in *The Trolley Car Family* (Clymer, 1947) that describes the daughter's awakening to new ideas and listed the things that she discovered were blocking her parents' independence.

This list was extended, using other books as sources, and then compared with their own list. This comparison provided material for a further examination of the circumstances that cause difficulties: working hours, family finances, lack of energy after work, the size of the family, and the state of its health. For the first time, the class faced the fact that their parents also suffered crucial disappointments, when they dreamed of doing things which they felt would never materialize as the years passed by. Reading *Triumph Clear* (Beim, 1946) helped with this new concept. In this story a victim of paralysis gradually faces the fact that she may never be able to dance again. In reading this, it was necessary to be careful not to destroy the students' own hopes for the future since several were not too certain of their own future regarding education and jobs. At least, they might be able to say to themselves, "If I can't be a nurse, I may still be able to work in a hospital."

In the meantime, on their own initiative, the students talked with their parents about their hopes.

Last night, I asked my mother if she used to want to be something very much, and we talked, and I understood more than ever before and I felt much closer to her than ever before.

I asked my mother, too, when we were doing dishes. Usually, she says "Oh, silly girl," but this time she talked about it. She said she wants lots of money so she can help my father provide for us. That's all she wants—to help father.

We had a little talk, too, and I'm glad I'm going to be a teacher and Ida a nurse because that way we'll please both parents. I guess they didn't get what they wanted, and now they want us to go ahead and do the things they couldn't do.

My mother told me her ambitions are different now. They used to be for herself; now they are for me. She wanted a nice house and an easier life, but now she doesn't think she'll ever get it.

This disscussion led to a consideration of opportunities and advantages they enjoyed that their parents had missed:

My mother was forced to leave school at the age of fourteen and go to work for seven dollars a week in a clothing factory. I'm fourteen now, and nobody even talks about my going to work. Both my parents want me to go through high school so I can have a better job. [*This student finished college.*]

My parents have to work hard in a factory. They don't want me to do that kind of work. They want me to study and learn how to do office work or something like that.

My father couldn't get an education in Europe and when he came to America he had to go right to work. Now he wants me to have an education. He says people think more of you if you have it.

PATTERNS OF FAMILY LIFE

It was easy to shift from the topic of hopes for the future to a study of how occupations affect the pattern of family life. Earlier compositions on this topic were full of complaints, such as rarely "seeing father because he goes to work when we come back from school," or "having to be very quiet and can't have fun in the house because he's asleep," or "he's a bus driver and has to work on Sunday so we have to stay home, too," or "both parents are working and I have to get my own lunch and eat alone."

To extend the conception of how jobs affect family life, the topic was started off with *Big Doc's Girl* (Medearis, 1942). It seemed important to bring out three main points: who earns the living, the effect of the job on that person, and the effect on the entire family's pattern of living. This story pictured a country doctor who must often take his pay in produce, whose wife must help him eke out a living, whose hours are so irregular that family meals are interrupted, but whose job brings satisfactions to the whole family through close contacts with neighbors and the high esteem in which they hold him. Then the class divided into groups to consider the same points in other books, such as *Linda Marsh* (De Leeuw, 1943), *Mama's Bank Account* (Forbes, 1943), *Gid Granger* (Davis, 1945), *Petar's Treasure* (Judson, 1945). *Linda Marsh* gave them a picture of a family in which there is no mother; the father must be away from home for long periods of time, and the oldest girl must take over many duties. In *Mama's Bank Account* the family must take in boarders to help finances. *Gid Granger* shows life on a farm, where all members of the family contribute to its upkeep; life here is totally different from anything these students knew. *Petar's Treasure* gave an idea of the struggles and deprivations of an immigrant family. The class discussed variations in the role of the breadwinner and how his job affects him and the rest of the family.

These three points were then applied to their own families, and the students began to use a new perspective. They spoke of father "getting no companionship" instead of "father coming home crabby." They even took it on themselves to discuss these matters at home in order to let their parents know that they understood, for example, that it was not easy "being a barber and standing on your feet all day."

This study also affected the students who had given very little thought to their own futures, in that they began to talk about what they wanted to be. Of their own accord, they paired off to go to the library to find out about careers, their advantages and disadvantages. Several reported their findings to the class. They became interested in a radio program that explored careers and sent for circulars, which they posted on the bulletin board "so they could help others decide." Groups gathered at the bulletin board at various times to see what others had brought in. Talk became serious. "If I become a carpenter, even if I have to work hard all day, at least I'll be home with my kids at night and I'll be able to see them." This exploration of careers was an entirely self-initiated activity in which the teacher took no part. Study of occupations brought up many considerations of how jobs affected what families do together and what would turn a chore into fun, such as housework, preparation of meals, and budgeting of time and money.

The last topic was what families do for their children. First, the class wrote on the topic. Most of them mentioned food, clothing, and shelter; many mentioned "teaching how to tell right from wrong," "the value of money," "helping you when you are in trouble," "love you," "cheer you up," "praise you," "teach you honesty," "teach you habits of cleanliness." In this context, the class examined acquiring beliefs, such as religious beliefs and aspirations; culture; ways of feeling about different things; and skills such as keeping house and taking care of younger children. This topic became so complex that it became a study in itself. The class also examined the ways in which families provide security, etc. For one illustration, an incident was used from *Mama's Bank Account,* in which Katrin discovers that there is no bank account. The students appreciated the fact that the mother invented a bank account to give her children a feeling of security, but, at the same time, inventions like Mama's conflicted with their desire to be considered grown-up and to be taken into partnership.

> HOWARD: How would you have felt at finding out about the bank account?
>
> GWEN: I'd feel so proud that my mother wanted me to feel secure.
>
> GINGER: If I thought she had a bank account, I'd feel bad when I found out the truth. But then, on the other hand, I'd feel good because now with my new money she can start one for real, and she wanted it so much. Now I'd be able to give it to her.
>
> HELEN: If your mother didn't want you to always be worrying, of course, she would do it. But when I found out, I'd feel ashamed of me because so many times I did something wrong to make her pay more.
>
> FAITH: I'd love my mother even more for sacrificing and keeping so much to herself.
>
> JENNY: I'd feel sad that all her life she tried so hard to protect us children.
>
> GINGER: I'd feel hurt that my mother didn't trust me. Most girls my age want their mothers to be close to them.
>
> HELEN: Mama said, "Is not good for children to worry."
>
> POLLY: Maybe you're not the kind that can understand, and that's why Mama wouldn't tell you.
>
> HOWARD: As children get older, they should be let in on family troubles.

Following this discussion, the teacher read "The Gift That Mattered" (Marx & Marx, 1948), a story of two families. One has comfortable means but a rather detached attitude toward their child; the other is poor but close to their children. The class realized that "even if you aren't rich you can have security." They analyzed what caused insecurity in the rich family and security in the poorer but larger and more closely knit one.

Many factors that cause insecurity, such as drinking and divorce, were brought up.

> Maybe if a father would see that his children will suffer, that they'll have to face things at school, and all—then maybe he'll stop drinking.

> In the fifth grade I had a very good friend. She was so jolly. The past couple of weeks she's been acting dull, goes home alone, doesn't wait for us. So one day I asked her what was the matter. She said her parents were going to get divorced because the father was drinking.

> I was small when my parents were divorced, and I couldn't understand what it was all about. Books should tell children what it's all about.

Finally, the class read "Yours Lovingly" (Courtright, 1947) to see how it feels to have no family. This is a story about an Indian boy who has no family. A reservation agent gives the lad the first affection, interest, and gifts he has ever received.

Again, the class analyzed the elements that foster security or lack of it and then brought the discussion back to their own families:

> IDA: My mother doesn't like to have me worry about money either. I worry, and my mother says not to because we have enough.
>
> LEO: My mother always showed us there was money for next month's rent, and we wouldn't be kicked out.
>
> SAUL: In our family we each have a bank account.
>
> CELIA: My parents took out policies in case something happens to them.
>
> NORA: My father has a steady job. The next door man—he changes jobs every week, and his kids don't have security.
>
> VICTOR: My mother isn't living with us, and my father got us a charge account at a store in case he is sick. We can buy food even if he's sick.
>
> GRACE: Even the sounds in the house make you feel secure.

WALTER: When the house gets too quiet you know there is something wrong.

ALICE: My parents bought a phone because I'm afraid when I'm alone.

JENNY: Just by their being near you makes you feel secure. My brother and my mother were at my aunt's once, and I woke up, and no-one was home, and I began to yell and cry.

MARK: When my sister is downstairs she keeps calling my mother just to hear her yell back.

IDA: When we were younger my mother used to come into our room and tuck us in bed.

TIM: When my mother leaves us alone, she says, "Here's the telephone number where you can get in touch with me if you need me." She always lets us know where she is, and that makes you feel secure.

GINGER: It's funny, but even a little sister can give you security. Lots of times my parents go out together and leave me alone at night with the kids, and it's dark and everything is mysterious but I cuddle up close to my sister, and just feeling her beside me makes me feel better.

HOWARD: When parents just love you, even if they scold you for doing wrong, that gives you security.

LOUIS: When I was in the hospital my mother stayed with me all night so I wouldn't be afraid.

For a final activity, the class considered the question, "What makes a democratic family?" *Caddie Woodlawn* and *Mama's Bank Account* were used to start the discussion. In the first book the family decides whether to move to England or stay in America; in the second book the family decides how money will be spent. This ended with a discussion of the kind of family they would like to have fifteen years hence. Several students had fairly good ideas about what they would have to be in order to have such a family:

I would like my children to be able to come to me and talk over their problems. I won't just say "yes" or "no."

I would like my whole family—kids, too—to get together and decide about important issues. Then my kids won't have to worry. They'll know they'll have a part in deciding, too.

If everybody reasons things out together and decides what jobs each has to do, that makes things run more smoothly.

That kind of thing makes better citizens some day.

I'll teach my kids to decide some things for themselves so they can see what happens.

I'll want the house to belong to everybody so friends can come in and so the kids can have parties.

I'll teach my children about prejudice and let them have all kinds of friends.

If parents would start when the kids are very young, and really make it seem silly to be prejudiced, and make them take everybody else in a natural way, then they would grow up that way.

Family has to understand that there's teamwork and everybody pitches in; then you can get done faster, and everybody can have a good time.

I'll want everybody to be a sort of a partner in the family, even the small ones, and share good and bad.

This exploratory sequence demonstrated that it is possible to use literature to develop a program of study, provided that the literature is used to elucidate certain issues, and provided that the incidents in this literature are used as starting points for analysis by the students. It also demonstrated that the combination of reading, writing, and discussion provides an opportunity for rotating the intake of new information with a personalized synthesis of what is learned and with an application of insights thus gained to modify both the attitudes and the behavior of students.

This experimental sequence helped the teacher to formulate a more systematic sequence for subsequent teaching. Simply stated, this sequence consisted of the following steps: (1) finding out by written work and open discussion what the concepts, feelings, and skills of students are; (2) reading a story or two for analysis of the ideas one wishes to consider; (3) letting the students work out these points in small groups with the help of books; (4) discussing, analyzing, comparing these points in class; (5) applying the new, broader view to look at their own family situation.

In evaluating the new content and procedure used in this unit, the teacher decided that students had progressed in skills as well as in understandings. The students had read and written more than ever. They were more critical in their reading and had developed a fluent style of writing.

In addition, perhaps for the first time in their lives, these students had taken a real look at their families with the purpose of appreciating what each member contributed, what problems and what satisfactions family life provided. Some were keen enough to sense that the family is a wonderful laboratory for learning how to get along with other people. They thought it an adventure to try out at home each new idea gleaned at school. Ginger was one of these. Time after time she encouraged the others: "Yes, it'll work. I tried it out at home." But more significant, these students saw themselves as important members of the family, and if they were not, they knew that there were ways of bringing about change. It was, of course, equally necessary to learn that some things could not be changed no matter what was done. Some made earnest attempts at democratic decisions at home and failed. But the very fact that they had attempted, that they were aware of alternatives, was in itself desirable. If they could do nothing today, there was the future.

Most students also saw that conflicts are universal and that some can be solved while others cannot. For some, this simple realization alone took the edge off the fears they had, such as a divorce between mother and father. They learned ways in which understanding of others' problems helped ease conflicts.

Finally, the class extended their horizons through having had an opportunity to look at other families—families with problems like theirs. The attempts to discover the circumstances that brought about differences made for greater understanding, and less condemnation of what they found in their own families.

CHAPTER XI

The People of America

The sequences described in the preceding two chapters were studied largely in literature classes and during the two guidance periods each week. These subjects permitted a fairly flexible organization of content based on students' problems. In both it was possible to experiment before the new structure emerged.

The problem in social studies was different. Here the sequence and an organization had to be spelled out in advance. Moreover, the objectives the teacher had in mind, the organization of content, and the sequence of learning experiences had to be fitted into one integral whole. To do this, the teacher needed to consider both the psychological continuity of learning as well as the logic of the subject matter. It took some time to develop such a plan. The teacher finally developed a "course" in American history which encompassed four large topics: The People of America, The Westward Movement, Industrial Development, and The Rights of Man. These four areas covered important aspects of American history and at the same time permitted emphasis on human relations and human rights, which these students needed. This chapter describes in detail the methods of planning and teaching the first topic and touches on others only lightly.

These eighth-graders had already studied the periods of exploration and colonization in the seventh grade, so it seemed wise to shift the emphasis to the study of people who came later to this country. Their first task was to decide which of the many ethnic groups in the United States to study. In making decisions like this one, student interest alone is an insufficient criterion. Students' interests are likely to be limited to what is familiar to them. Therefore, before she took up the matter with the students, the teacher set up criteria for selection. Several were appropriate. The class could choose the largest ethnic or racial groups in their own city or in the United States. For a contrast, it seemed necessary to include a religious or a racial minority group plus people who arrived early in our history and those who came later. It seemed important to include groups of people about which the students knew very little and which they most likely misunderstood. The final list of groups of people to be studied consisted of Italian, Polish, Russian, Irish (all of whom resided in large numbers in the city), Spanish-speaking (who represented special problems elsewhere in the United States), and Negroes (an important racial minority in the city as well as in the nation).

It would be possible to compare and contrast all these groups, and for this purpose a common set of study questions was needed. These were set up as follows:

1. From what places did these people come and where did they settle? This question would allow investigation of the geographic distribution of the origins of the American people and possibly, of the reasons for the clustering of the ethnic group here.

2. Why did they move? This question would permit an exploration of the reasons why these people moved and would reveal that some people left their country because of difficulties at home, others because they were seeking improvement or advantage in America and still others unwillingly as slaves. Such exploration presented an opportunity to penetrate beyond the stereotyped notions about the reasons for immigration usually presented in the textbooks.

3. What problems did these people have and what adjustments did they have to make? A consideration of this question would allow the students to see what is involved in giving up a life in one land and beginning it again in another

4. What did they find here? A study of this question would help depict the advantages and disadvantages of life in a new country in sharp contrast.

5. What type of work did the newcomers do? This study would help the students to appreciate the difficulties newcomers usually have in finding suitable employment as well as the range of skills they have contributed.

6. What adjustments did they have to make? Answers to this question would bring to the fore the opportunities to be found in America as well as what people must give up in order to take advantage of these opportunities. This ques-

tion might also give students a chance to consider the American ideals and standards in a fairly tangible way, and perhaps set up standards for the kind of world they would like to make. It could lead to a thoughtful re-examination of their own values and those of society.

7.   What contribution did these people make to American life and culture? A study of this question would permit the class to see more clearly how American life has been enriched by importation of all sorts—from foods to skills to additional hands to build the country.

The teacher made an effort to "take the students with her" in planning and starting the unit. She began with their own experiences. Most of the students had moved at some time or other. She opened the study of why people came to America with a discussion of why they themselves had moved, what they faced when moving, what worries and anxieties they had, and what adjustments had to be made in starting life in a new community. The purpose of this activity was primarily to create motivation. It seemed possible also that a consideration of the emotional problems in connection with moving might lend reality to the phrase "hardships of immigrants" which appears so frequently in reading material and means so little.

The discussion of moving took three full periods. Because these students had had little experience with discussions, it was necessary to establish a climate for participation: each student needed a chance to talk. The teacher took little part in the discussions, but recorded the gist of each person's statement on the blackboard, classifying the items under the headings of the study questions: who came from what place and where they moved, reasons for moving, problems encountered, what they had to do to help, and what adjustments were required in the new place.

A variety of reasons emerged:

We needed more room.

The landlord sold the house, and the new landlord wanted our flat for himself, so he kicked us out.

We came from another city when my father got a job in the aircraft industry.

My uncle died and left my mother his house so we moved into it.

Our house burned down.

We sold our house and were going to buy another one, but prices got too high.

We were living with my grandmother and when the new housing project was built we moved there.

We used to live in a house that they said had to be torn down because it wasn't a fit place to live, so we had to move.

We moved down to the first floor because my mother couldn't climb the stairs.

When we moved, the other family didn't have their things out of the house yet, and we couldn't move in. Another time we moved, we had trouble with landlords because they didn't want children and we had no place to go, and I remember being very tired after walking and walking. I sat on the suitcases and waited for my mother and father. I was so tired.

We moved from Jamestown to Freeport when I was little. I was afraid of the big trucks in the city and all the noise. I was afraid to go to the big new school and I was afraid of making new friends and wondered whether the children would be my friends.

My dog was so big we couldn't fit him in the car. He keeps jumping up, and he had to stay still, he's so big. We had a problem finding a house, too, and when we did finally find the house, we couldn't get the piano in the doors. We had to shinny up the porch and then take down one door after another till we came to the room where we wanted it.

We had a nice big divan. I liked it so much because I could lie down and be so comfortable. But my mother said we couldn't take it with us and I cried and cried when they took it away.

The children knew the countless tasks that moving families must take care of. Some were routine. Others were troublesome enough to be listed also under worries: look for a house, pack furniture, sell unnecessary things, arrange for movers, say goodbye to old friends, transfer to another school, make new friends, paint the inside of the new house, connect the stove, arrange for installation of telephone, notify the electric and gas companies and post office, get a new milkman and a new family doctor, arrange for payment of rent, learn how to get around in the new town, find out where to shop, register to vote, and find sources of recreation.

As the students worked on these listings, two problems cropped up. One concerned the ability to differentiate and to classify: the items on reasons for moving and problems of adjustment often overlapped. Also, it was hard for them to grasp the concept of adjustment.

OUR FAMILIES COME TO AMERICA

When the listing was finished and discussed, the students were given an assignment to interview their parents, grandparents, a neighbor, a relative, or a friend who had come to America from another country. This assignment served two purposes: to sample a variety of ethnic groups—since these children had widely differing backgrounds—and to give the students a chance to relate their own personal experiences in moving to those of people they knew.

In this neighborhood, many people were sensitive about not being accepted because of their foreign background. To put the students and their parents at ease about the assignment, the teacher told a story about her own father. When he was only fourteen he ran away to avoid being drafted into the Czar's army. Alone in the dead of night, he found his way to the German frontier. Later he reached a port and boarded a ship to America. Since the teacher wanted the interviews to cover many points of information, she covered many points in her own story. To create a model, she tried to describe vividly the fears and worries of a young boy escaping from his homeland. She then told where he settled in America, what he found in America (such as the opportunity to go to night school), what kind of work he found to do, etc.

The study questions itemized above supplied the points to investigate. Discussions of these investigations took at least three periods. The interviews ranged from exciting and colorful accounts to lists of bare facts.

The class drew up a list of the nationalities represented in the class: Italian, Polish, Russian, Irish, English, Scotch, French, French-Canadian, Lithuanian, German, Swedish, Spanish, Portuguese, Finnish, Danish, various combinations of these, and American Indian. The teacher noticed that the students were quite aware of the prestige hierarchy of the ethnic backgrounds. For example, if a child had one Italian and one Irish parent, he told the story of the Irish parent. Several others of mixed parentage did the same thing. The German side was preferred to the Irish side and the French side to the Irish. The two Jewish children felt safe enough to talk about the countries from which their parents came, but to the question of why their parents left, they only answered "persecution," and offered no details.

By this process the class compiled a long list of reasons why people came to America:

> They heard others tell wonderful stories about America.
> They heard others talk about coming.
> To make a better living, to have a better life.
> To see the world—for adventure.
> They wanted their children to be born in America.
> There was not enough food in Europe.
> To visit, but they liked it and stayed.
> To have freedom of religion.
> To avoid serving in the Czar's or the Kaiser's army.
> Fear of being punished for talking against the government.
> To follow the husbands who came first.
> For better education.
> To start life over when everything was lost in an earthquake.
> To get better medical care after one baby died.
> To avoid being bombed in World War II.

The students also told gruesome tales about people's fears and the lack of food in Europe. These reasons were to be compared later with reasons that other people had or with those given in texts. The places from which their parents or grandparents came were located on the map as were the places where they settled at first. Most had landed at Ellis Island in New York harbor. The students learned much about routines at this great port of entry. From New York most of the newcomers had moved to New England. Some had gone first to Pennsylvania, New York State, New Jersey, Virginia, and North Carolina.

In spite of some difficulty, a great deal was learned about what worried the newcomers:

He didn't know American money and didn't know if he
got the right change when he went to the store.
They had trouble about the language and money.
Looking for a job and finding an apartment.
Couldn't find the relatives they were looking for.
She was very lonesome.
She had to lie about her age to get in.
They couldn't find enough work, and the children had to
go to work to help.

The reports also contained remarks about what in America impressed the newcomers:

People had too much sweet stuff—junk.
The faucets in the house.
They were surprised at all the noise and cars.
There were so many conveniences here.
Everyone seemed so dressed up.
They could go to night school and get an education.
There was lots and lots of food to eat.

It was fairly easy to obtain stories about the jobs their parents
or grandparents had to take in America, but few could obtain information
on work they had done in Europe. One child learned that when her
grandparents came "even the children had to work in a candy factory
as soon as they were old enough, 'cause they needed the money." Others
had parents and grandparents who took jobs on railroads, in taverns, in
mines, in tobacco fields, or in the city street-cleaning department. One
girl, whose father was a painter's apprentice in Europe, described his
difficulty in finding work here because he came during the depression.
Some were farmers in Europe, but did not own the land they tilled; they
had come to the United States to buy a farm, but they had to continue
working in a factory, and the farm was still a distant dream. Women had
to serve as housemaids, seamstresses, or tobacco field hands. A job was
a job. However lowly the job in America, it was better than the job in
Europe, the children were told.

The newcomers had to make many adjustments. Students reported
that, although their mothers went to work, there was still not enough money
to keep the family going. The newcomers went to night school to learn
to speak English. They had to live with people who came from the same
country, but gradually they spread out. Others described the crowded,

inadequate housing conditions, the pinch-penny saving for years, and the purchase at long last of a house of their own. One child told of the kindness of neighbors who helped the family learn English and told them where to shop. Some had relatives who helped tide them over the bad times; others became resigned to the fact that there "wasn't gold in the streets," and that they might never own their own piece of land. Another concluded, "Our family, even in my grandfather's generation, helped keep America's factories running."

After this discussion a short period was devoted to determining what was similar and different in the stories of their own moving and the stories of the immigrants. For example, in both cases it was necessary to change occupations, but only those who moved to another country had to change their language and to buy new household equipment. Moving to a new country also usually brought greater trials and dislocations than did moving within the same country.

OTHER NEWCOMERS

The next step was to help develop sensitivity to the problems of moving of a greater variety of people. Without an emotional insight into what is involved in migration, the factual information about immigrants and immigration would yield relatively little meaning. The material in the text was both too general and misleading. It created an impression that only outstanding individuals and outstanding contributions had helped develop America. For the groups of second-generation immigrants it was important to learn what the common people like their parents had also contributed.

For these reasons it was necessary to turn to fiction. "The Citizen" (Dwyer, 1935) was the first story read to the class. It is a story of Ivan and Anna from Russia. It tells about their intense desire to be free and to own their own land, and about the hardships they endured in escaping from the tyranny of the Czar. This story was chosen because it was one of the suitable ones in the available anthology and because it described people who come to America relatively late and whose experience closely resembled the experience of the parents of these students.

At the beginning of the year only a few suitable stories were available. Furthermore, the students' reading skills were too poor to allow them to absorb the feeling of the story. For this reason, the teacher often read the stories aloud to the class. But whether the stories were read to the class or were read by them, the usual procedure was to follow each reading with a discussion of the class's reactions to the story. These discussions offered students a chance to express their views and to identify with the characters in the story.

The comments on "The Citizen" follow:

I liked the way they saved. They didn't just dream. They saved.

I liked the way he learned that police in America help you instead of being against you.

She was so thrilled when the cop helped her across the street.

Some people start dreaming to do something and start saving and it takes too long and they give up. And then spend the money on other things.

There was something about the earthenware pot that seemed very realistic. Maybe my grandparents had to do something like that to get to America. Maybe they had a dream too.

They were sure that the ship would not sink. People don't think bad things are going to happen to them.

I'm sure glad I'm an American and don't have to go through all of that.

The class then turned to the original questions used for interviewing and talked about the reasons why Ivan and Anna came here; for example, Ivan wanted a job in America, "a chance to do things where no one would jeer at them," a place "where they wouldn't be afraid to speak their mind." One student wanted to know how the Czar could keep people from being free. Others who were better informed told him about the Cossacks; another mentioned the threat of Siberia. Some had read *Katrinka* (Haskell, 1915) in the lower grades and remembered illustrations from it.

"The Citizen" gives the impression that Ivan and Anna adjusted quickly and that everything in America was wonderful for the newcomers. For contrast the teacher read "Theresa Follows the Crops"

(Lambert, 1947). This story gave an opportunity to explore the feelings of people who are not accepted. Theresa's family is Mexican, unaccepted even by other Americans who also follow the crops. Because the family moves around so much, Theresa knows what it means to be unwanted in a new school, but she wishes to go to school in spite of this. Her new teacher helps her find a place among her peers.

Since there were several newcomers in the class, the teacher asked the class to consider how one feels about going to a new school. They said:

> You don't know what to expect. You're afraid they'll laugh at what you do.

> It makes you kind of nervous.

> He feels not wanted, and he doesn't want to mix in where he's not wanted. And the teacher is acquainted with the old ones, and he doesn't know her either.

One child soon brought this exploration to a head by asking, "Well, I'd like to know why children weren't friendly to Theresa in the first school."

RITA: They didn't know her.

MARK: That's not why. I think they thought they were better. They thought she was poor. They looked upon her as if she was a rag.

TOM: Then the teacher in the new school helped. She told about the dress and aroused interest in her.

EDITH: She probably felt she wasn't like other kids. Just stuck off on one side.

GINGER: When you're new like that everybody stares at you and makes you uncomfortable.

TEACHER: When you came to this school, did anyone help you feel any better by anything that was done?

HELEN: The children came over to me and invited me to their committee they were forming for work in the room. [*The teacher and the class had decided what committees would be necessary to do routine tasks and to keep the room in order. Names of the committees were listed on*

the board, and the students signed up for what they wanted
to do, since at this early date no sociogram had yet been
made.]

GWEN: Jenny showed us around the school the first day in
our noon hour.

LOUIS: You helped us by letting us travel together whenever
you needed an errand done.

Discussion was then focused on how Theresa must have felt and
what her classmates might have done to make her feel better. Next, the
points related to the study questions were identified, but this time comparisons were made with "The Citizen." For an assignment, the students
wrote a paragraph comparing the two stories on what newcomers found
in America.

The teacher thought another story was needed on individuals who
came to America at an earlier period. Since no suitable story was available, a chapter was read from *They Came From France* (Judson, 1943),
a story of the settling of Louisiana. This story offered many contrasts to
the previous two and provided good material for comparing the three on
most of the study questions.

WHO ARE AMERICANS

To discover what the students knew about being an American, the
teacher asked them to describe who they thought were American. The
answers varied. Some said, "We are!" others, "Citizens." Citizens were
defined as "People born here." "Are they the only ones?" "No, if you
come from another country and took out citizenship papers you are also
a citizen," said some. Others thought only those born here were "real
Americans." To settle the point, three students volunteered to look for
further information in the library. The next day the teacher pushed the
issue a step further by asking whether immigrants who come to America and are not yet citizens are Americans. There were yes's and no's.
Returning to "The Citizen" the teacher asked, "What kind of American
do you think Ivan is, just knowing what you do about him?" That provided another focus for their thinking and elicited such answers as:

He will fight for justice, like when he beat up that guy
who turned the hose on the old lady.
He'll stick up for what's right. He's not a coward.

He's strong and can do a lot of work.

He wanted freedom so much. He knew what it meant not
to have it and he'll appreciate freedom.

The class went on to discuss why some of their parents are good
Americans even though they were not born here. The answers did not
come readily, but finally they said:

My father's work has helped to keep the streets of our
city in good condition.

They worked in America's factories.

They had children who went to fight for America in this
war.

They made war materials.

She raised me, and I will be a good citizen when I am
older.

They have contributed by giving their hard work.

After this introduction, it was time to start the study of factual material.
This aspect of the work required the teaching of a whole new set of study
techniques. Students were accustomed to using a textbook and knew only
how to memorize the facts and make outlines. To answer the study
questions required the use of many books and involved a new way of
selecting information and taking notes. Teaching a new method of note-
taking and information-getting while using new content gave the students
too many new things to learn at once. Tackling one new thing at a time
is likely to produce better learning. A new skill is learned better with
familiar material; then it can be used to learn new material. The teacher
borrowed a set of seventh-grade social studies textbooks which the students knew and reviewed the account of the Dutch colonization because
it was the shortest. Then the class was ready to find answers to the study
questions with which they had already worked in connection with their
interviews. This was an exercise in selective reading and in the use of
the index to train them in skills they would need in the study to come.
The answers were compared with those found in talking to parents.

The next step was to teach them how to take notes from references.
By this time a classroom library was assembled: ten copies of *One Nation*
(Stegner, 1945), five issues of *Building America, Our Country and Our
People* (Rugg, 1934), *One America* (Brown & Roucek, 1945), and *A
Nation of Nations* (Adamic, 1945), *One God* (Fitch, 1944), several arti-
cles from *Life, Time,* and *Common Ground,* pamphlets on racial and reli-

gious groups, which were obtained from various organizations. This collection included books for both good and weak readers.

It was necessary then to decide which groups of people the class would study. A list of nationalities represented in the class was already on the board. To this the students added the Dutch, Indian, Mexican, Japanese, Chinese, Greek, Norwegian, and Negro. Since it was not possible to study all these groups, a selection was necessary. For this purpose, the class had to develop a basis for choosing, such as which groups were the most numerous in the city, against whom there was the most prejudice, which were the most interesting to them, and, finally, the groups on whom material was available.

First, the class discovered that they did not know which groups were the largest in the city. One student volunteered to call the Chamber of Commerce for this information and reported that the four largest groups in order of size were Italian, Russian, Polish, and Irish. The students were amazed at the large number of Russians. The teacher pointed out that this number probably included Jews, since many people whom they classified as Jews had probably come from Russia in the early 1900's.

All four of these groups were finally included. The teacher wanted to eliminate the Russian or the Polish groups because their problems might be similar, but the several Polish students in the class would have none of that. The children who argued for the Russians said they could do double duty by studying the Jews also. Negroes were chosen for a group other than white, although there was a bit of grumpiness about leaving out the Chinese and Japanese. Finally the Spanish-speaking were selected to represent a group of people that was important in another section of the country. Six groups was a satisfactory number, since the class could be comfortably divided into six committees. The teacher finally added Japanese-Americans as one group on which to practice the way of using multiple references with the whole class before launching committee work.

For orientation to the study of Japanese-Americans, the teacher read to the class a chapter from *The Moved-Outers* (Means, 1945). This book tells the story of a Japanese-American family sent to a relocation camp after the bombing of Pearl Harbor. The author describes their feelings at the display of hostility by other Americans. One student asked, "Why did they do that to them?" A boy who had heard many tales of Japanese atrocities insisted it was necessary because of saboteurs; besides, "It was what we should have done anyway. They did worse things to us." The argument became heated, and it was decided that the class was arguing with too few facts at its command.

At this point the teacher passed out the ten copies of *One Nation* (Stegner, 1945). Three children shared each book. The teacher explained that the class was to find information that would be helpful in understanding the points that had been planned for investigation. Information on those points would add to the understanding of the whole problem. The class was also informed that they needed to learn how to gather information from more than one book, since no one book was likely to have all the necessary information. Together the class took notes from *One Nation* on Japanese-Americans. The class practiced selecting only those facts needed to answer the questions at hand. Then, since no other multiple sets of books were available, the teacher read aloud from one book, helping the class find what was pertinent. Finally, she distributed a number of different books. Two people worked with each book. The teacher helped each couple in turn, and when everyone was finished, the class worked together on the problem of constructing a report from the information gathered.

Following this practice session, six students volunteered to meet that night and to prepare a report to be presented to the class "just for practice." The class had done some role-playing in literature class, and was intrigued with the idea of acting. Before the six volunteers went home that night, they asked whether they could play out the story. The teacher agreed but stipulated that the presentation had to be based on facts. The next day the group enacted a series of family scenes and did a creditable job. One showed a family on a boat, talking about why they were coming to America; another depicted their difficulty in finding a room in Little Tokyo; still another showed them looking for a job, and portrayed the antagonism they encountered. In the fourth scene they at last rented a very small store, but in the very next scene they were dragged off to a relocation camp, and their store sold. The scene on life at the camp showed how unhappy they felt about not being considered Americans in spite of all their efforts. The next scene depicted their rejection when they tried to go back to their homes on the Coast after the war was over, and the final scene showed their decision to settle in another part of the country.

The class now returned to the original argument about the West Coast Japanese in relocation camps, the question that had been raised during the discussion of *The Moved-Outers*. There were still such arguments as "Well, we couldn't watch all of them." But most were now able to cite the good record of Japanese-American soldiers; the fact that the Japanese were invited to come to America originally to do menial tasks that Americans scorned; that we were at war with other countries, too, but did not put into camps people who had originally come from those countries; that "before you put people in jail you're supposed to prove them guilty"; "that these people are easy to tell apart" so they were "picked on."

One child then asked *why* people in some sections of the country disliked the Japanese. "They are clean," she added. Others gave explanations such as that when jobs were scarce people blamed them for working for low wages, that at first they did not compete for jobs other Americans wanted, but later, by working hard and saving little by little, they did manage to "come up."

One other question was raised—the meaning of a statement in their books on the citizenship of first-generation Asiatics. Three students were chosen to look in *What Shall We Do About Immigration?* (Davie, 1946) for information on quota laws and restrictions against Asiatics. The committee was to report to the class.

After this practice run with the whole class, six committees were formed, each of which was to study one of the six groups of people. The question now in the teacher's mind was how to compose the committees. The teacher had the information on the students' sociometric choices, but, if committees were formed on this basis alone, students' interests in certain ethnic groups would be disregarded. Finally, she used a device that combined sociometric choice with interest in subject matter. She explained to the class that first she would choose only one person for each study group and then a second person for each study group, and this would be continued until the committees were set up.

"Who would like to study Italian-Americans?" she asked. Several hands went up. From these the teacher selected a person whom her sociometric chart indicated was a center of attraction for several others. This procedure was repeated for each topic. When it was time to select the second person for each committee, the teacher again asked who would like to study the Italian-Americans. Several hands that had been up on the first round were not raised because these students were more interested in working with a certain person who was now on another topic. To fill the rest of the committee membership and before the last round the teacher selected students she knew to be unchosen.

After the committees were composed, seats were rearranged so that each committee sat together. The class then discussed what procedures were necessary to insure the success of committee work. It was decided that it would be best for each committee to elect a chairman. The class listed the duties of a chairman and the qualities needed to carry out those duties, such as, that a chairman "must be fair," "shouldn't be a big boss," "should let others help decide issues." Immediately after the discussion, each committee balloted for its chairman.

On the work table the teacher had laid out books, pamphlets, folders containing newspapers and magazine clippings arranged according to the peoples to be studied. The students were warned that materials on some people, especially the Irish and Polish, were very limited, and that if they found that the classroom library had insufficient information, they would have to consult the public library. Meanwhile, the teacher had arranged with the branch librarian for a special reference shelf for the use of her class. The students took books from the work table back to their seats and were given time to thumb through the materials. A critical point had been reached. Topics had been chosen; committees had been formed; and the students had explored some of the literature. It was time to dig into research.

In previous years the teacher had simply passed out the material, given the "go" sign, and then worried about why committee work was not successful. This time she did not want to risk another poor performance. Committee work can be slipshod, and, to be successful, it requires careful step-by-step planning and many new skills. The teacher has to be alert to foresee and forestall trouble.

After a period of browsing the class was reassembled and faced with the problem of how they were going to proceed. Each committee wanted to do something different. Some wanted each member to hunt through all available sources for information needed to answer the study questions. Others thought they should divide the books and pool information. Since these students had already worked on committees responsible for room routines, the teacher had enough confidence in their skill to let them proceed as they wished.

Next day the difficulties began. Tears were shed by one girl whose feelings were hurt. Her chairman had set deadlines for each member to finish his book so that another student could use it. This girl did not understand her directions and said that the chairman spoke to her "rudely" instead of "just telling" her. This called for a little sociodrama session on how one can point out errors without hurting feelings. To prevent any tears from the chairman, the teacher explained how difficult the task of the chairman is, how much responsibility the post carries, and how easy it is to become overanxious about the success of a committee venture. After the sociodrama the students concluded that "a lot depends on your tone of voice," and "you can avoid trouble by putting a slip with the date in each person's book." Other difficulties had to be ironed out too. One chairman gave a member thirty pages to read in one night. What was a "fair" assignment for homework? "Who is to decide how much each person does?"

Everything was quiet for a day, then more complaints—"I can't find a book," "I used all we have," "The library doesn't have *good* books"—all of which were valid. Some committees had few suitable materials and found a trip to the main library unrewarding. Most textbooks told the story of each group in one highly concentrated paragraph of generalizations. The teacher gave the most difficult books, such as *A Nation of Nations* (Adamic, 1945), to expert readers and helped individual students with interpretation. She passed out to others whatever fiction she had on the topic.

Since many books were too difficult for the students, the teacher had to watch for misconceptions and misinterpretations. One boy listed in his notes, "The Negro is inferior," and insisted that was what the book said. Upon checking the reference, it was found that the statement said something to the effect that "The Negro is too often considered inferior because . . ." and went on to list hardships Negroes are often forced to endure. Since two other committees—those studying Italians and Jews—were having the same kind of difficulty, class time was taken for a lesson on interpretation. The trouble lay in the fact that the students were trying to pick a phrase to jot down, instead of reading a paragraph and interpreting it as a whole.

The committee that had the least material finished their study first. They were ready to plan their presentation. Since the other committees had a clear enough idea about their materials, it seemed wise to hold a session on planning how to report. The class discussed ways of presenting their findings that would invite participation and be interesting to the rest of the class. Several suggestions were made: to report factually, but to offer illustrations that would add to interest; report through a sociodrama, a panel discussion, a "radio" program, the tell-and-read method, and by drawing pictures. Each committee discussed these suggestions and chose its own method.

Before each presentation, the teacher read to the class a story on their particular group of people. This was done partly in order that all students could start with some information in common. Building emotional readiness to react to the reports was another purpose. But the teacher also needed the reactions to the story to diagnose what the students did or did not understand about the people they were studying.

The teacher tried to choose stories that sampled different problems and showed several types of adjustment. "Prelude" (Halper, 1945) was about Jews, but it also gave the class a chance to discuss overt prejudice; *Michael's Victory* (Judson, 1946) showed the hard work the Irish had to do and the low wages they received for it; *Blue Willow* (Gates, 1940) and *The Very Good Neighbors* (Eberle, 1945) stressed hardships of Spanish-speaking people in finding a job and home; "After You, My Dear Alphonse" (Jackson, 1945) brought out racial stereotypes; "Things Greater Than He" (Kreis, 1945) described the feelings of a child left out because of his race. These selections included a few stories that dealt with groups no committee was studying if the story described an important problem of adjustment, such as difficulty in finding a job or learning a new language. When no story was available—there was none on Polish people—records from a series called "Americans All—Immigrants All" (U.S. Office of Education) were played.

For the study of problems and adjustments, stories seemed more satisfactory than recordings. Recordings cram too much into a short space of time and therefore tend to scatter interest, and the class discussions following these recordings were also scattered. Although such records were better than nothing, they did not really serve the purpose for which they were being used. Recordings were more useful as devices to stimulate the formulation of conclusions after all reports were given and the class was ready to form conclusions.

Since these stories were used primarily to create insights with which to interpret the facts from the reports, it is interesting to analyze what they did and how they did it. For example, "Things Greater Than He" (Kreis, 1944) was read and discussed as a prelude to the report on Negroes which followed a day later. In this story a Negro boy decides to give his white school chum a stamp collection that his friend has wanted. As he arrives at the house he finds a birthday party in process, a party to which he has not been invited. The mother of the boy meets him at the door and does not invite him in. As he backs out he looks at himself in the hall mirror and realizes for the first time that he is different and therefore not acceptable.

The following are excerpts from this discussion:

TEACHER: What do you think of the story?
ELLA: He was a Negro, and that's why they didn't invite him.
ALICE: Bob couldn't be too much of a friend if he didn't invite him.
PRESTON: It was Bob's mother that caused it—that feeling.
JOEL: She thought she was better than him.
DAN: Just because he's black they think there will be trouble.

FRED: He thought if he brought a present he'd be invited.

CORA: No, he didn't even know about the party. He was being thoughtful in bringing it.

MARY: Bob didn't invite him because he was afraid that others couldn't come if he did.

WALTER: But they played together, all of them in the schoolyard.

FRANCIS: Maybe he didn't invite him because he'd feel out of place.

VIVIAN: It wasn't right of the mother to not even say "hello."

PEGGY: If I was having a party and had a best Negro friend and my mother said I couldn't have him, I wouldn't want a party.

MAX: Maybe the mother never saw a colored boy before.

LEO: The story said she didn't even look at him. She didn't want him.

HANNAH: If the mother invited the Negro boy, the neighbors would gossip and not let Bobby play with their kids.

PEGGY: The kids wouldn't want to play with Bob if he invited him.

CELIA: But they had been playing with him.

MAX: Even though you play in the yard, it makes a difference inviting him to your house.

AMY: If they were friends, why didn't Bob say, "Come in," when he brought the present?

VIVIAN: Bob's mother pulled Bob away.

MAX: Some Negroes are good kids. I lived near them. I don't think she would know if he was nice or not.

GRACE: She must have known him. Her son talked about him.

ELLA: Maybe he didn't. Maybe he was afraid to tell her about him, because she'd stop the friendship.

ALICE: She could at least have asked him in. It would at least make me feel better to be invited in.

VICTOR: But he didn't live in that kind of surroundings. When he went into the hall—the great big mirror—you could tell.

CORA: His father was a preacher and that would make him middle-class.

PEGGY: Maybe Bob's mother heard a lot of stories about Negroes—what they do and everything—he'd steal the silver and all.

Thus far the students had brought out their own stereotypes, putting them into the mind of the mother in the story. Their suggestions were an illogical combination of sympathy and lack of realistic insight. To force the issue, the teacher asked, "How would you feel if you were Jonathan?"

ETHEL: I'd feel the white people didn't want me.

SAUL: He knew it was the mother's fault.

ELLA: I'd feel hurt and unwanted.

NORA: I'd be confused and not know whether they were my friends or not.

ISABEL: I'd think they thought I'm not good enough for them.

CORA: I'd feel sorry that I was ever born. [*This girl was Italian and refused to divulge the fact.*]

FRED: I'd feel like getting revenge.

WILBUR: I'd wish I was a white person.

AMY: He'll grow up to hate America.

NORA: He'll grow a hatred toward people.

VICTOR: No, I'd grow up wanting to teach them that Negroes are just as good. I'd do something to prove it.

CELIA: I would *expect* that kind of treatment. We hung around together.

ELLA: The mother tried to tell him it was too far, but she was afraid he'd be hurt by his color.

VICTOR: Then why did she let him go in the end?

ELLA: He's got to find out some time.

VICTOR: Not by being hurt!

ELLA: Sometimes that's the best way.

WALTER: You'll find out without getting hurt.

ELLA: How can you without being hurt! Not a thing like that!

VIVIAN: I think he should learn it gradually.

VICTOR: If he learns when he's young, he'll think whites don't want him.

CORA: And that will discourage his whole life.

ELLA: If he learns when he's older, he'll become a criminal. He should learn it early.

PRESTON: If he learned it when he's young, maybe he'd try to change the white attitude.

WALTER: If you learn someone doesn't like you, you don't become a criminal.

ELLA: But you'll have an awful hatred. . . .

PRESTON: Down South they don't like *any*. [Preston had just returned from a visit to the South.]

CORA: The whites have always hated them, at least for a long time.

PRESTON: There's still a future to look to. You don't always have to look to the past.

APRIL: How'll he feel when he goes back to school the next day?

The teacher noted that not one person questioned why it should be necessary for a child to learn what it means to be unwanted because of color. She could not resist putting the question to the class, but got no reaction.

The report on Negroes was presented as a straightforward account because the committee felt that their material was so interesting and the illustrations so vivid that no "dressing up" was necessary. It covered a multitude of topics: importation of slaves, present-day migrations from the South to the North, discrimination in housing and employment. In the discussions that followed the panel reports, the class raised many questions and challenged the panel on many issues, such as the FEPC and reasons for needing the Thirteenth, Fourteenth, and Fifteenth Amendments. The excerpt below is from the discussion of voting and poll tax.

LEO: You said the Negroes were made citizens, and they could vote. Then you said they can't vote.

SAUL: They can, but they haven't got the money for the poll tax.

LEO: Whatzat?

SAUL: It's a tax they have to pay to vote.

AMY: When Negroes voted, the Ku Klux Klan scared them and kept them from voting.

STEPHEN: They *could* vote by law, but the whites thought of ways to stop them.

VICTOR: What's the good of a law if they can't use it?

GRACE: *Some* will manage to vote if the law is there.

ELLA: They were chased away. By law you can vote, but if you are chased away, you *can't* vote.

SAUL: If they came up North they could vote, so it does help to have that law written down.

ETHEL: But why did people down South try to stop them?

GRACE: It's about Jim Crow. *(Explains again)* They don't want them to get ahead of them. *(Reads from* One Nation [*Stegner, 1945*] *to verify.)*

WALTER: I read that practically every state in the United States at one time had a poll tax.

DAN: This book says that the Fifteenth Amendment says that they can't take the right to vote away. How come they do?

STEPHEN: If the poll tax is a law, why can't another law stop it?

WALTER: In the South the white people make the laws for their state, and they're not gonna pass another law like that. And besides the federal government can't make laws for the states.

STEPHEN: But it concerns the whole United States.

SAUL: In the South, they didn't want the Civil Rights Bill to go through because the federal government will have control of that instead of the states.

STEPHEN: I heard on the radio that they are going to try to destroy the Ku Klux Klan.

CELIA: *Negro Americans, What Now?* [*Johnson, 1934*] tells about Negro cases that were thrown out of court just because they were Negroes. They didn't even get a trial, and they are citizens.

DAN: In this book [The Nation's History, *Leonard, 1931*] it told about the poll tax, too. Everybody has to pay—whites and Negroes, not just Negroes. But if a white man is poor and he can't pay, there's a Grandfather Clause and he can vote.

LEO: A *what!*

DAN: A Grandfather Clause. If your grandfather voted, so can you. But the Negroes' grandfathers were slaves so they couldn't vote.

These open discussions served many purposes. The teacher could appraise what the students had learned, and it was evident that they had not only acquired a wealth of facts but also could use them precisely in reports and arguments. The teacher reported that this reminded her of a time not so long ago when she was reluctant to give up the textbook and page-by-page fact-learning because she feared that the students would learn less without the aid of the text.

The introductory stories had given the children a chance to identify with Negroes. It was evident in many questions and in the discussions that followed the panel reports that these experiences helped them to consider feelings as well as facts. There is also evidence of an intelligent selection of the relevant facts and of using them productively in supporting points made in the discussion.

Evidently the impressions gained from reading of literature were integrated also and used to illustrate points, as the following excerpt from the same discussion sequence demonstrates. For example, while a week before, Jonathan baffled them, he now supplied a personal perspective to the problem Negroes face:

ISABEL: You talk as if the whites are big shots and the Negroes are such humble people. In the sixth grade, when I lived in another city, there was a big bossy Negro girl who always picked fights to show she's a boss and a big shot.

TEACHER: Has anyone any explanation to offer for such behavior?

ALICE: Maybe they felt unwanted and so they got attention with fights. Maybe when they were young, like Jonathan in that story, they were pushed around.

MAX: At first, I used to fight with them but if you're good to them, they'll be good to you.

ALICE: But nobody was good to them maybe.

PRESTON: Maybe they feel they are getting back at whites for picking on them all those years, ever since they were very little kids.

STEPHEN: Some colored kids were coming with wood one day and started calling us "white trash" and throwing wood at us. We never did a thing to them. We never even saw them before.

GRACE: They must have met up, plenty of times, with whites that called them "Negro trash." Maybe it just happened, and, if it did, they're not going to be happy to see you. If you tease a dog—a nice friendly one—he'll get mad too. This girl I know went by one and he bit her and she wasn't even there before. How long do you think little Jonathan is going to stay friendly and take it? Just how long?

AMY: I read a book that explains why a little colored girl pushed a little white girl. (*Reads to the class from* Willow Hill.)

In the course of this unit there were also incidental opportunities for training in work habits. For example, students learned to use facts to substantiate their statements. When the students reached a stalemate in an argument the teacher usually asked them to find the place in one of their books which explained the point. Generally nothing more was necessary. The teacher made this demand repeatedly in order to cultivate in the students a habit of demanding proof of others and of offering it themselves. For the time being, facts in books were accepted as proof. Later on the class learned that some printed materials are closer to the truth than others. This study came after they had had more experience with publications of varying quality.

From time to time matters requiring critical evaluation of information were introduced. One such matter involved fallacies about how the law of supply and demand works. The class was discussing why some people want to "keep the Negro down." By questioning the class the teacher discovered that practically all students felt strongly that they would have more if the next fellow (Negroes mainly) had less, and that they would have less because someone else (Jews mostly) had more. At such a point a simple explanation of the relationship between production and the ability of the consumer to pay can be an eye-opener. The teacher may trace a simple item like a candy bar from the manufacturer to the storekeeper. She can show what happens when people do not have enough money to buy that bar of candy and what happens when they do.

At other times, committees of two or three students were formed to investigate facts when discussions revealed a need for them. One such committee studied the question of Negro housing—the Ida B. Wells Homes in Chicago in particular—when someone said that only a few police were needed in that area. The students investigated the cost, to them and to others, of police protection and disease in slum areas compared with the cost of better homes and medical care. They brought back some revealing figures and pertinent items from the newspapers, one of which was running a series on this subject. The fact was brought out that each new group of immigrants is forced to live in slums until, after years of hard work at menial tasks, they save money and move out. Newer groups replace them in the slums, which become worse year by year. The Negroes have not yet had a chance to move out.

The class also spent some time in analyzing the style of reporting. Some members of the committee on Negroes were criticized for reading their reports poorly. They were told to "practice first next time." They were also chided for assuming that the rest of the class knew about the

Amendments and such terms as "Ku Klux Klan" and "Grandfather Clause." The committee members countered by asking, "How should we know they didn't know?" It was finally decided that the general policy henceforth would be: "If you didn't know it yourself before you read it, then the others don't know it either."

The other panel reports went less smoothly than the one on Negroes. In spite of the teacher's efforts to compose balanced committees, one committee was sociometrically unbalanced. The boys and girls divided into two camps and at the last minute presented their material separately. Another committee showed the effect of the chairman doing too much work and not "bringing the others with her." The presentation was in the form of a radio program, and the chairman had appointed herself moderator. The others, either because she had not consulted them or for some other reason, did not appear at the practice meetings, so the chairman assigned their parts and worked with them for two hours the night before the presentation. Of course, things did not go well. But the report did serve as a good lesson on how a breakdown in teamwork can cause a complete failure of an otherwise well-prepared report. Other criticisms included such technicalities as "They didn't talk loud enough." Many of these difficulties, like lack of skill in oral reading, needed special work, and were dealt with in the English period.

The procedure for other committee reports was much the same: reading and discussing a story; the study; the committee report; then class discussion, first, to clarify the issues at hand, and second, to compare findings on common questions. These comparisons were made after each report, for they gave the only chance to note the differences in adjustment of the early and late comers.

Each committee report raised new issues. For example, during the discussion of the Italian-Americans, someone mentioned that they were used as strikebreakers; on the other hand, no one pointed out the language handicap of these immigrants. Reading a chapter on the subject from *Anything Can Happen* (Papashvily & Papashvily, 1961) clarified this point. In the course of discussing Jews in connection with an incident in "Prelude" (Halper, 1945), the issue of community responsibility for protecting all people arose when one child said, "My mother says to mind my own business."

To get a clear picture of the movement of each nationality group from their place of origin to the United States, students drew a map of the world, with America sketched in the center, on a large sheet of paper in the back of the room. The students had two good maps to help them in this job, one from the Friendship Press and another from the Council Against

Intolerance in America. Each committee marked on the map the country from which its group came and the places in the United States where the newcomers settled, connecting the two points with colored string. Each committee used string of a different color so that the movements of each group stood out.

HOW NEWCOMERS HELPED

One model map was a pictorial representation of the work in which Americans were engaged. This map suggested a study of what the newcomers contributed to America. Since in previous years the study of contributions of various minority groups had been made from textbooks, discussions had always centered on the contributions of famous individuals, such as Marian Anderson and Einstein.

The earlier study of the occupations that immigrants could secure upon arrival did not touch on their contributions, because the class had concentrated on their difficulties in getting jobs and the menial nature of the jobs they did obtain. To bring out an array of the less spectacular contributions, the class again turned to literature. This inquiry was not limited to the groups the class had studied earlier. Rather, books were selected which told about contributions made by newcomers, irrespective of the ethnic group to which they belonged. Six novels were selected from among those the class had read in the literature class.

Six students presented their findings. The class participated intelligently in a panel presentation, which helped them to use the information from the books in a way that differed radically from the purpose for which they had been read originally, such as description of family relations. The discussion that followed raised several interesting questions. One student wanted to know (in connection with *Blue Willow*, Gates, 1940) who would pick our crops if Mexicans were able to find better jobs. Another answered, "That's just the trouble. We want people only when we don't want a job ourselves, but we won't give them a break and let them get a better job." Another said that the least that could be done for the Mexicans, since they were doing something others did not want to do, was to give them a decent place to live and a decent wage. "Then people will be better off and that will help the whole country," was a third thought. A fourth child decided, "Then they will be educated and will invent machines to pick crops."

Another issue arose when one child told of Jewish contributions to charitable organizations. One boy simply refused to believe that any Jews were generous. The idea conflicted with his conviction that "Jews don't pay for what they get." Those who had been on the committee studying Jews were most vocal in their defense. These students read and reread portions from their pamphlets and became angry with the boy because he would not accept "proof."

To bring the subject of contributions directly home the teacher asked, "Do you think your parents gave anything to America?" Apparently the idea was new, even though it had been mentioned earlier. For a few seconds no one answered. Then one boy piped up, "Yes, they gave *me*." This struck the others as funny, but when the laughter quieted down, this statement turned out to be illuminating. One talked of becoming a nurse and helping people, another of becoming a carpenter. Then they discussed what their parents did, how their work was a necessary link in a great chain.

To wind up the study of the two topics the teacher chose two generalizations and asked the children to write their reactions to them:

1. People came to America to fulfill a dream.
2. People found some things that disappointed them and others that gave them great satisfaction.

Some children cited facts to support their generalizations. Others related the statements to themselves:

> I used to be ashamed to be part Italian. I was afraid people would make fun of me. I was ashamed because other kids were calling my girl-friend "guinea." Then I was afraid to tell I was Italian, too. When you have to take a pick-and-shovel job, people don't think much of you.

A few offered other generalizations:

> All nationalities get that way against a new nationality that comes in.
> You come and you are on the bottom, but you get a job and you can get on top.
> People want America to like and want them.

SOME PROBLEMS

Two important tasks remained. One was the study of immigration laws that the students had brought up earlier in connection with the subject of excluding Asiatics. It had been dropped with the understanding that it would be taken up later. The other task was to develop some understanding of the nature of prejudice as a psychological and social phenomenon. The students had indicated a need for this a few times when they asked, "What made the Southerners want to keep Negroes from voting?" "Why did people spread lies about Jews?"

It was decided to take up the immigration issue first, since it could be covered in a shorter time. Five copies of a Public Affairs Pamphlet entitled *What Shall We Do About Immigration?* (Davie, 1946) served as texts. Ten students worked in pairs to report on five aspects of the problem:

1. History of immigration in America
2. The quota laws
3. Asiatic immigration
4. Who wants restrictions of immigrants? Why?
5. Who wants relaxation of quota laws? Why?

The rest of the students sought information in books and in newspaper clippings that last year's class had collected on proposals made in Congress regarding immigration policy. A few went to the library.

When the information was presented to the class, the pros and cons of a more liberal immigration policy were listed on the board and clarified through discussion. Then a debate was planned. The whole class worked on the wording of the resolution: That the United States needs a more democratic immigration policy.

The students wanted to try a formal debate. The teacher was interested in debating mainly to round out experience with a variety of techniques for learning and communicating. Each technique teaches different skills. For example, the panel discussions require ability in oral reading, in presenting facts in an interesting way, in gathering and sifting facts, and in working together as a team. Field trips train youngsters to plan, to observe carefully, and to evaluate. Interviews require conversing with an adult, finding one's way about the city, and using a dial telephone. It may be hard to believe that an eighth-grader in a fairly large city had never used a dial telephone or for that matter any telephone, but it was true. One boy who had to telephone for an interview found making a phone call the hardest thing he had to learn. Maybe, the teacher thought, a debate had something to offer, especially at the end of a unit, when everyone was primed with facts and opinions.

The class decided that they should know the rules for debating. Together they studied the lesson on debating in the English textbooks, and outlined the procedure on the board to have it for reference on the great day. They had heard much about debating societies in high school and there was an air of excitement as they made plans. Their disappointment was sharp when they discovered that only six could participate as debaters, but the fact that they could choose the six debaters and could act as judges offered some consolation.

The next day the debaters arranged themselves at the front of the room. There was a painful silence. The debaters seemed frightened; the others expectant. In spite of the lesson the day before, the debaters had not caught the full import of the rules and wanted to challenge the opponent's statements immediately. When they discovered that once they had their say, they had to wait for the rebuttal, they were furious.

The pros won, though the cons had argued well. Then a few minutes were taken to talk about the class's reactions to debating. They didn't like it, preferring the panel discussions because debates "make you feel like enemies" and "don't give everyone a chance to talk." After the debate the rest of the class wrote individual papers on "which side they would have been on and why." A few still seemed concerned about immigrants taking jobs away. At the other extreme, a few gave wonderfully lucid arguments for revising United States immigration laws. In the middle were those who had come to feel that there was "something wrong" and were able to substantiate their feelings with one or two reasons.

THE STUDY OF PREJUDICE

The study of prejudice was introduced by reading "After You, My Dear Alphonse" (Jackson, 1945). This story describes a luncheon conversation between the mother of a white boy and his Negro friend. The mother reveals her stereotyped notions about Negroes.

First, the teacher opened class discussion by asking each student to write down his reactions to this story. Then, she asked, "What ideas did Mrs. Wilson have about Boyd's family?"

LOUIS: She got mad that his father is a foreman.

BARRY: She thought the mother should be working.

JENNY: She was trying to tell Johnny a big story about being big and strong. That's why she was disappointed when Boyd said his father is a foreman.

HOWARD: She was surprised because she had an idea that Negroes have big families. She was surprised when he said his mother is not working, because she thinks all Negro mothers work because the fathers don't have good jobs.

TOM: Already she had the whole story. She had an impression but everything was different.

MARK: She figured the father carried boxes and she was surprised that he was a little guy and she thought he loafed and the mother went out to work. She was surprised that the sister could be a teacher. She thought they could only be maids. And she was surprised when she found they only had two kids. She thought Negroes had a slew of kids all around the place. Boy, she had plenty of surprises.

HOWARD: She said to Boyd that he can have as much to eat as he wants. She figured he was so small because he doesn't get enough food.

FAITH: She really was prejudiced because she was surprised that the sister is going to be a teacher. Then she wanted to know if he was going to make something of himself. She thought his father must be cruel and didn't give him enough food.

GINGER: Look how much Irene eats and she's thin.

LOUIS: She thought Negroes couldn't be smarter than whites.

TEACHER: Where did she get all those ideas?

GWEN: She might have heard them in just one instance, and she thinks it's true always.

HELEN: She might get them from books.

MARK: She could get them from magazines and jokes—you know, the jokes about all the little kids running around. And magazines show them loafing and the houses dirty. And the newspapers tell about Negroes in police courts.

LOUIS: She got the first impression when he refused the clothes. Then she asked all the questions that showed the rest of her prejudices.

JERRY: Lots of people have those ideas.

POLLY: Other Negroes maybe were in the community and they were not a good example. Maybe she saw a dirty house. That's how she got the impression they all were like that.

GINGER: She may have read a book about people who start slums. Books have bad examples and don't mention the good.

TOM: She wouldn't believe the good things because she wouldn't allow herself to.

JENNY: The worst thing is that people believe bad things about a race that are not true of everyone in that race.

JUDY: Who starts all that funny business anyway?

HOWARD: Maybe someone wants to take his troubles out on someone else so he starts raving.

MARK: Yes, one person can do an awful lot of damage.

TOM: You bet! Look what Hitler did.

MARK: There's a lot of people who believe anything. If you told them the world was square, they'd believe you. That belief spreads.

JENNY: They believe what some powerful person says—someone who has power over the people.

FAITH: Last year in assembly we saw a picture about propaganda and how a leader succeeded in separating the people.

HELEN: Sometimes we pick it up from our homes and from movies and books and on the street.

POLLY: I got my prejudice about Jews from my stepfather. He came from New York and he has lots of prejudice about Jews.

FAITH: My stepfather thinks that all Jews want money and that Japs should be run out of the country.

MARK: When I was a little boy, I used to play with two white girls and a little colored girl. The white girl would say, "Don't put that whistle in your mouth. Maybe the colored girl had it in her mouth." I thought all colored kids had all the germs.

HOWARD: Or parents will say, "Don't go play there because Negroes are there."

JENNY: Just because some are bad doesn't mean all are bad.

LOUIS: In the paper once it told about five Negro prisoners who had started a riot and the guard shot them.

JENNY: But if white prisoners started it, the paper wouldn't say, "White prisoners started a riot." They just tell if he's Negro.

EDITH: We say one thing and do another. Like we all say people are equal, but we don't treat them that way. If a Negro becomes a lawyer, he has to just take Negro cases.

Next followed a study of the feelings of the victims of prejudice, of the effect of prejudice on those who hold it, and of how prejudice grows.

For this study, the class was again divided into work groups. Each was given a specific task. One group was to examine and report on an article from *PM* describing a study of prejudice in textbooks; another was to report on certain sections of *Probing Our Prejudices* (Powdermaker, 1944); a third was to form a panel on *Keystone Kids* (Tunis, 1943) with the task of talking about how the underdog felt; a fourth was to form a panel on *Somebody Else's Shoes* (Lowe, 1948) to tell about the effect of prejudice on the character of the prejudiced girl. The fifth group was to prepare a discussion on the filmstrip *About People*. To test the effectiveness of mastering group skills, all groups but the last worked entirely by themselves. This group needed help because showing a movie was a new experience for them. They had to learn to run the machine, to talk while the film was being shown, and to encourage group participation. All reports were discussed thoroughly. Sometimes it was possible to hear two reports in one period, but others took a whole one. *About People* took two periods. It was a long film that had good content and new ideas.

Finally, the class read the cartoon pamphlets "They Got the Blame" (Gould, 1945). The students were most impressed by the tie-up between the scapegoats of today and witches, the scapegoats of another day. The class concluded:

> If people are easily led and if they believe everything they hear, the whole country can be aroused against a small minority.
>
> People that are blamed aren't always the cause of the trouble.
>
> People who don't want to blame themselves, find someone else to blame.

The final discussion in this unit was on the topic "What we can do to make the kind of world we want." First little buzz groups were formed just to talk. This was done partly because the teacher assumed that in smaller groups talking would be easier for some students. Then the class pooled their suggestions. Someone asked, "How can you fight everyone else who doesn't think the way we do?" Another answered, "If everyone does a little bit—as much as he can—they'll learn." But a third countered with, "That's too much waiting—till you get everybody to learn."

Then the suggestions became a bit more tangible.

> In high school we'll meet other kids and tell them.
>
> When we had our school elections a Negro man got lots of white votes. We can help in votes, later, too.

When we vote, we can get people in who will work for better homes for everybody.

We have to let people know that if we paid more money for good homes and schools for everybody, we'd save money on police and it would be cheaper in the end.

We have to support the FEPC.

We can help fight prejudice by not talking against minorities ourselves.

We can take time to find out the truth before we talk.

We can band together for good as much as others band together for the bad.

We can help by talking for minorities when someone talks against them.

Let people know that prejudice leads to war.

We mustn't stand on the sidelines and let things happen.

We have to think of people as people, not as special kinds.

It will take a long, long time but we'll teach our kids and they'll teach their kids.

THE RIGHTS OF MAN

The last unit was on Rights. For it they used such sensitizing materials as *We Have Tomorrow* (Bontemps, 1945), *The Girl Who Ran for President* (Kerr, 1947), *For the Rights of Men* (Carmer, 1947), *The Railroad to Freedom* (Swilt, 1932), *The Good Crop* (Emerson, 1946), *Joe Louis: American* (Miller, 1945), *Anything Can Happen* (Papashvily & Papashvily, 1961), and *Freedom Road* (Fast, 1946b). The teacher screened *Freedom Road* carefully and read only parts of it to the class.

The right to vote was chosen for intensive study. That right had the longest history; its development could be traced through the history of the United States. The study focused on how it came to be a right and who still does not have that right.

The class studied the landmarks in the gaining of civil rights, from the Magna Carta and the Petition of Right on to the present day, and the setting of the early struggle for rights and the conditions that led to it. This struggle would form a basis for contrast with conditions at later points in history. The selection of American landmarks in the struggle for right included: Mayflower Compact, Act of Toleration, House of Burgesses, Fundamental Orders of Connecticut, Bacon's Rebellion, Declaration of Independence, War of Independence, Constitution, Bill of Rights, the

Thirteenth, Fourteenth, Fifteenth, and Nineteenth Amendments, Roosevelt's Four Freedoms, FEPC, and the Civil Rights Bill.

The filmstrip series *Our American Heritage* (Reader's Digest). helped with the study of this part of the unit. An effort was made to see how many individuals and groups worked to gain those rights and how others worked to take them away. An attempt was also made to show how rights are won, sometimes by war, at other times by laws, and how individuals can be a great influence in rousing public opinion (*Citizen Tom Paine* [Fast, 1946a] brings out this point), while other individuals and groups can do great harm in denying rights to others.

The next attempt was to develop an insight into what must be done before unrealized rights, such as the right to have a job, may be attained for all. Students often take the rights they have for granted. They think that rights "just come." The study of the historic struggle to establish civil and human rights gave this group a picture of the ups and downs in the terrific effort that man must make to gain them. Studying the problem in this context helped them gain a perspective in which the struggle for the extension of rights in America was seen as part of a greater one going on in the world today.

In groups, the class studied about other rights that mankind was struggling for during the same period: the right to free speech, free press, free education, and religious liberty. They learned how these rights were acquired, how they were taken away. For this part, they used such pamphlets as *Religious Liberty* (Williams, 1941). They also had a few copies of "The Democracy" (Macmillan) series. The teacher read to the class such stories as *Citizen Tom Paine* (Fast, 1946a) to show how people organize to gain rights; *Freedom Road* (Fast, 1946b)[1] to show how they feel when they are fighting for the rights of others; *Anchor Man* (Jackson, 1947), *Tradition* (Emery, 1946), *The Moved-Outers* (Means, 1945) to show how they feel when they are denied rights that others have.

In connection with this study, the class also visited the state capitol to watch the legislature in session, to listen to a public hearing, and to see where the state supreme court makes its decisions. Before the visit, the class examined the process by which a bill becomes a law. This background, the teacher hoped, would enable them to understand what was going on regardless of what stage a bill happened to be in when they arrived.

As a culminating activity for the year's work, the class constructed a huge time-line, marked off by periods of fifty years. They were given two

---

[1] Adult novels like these should be read critically by the teachers before selections are made for class use.

days to look up the dates of events they had studied and enter them into the time-line. The final chart was a mess because almost every student had something to add. The class, however, felt a great deal of satisfaction when they opened their books to the appendix, compared their list of important events with that in the text, and found that they had included them all and then some.

CHAPTER XII

What Happened

It is difficult to assess the results of the kind of program we have been discussing. Such a program can be assessed only in terms of what happens to the students for whom it is designed and in terms of the particular objectives for these special students. Evaluation of such a program, therefore, depended heavily on examining what these students said, wrote, and did.

EVALUATION OF THE EIGHTH GRADE

The eighth-grade teacher accumulated fairly systematic data and described her efforts as follows:

> I recorded their discussions in detail and kept notes on difficulties with skills and thinking as well as on progress as we went along. I saved papers that children wrote and compared them to see what changes in insights and attitudes they revealed and what growth in skills they showed. I kept records of what they read and on their reactions to books. Sociometric questions were given several times a year to record new patterns in group relationships and changes in reasons for choices. A detailed class log permitted me to assess the changes in what happened in class. Over fifty class discussions were recorded verbatim. They were analyzed for evidence on attitudes, insights, and thinking. I also did my best to combine information from many sources: my own observations, parents' comments, and remarks by children in their conversations with me after school to note which tendencies appeared in all. In this manner I gradually

accumulated insights on what happened to the students: what they knew, believed and valued, and what they could do or think. My conclusions were based on the data these devices supplied.

Naturally, this evidence was not entirely objective. The data from reading records and sociograms was fairly compact and comparable: I could count the number of books read and assess their level of maturity; I could trace the broadening in patterns of acceptance and maturing of reasons for choices. Other materials—writing, classroom discussions, and observations called for judgment rather than a quantitative analysis. There was no time to subject these materials to careful quantitative analysis. I could only study them and note changes.

Subsequently these data were subjected to a more careful quantitative analysis. Much of the material included in this chapter and in those preceding was derived from this analysis (see Taba, 1955).

Relatively speaking, assessing growth in academic achievement presented no problem. The records of classroom discussions provided abundant evidence of the students' knowledge of American history. These records assured the teacher that the students had a fairly coherent idea of the main events in the making of America. Even though chronological sequence was not followed, the students had examined several periods of American history in connection with each topic, searching for relevant points, relating ideas and facts, and making comparisons. Furthermore, approaching the study of history by marking off the landmark events helped them to gain a rational basis for reconstructing historic events. They could tell in which period of history a given event could possibly have occurred, what significance it had, and how it affected the course of other historic events.

Reading and Writing

At the beginning there was some concern that the students might not get sufficient practice in reading and writing, but their work exceeded all expectations. By the end of the year, many students had advanced two years in standard reading scores. The amount of reading increased also. These students read many more books than any class had before. Students who said they had not read a book "on their own" for years were now reading one a week and liking it. It was not uncommon for some to read two or three books a week. One parent commented, "I don't know what's come over her. She never used to read. Now I can't get her to take her nose out of the book."

This change in interest in, and attitude toward, reading resulted largely from the practice of not assigning reading, but allowing students to talk about the books they had read and to recommend them to others. Because these books satisfied immediate needs and answered questions important to them, the students usually talked about them enthusiastically. In time, they began to regard reading in an entirely new light. Books were there to answer questions, to provide ideas, and to enjoy. Often, when questions were raised in class, students answered them by recommending books on the subject. This change in orientation to books was also reflected in requests to the teacher for book recommendations. Instead of asking the teacher for a "book with excitement" or "about horses," as they had earlier, the students looked for books to answer questions on specific problems, such as: "I want a book that tells how families can get along."

This wider reading, focused on specific purposes, induced students to evaluate sources for their adequacy and to differentiate sources that supplied facts from those that gave opinions or described feelings. All this, of course, changed the way in which information from reading was used: it was applied to solving problems instead of only being committed to memory in order to pass a test.

The students' skill in writing also increased markedly, not only in mechanics but even more in the ease and effectiveness with which they expressed themselves. They began to speak and to write more coherently, more fluently, and more interestingly. Students who at first found it difficult to write more than a sentence or two, who had always dreaded writing themes, now began to write with a fair degree of skill and in some cases with enjoyment and originality. Spelling began to improve with very little formal practice. Because students wrote for a purpose, they were anxious to write well. They composed individual spelling dictionaries to avoid misspellings, a device that worked beautifully as a substitute for spelling drills. As the students acquired new and exciting ideas, talked them over in school and out, they gained confidence because now they had something to talk and to write about.

Two examples of writing are given below. One is a theme from the last set of papers written in Social Studies, in which students wrote their reactions to the story "How I Found America": why they thought the author wrote the story, what they thought of her reactions to America, and what caused the change in her feelings. The other is a personal reaction to a sophisticated story in *Harper's*—"The High Hill" (Deasy, 1948)—that deals with the problem of social isolation in the first grade.

I think the author wrote the book to show the feeling an immigrant has for America and the way they are received, the way some people made them work for almost nothing, how they thought America was so wonderful and then found out what they thought was the real America in the slums and sweatshops because they couldn't see the other side of America. It shows how one person cared not for the others, each striving to keep alive, each becoming a stranger among friends. People grow within themselves knowing they are nothing America wants. Unless something happens to change their minds they live and die, as they think, without a purpose to fulfill.

I think her reaction was a natural one, although at first not complimentary to American ideas of freedom. I don't think anyone living under those same conditions would have acted much differently. Anyone who had to live in slums, who worked hard night and day in a sweatshop would not believe America was the land of freedom. America *is* a land of freedom, but only if you are accepted by Americans and have a decent living.

I think she changed when the American listened to her story and encouraged her to talk. I think this was the important factor in changing her idea about America. If there were a few more understanding people like her in the world it would no doubt be a better place to live. Now she had a gleam of the true America. Now she could help make the great American idea of freedom for all people come true.

* * *

It was a beautiful story! I wonder, are all teachers like Miss Farrel? Could there be more people in this world like her, wanting to do those same things and having dreams like hers? If so it could be too wonderful. And I felt so happy when those dreams were fulfilled, just by a little unwanted child. It was justice. A justice that can never be served in a world court of law and man. It goes deeper than that. And are there more like Sisley? I know from personal experience that there are. Dreams and prayers and hopes can come true if each and every one of us tried being a small portion of Sisley. She was definitely a democratic person. It's good to be like that in the "valley of childhood." She'll have that quality always. We all know, of course, that there are thousands of Elvy's all over the world. I myself was an Elvy. Bonnie, Ginger, Helen, and Harriet were the ones named Sisley. Especially Harriet. They've helped me come a long way. Since I started school all the way up to the fifth grade my name might well have been Elvy. I was first thought of as—well—I just didn't seem accepted.

I think there are many like Miss Janieck. The way of talking and the feelings.

Margot may in time lose her feelings toward kids like Elvy. I hope so. For if that's the case then there would be brotherhood and lots and lots more of love.

Class Discussions

Perhaps the most dramatic change occurred in the quality of discussions. The chief problem at the beginning of the year was to elicit any response at all, and later, to talk coherently and logically and thoughtfully. At first the students simply gave some kind of thoughtless response to the teacher's questions. The responses were also addressed exclusively to the teacher and never to the class or to individuals in it.

A typical discussion early in the year ran something like this:

TEACHER: Why do you think the author wrote this book?
STUDENT: Because it is an interesting story.
TEACHER: What do you suppose made that girl behave that way?
STUDENT: Because she wanted to.
TEACHER: Why did she want to?
STUDENT: She just decided she did.

A bit later, participation increased but still the students did not focus on any topic very long, and only a few took part at any one time. The discussion pattern was that of an argument, of pitting one against another, as the excerpt below shows:

GIRL 1: If a boy doesn't come from a good family, I don't think the college should admit him.

GIRL 2:   Why not? I don't agree with you. His *marks* are good.

GIRL 1:   But he's not good, even if his marks are.

GIRL 3:   What makes you think this boy isn't good? Even if a child lives in the slums, he can still be good.

GIRL 1:   I don't mean about slums. I mean his family. If he doesn't come from a good family, he won't be good, and he shouldn't be in college.

BOY 1:   If my parents get drunk every night, I can still be a good kid.

GIRL 1:   But those parents will lead you wrong.

GIRL 4:   It's not the kid's fault. He's only small, and he can't tell his parents how to bring him up.

GIRL 1:   I didn't say it was his fault, but he still didn't have a good influence and he shouldn't be in college.

GIRL 5:   It's not his fault, but you are still punishing him because of it. You should let him in that college if his marks are good and then put him out later if his character isn't good.

BOY 2:   If my parents were drunk, I'd want to go to college and prove I was different.

GIRL 1:   But all kids don't feel that way when they come from a bad home. They're bad too.

BOY 2:   But you don't know which way he'll be or what he's like.

BOY 3:   Sometimes a kid learns from parents' mistakes and he won't be that way.

GIRL 1:   But still they've influenced him. It will bother him and his marks will go down, and he'll be kicked out anyway. And he's not a good influence on the other kids in that school if he didn't come from a good home. I still think he shouldn't be in college.

BOY 4:   What if he keeps up his marks and ignores his father?

GIRL 1:   That's just a chance.

Throughout the discussions, opinionated comments such as the following kept cropping up:

Any mother who wants to give plenty of time to her kids, will.

He was a coward for not being able to take a ribbing.

I wouldn't associate with anyone who is that loud.
If her house isn't clean, she won't be clean either.
If he doesn't have a good job, it's because he didn't try.
He should have sense enough to know better.
He's a sissy, and I don't blame the other kids for not letting him in the game. He doesn't know how to throw the ball anyway.

As time went on, many changes took place. First, participation increased. More students learned to talk freely in class. The students also began to listen and respond to each other, instead of only reacting to the questions of the teacher. They learned to focus on central questions, to follow a thread of an idea, and to offer lively contrasting ideas without getting into fruitless arguments. They learned to develop each other's ideas and to articulate important concepts.

The discussions later in the year also demonstrated their capacity to analyze human behavior, how it is caused and how it is learned. Above all, these students, who in the beginning of the year had a great difficulty in understanding the positions, views, and feelings of others, began to demonstrate a rather unusual sensitivity and capacity to identify themselves with feelings and views that were different from their own. There was less dependence on conventional clichés that substitute for thinking about other people. The analysis of the characters in books and their behavior showed a remarkable depth of perception as well as the ability to relate facts from other sources to the content of the story.

The two discussion excerpts below demonstrate these changes. Both were discussions of incidents from the story, "The High Hill," referred to above. This story tells how prestige and power are gained in a schoolroom. It is about Elvy, a new pupil in the first grade. She is a physically handicapped child from a large, poor family. Miss Farrell, the teacher, seats her near Sisley, a leader in the class. Elvy is completely isolated and no one but the teacher pays any attention to her. On Valentine's Day, Elvy removes Margot's valentine for Sisley from the box and signs her own name to it. Margot accuses Elvy of stealing. Later, the teacher's ring is missing and suspicion falls on Elvy. She neither admits nor denies taking it, and her fearlessness wins her prestige among the children. They admire her for being able to do what they would not dare to do. Later, when the ring is found, the children conclude that she "didn't dare" take it and are ready to subject her to the treatment they gave her before. This story describes subtle psychological relations and invites moral judgments. The teacher read it primarily to see what gains the students had made in understanding interpersonal behavior and in objectivity.

The first discussion pools perceptions of the story but also develops the concept of power—how it is gained and maintained:

TEACHER: What do you think the author was trying to show?

EVELYN: The story went along with the idea of the left-outer. It's about a teacher who wants the children to mix. The other teacher didn't think that that was important. Sisley finally reached the top of the hill. And I think the teacher felt she had reached it, too.

IRENE: I thought it was Elvy who reached the top of the high hill.

HARRIET: I think Sisley was at the top, and Elvy was trying to get to her.

JENNY: It showed that Miss Farrell was not happy when Elvy was worshipped by the other kids for doing something daring. She didn't want them to worship her. She just wanted them to be her friends.

TOM: She was afraid that if that business kept up, Elvy would think she had to steal to keep up her title, and then she would go from bad to worse.

GINGER: They sort of made her a queen because when she was facing them in the yard, she stood up to them and said, "I wouldn't be afraid."

HOWARD: That's true of lots of kids. They admire kids that have guts and nerve. They don't care what they do as long as they have guts.

IRENE: That's funny though. If I stole your ring, I'd not expect the class to envy me, and I wouldn't think they'd hang around me or even want to associate with me.

POLLY: What really happens is that she gets so much power that she can influence a crowd until they are scared to refuse to do what she says. She steals more and more to get more and more power.

TEACHER: Have you ever known anything like that to happen in important world affairs?

TOM: Hitler got his power by talking himself into it.

TIM: It was more than that. He promised people that they would have power, too.

FAITH: I read a book on Mussolini. He did one deed, and they put him on a pedestal. Then he got more and more power. John Dillinger became a leader of the underground in the same way. He got a little power and then he got more and more and then people continued to follow him because they were afraid of what would happen to them if they refused.

JENNY: But in this story they admired her even though they feared her.

GINGER: Out our way one boy is strong and bigger and older than the rest, and they obey him because he punishes them if they don't and he hurts them.

TEACHER: Why did the children turn against Elvy when they found that she didn't steal the ring?

IRENE: That's what I want to know.

JENNY: When they found out that she was not daring, they didn't admire her any more.

HELEN: They found out that she was just like them. They didn't want an ordinary person for their leader.

HARRIET: They had no fear of her any more. She was just as afraid to steal as they were.

POLLY: They never liked her before, until they found she was daring. Now that they realized that she was no longer what they thought she was, they didn't look up to her.

IRENE: Margot was the one who started the prejudice against Elvy. She's the one who said, "You didn't dare."

In the second excerpt, students are dealing with the concept of social learning and reveal a maturity in understanding this concept that would do credit to adults: how behavior is learned and modified, what role fear and punishment play, and what "telling" accomplishes. They also express trust and freedom by openly recounting their own childhood misdemeanors which, until now, evidently had remained their own secrets:

VIVIAN: She was too young to understand about stealing.

MARY: It's real that when one person steals, they'll be blamed for everything that happens.

TED: Vivian, how come Margot knew about stealing and Elvy didn't?

VIVIAN: She knew but she didn't understand!

GRACE: Vivian, you are taught about stealing from the time you can talk. You should know. You learn it in school, and you learn it at home and at church.

VIVIAN: There's a little girl in our house. She just takes things she likes. She thinks they are hers. She doesn't understanding about things belonging to people.

PRESTON: Elvy didn't have the intention of stealing. She wanted to give Sisley something nice. She liked her so much.

CELIA: Little ones don't really understand stealing.

NORA: Some people grow up ahead of others. She just didn't know any better yet.

CELIA: This kid had no friends. She had to get them. That was her way.

PEGGY: Did anybody in this room ever steal when you were little?

SEVERAL: Yes.

PEGGY: Did you feel cheap?

VIVIAN: Not until I really knew that what I did was wrong.

NORA: In the five-and-ten-cent store, there were such lovely baby-doll shoes, and they had a lot of them, and we couldn't help it—we took them. But at that time we didn't think we did so wrong. Now we think it was terrible. When I came home my mother said, "Where did you get those little shoes," and from the excitement in her voice, I knew something was wrong. *Then* I knew it was wrong, but not *before* even though I was told before. When my mother yelled and was so upset, *then* I knew it was wrong.

CELIA: I once stole a Mother's Day card, and I didn't think it was wrong because it was for her.

GRACE: Your mother took you places, and you saw pretty things. Did she ever let you take them?

NORA: The other day, a four-year-old boy was near me, and I said if his little three-year-old sister falls down, he should pick her up. And he said, "Why? She can pick herself up." He didn't understand really. I can tell him, and he'll repeat it, but he doesn't understand. Sure you tell them, but they don't understand. Not until something happens that they are old enough to realize. Not just explanations. Not until they feel the difference.

GRACE: If you explain right, the child won't forget.

NORA: That little boy's mother tells him to say, "Thank you," but he forgets. His mother has to remind him. He doesn't realize why he has to say it. He doesn't realize about politeness, and what people will think of him if he's not polite. He's young yet.

JOEL: He's so excited he forgets.

NORA: Yes, and pretty things make children excited, too. And they forget.

VICTOR: When the cop says, "Don't steal," little kids are scared, but they don't understand. They're just scared.

NORA: My mother told me to bring those shoes back, but I didn't. I was scared and hid them in the cellar. Scaring doesn't do any good. It's worse. [*The class discussed what a mother might do under such circumstances.*]

JOEL: I saw a mother in the five-and-ten-cent store make her child put the toy back. They learn that way, but it takes time.

PEGGY: I have a whole bunch of toys still in the cellar that I used to "borrow" from kids and hide them.

ROY: Once I took a harmonica and said Joel gave it to me, and he told my mother he didn't. Was I in Dutch!

GRACE: These kids are still stealing at age four or five. If they were properly taught and the mother spanked their hands, they'd soon stop.

NORA: Slapping hands doesn't make you understand!

GRACE: If you begin at age one when you start to walk, and by age three after you've had to bring things back, you'll soon stop.

NORA: My goodness, Grace! Age one! That's an infant. That baby doesn't even know what's to put in your mouth, let alone what's stealing. If he doesn't know what's good to eat yet, how can he know what belongs to him and what belongs to someone else!

Dealing with Interpersonal Problems

As the chapter in diagnosis indicated, these students were beset with many interpersonal conflicts with their peers, siblings, and families. A large portion of the program centered on helping them acquire a rational perspective toward coping with these problems. It emphasized the analysis of the factors that lead to conflict and of the causes of behavior, and the understanding of the role feelings play in behavior.

Evidence in the records as well as observations and writing indicated that a great deal of progress in dealing with interpersonal relations had been made. First, the students began to understand that behavior is caused and learned. They began to see that people's behavior is often the result of their past experiences. This was revealed in one instance after another. They began to analyze the restrictions that their own foreign-born parents imposed on them because of their "upbringing"; they analyzed the behavior of a Negro boy who abused one of their crowd because of what others had previously done to him; they began to regard the "showing off" of other children as a result of too little attention and acceptance at home and in school. This kind of thinking appeared to be an important factor in helping them accept differences in their own group as well as in members of their own families.

They also grew in the ability to see behavior as causing reactions in others. At the beginning of the year the students interpreted the behavior of their parents, siblings, and friends only in the light of their own feelings: younger siblings were "pests"; parents were mean. Gradually they came to see that what their parents, siblings, and friends did was partly caused by their own actions and feelings. When a classmate persisted in annoying them, for example, by "cutting up" when they were working in small groups, they analyzed his behavior in relation to the treatment they had accorded him. They had let him know that "he never could do anything right," and therefore had tried to keep him out of any serious group work, although he was acceptable when "crazy things" were going on because he was "the craziest of all." In other words, they realized that he was behaving as they expected him to behave. He had not yet learned to discriminate in choosing the time and place for his "crazy" conduct, because he had not had a chance to discriminate. They had not even given him a chance to show whether he could do "anything right."

A similar growth took place in their ability to identify with people who were different from them. At first, identification with others had to be artificially encouraged through stories and through the "if-I-were-that-person" technique. Later, the same phenomenon began to appear spontaneously. This skill carried over into discussions in and out of school, and into relationships with one another and the family. While these changes may seem like small steps, they represented milestones of progress for these particular students.

Shifts took place also in their ability to think through interpersonal problems, to consider a variety of positive solutions, and to apply their understanding with some degree of personal satisfaction. One girl, for example, found weekends with her family very difficult because of confusion and contention at home. During the weekends her mother, grandmother, and stepfather were all home together, weary from the monotony of machine labor in a factory. All three were good cooks and anxious to do the cooking, since this task was more creative than dishwashing. One would start and the others would come into the kitchen and begin stirring together ingredients for another recipe—a natural source of strife. By her insight the girl helped to forestall the up-to-now inevitable battles over the family menu. She led her family to see that taking turns would solve the problem; she even helped them plan a schedule of hours. At each meal she learned to provide some satisfaction for each of them. Later she organized a clean-up crew; teamwork in cleaning up provided a measure of fun. She even learned that there would be times when all her efforts were futile and that then she herself must stand ready to carry a greater share of the monotonous tasks.

Students also learned that many solutions to their problems lay in their own hands, that they themselves had the power, at least in a limited way, to change things for themselves and others once they understood that conflicts rose from situation factors that could be altered. One girl felt uncomfortable because of the silence during dinner and the rest of the evening. Her father was an elderly man, and she was the only child left in the family. Once she understood her parents as human beings, she arrived at the point where, for the first time in her life, she could bring herself to ask her father whether they couldn't do something together. She was surprised when he answered readily, "What would you like to do?" Having no ready answer, she returned the question to him. Although she was disappointed when he suggested addressing greeting cards together, she fell in with his plan and they shared an experience that was pleasant enough to surprise both of them. From this point on, her life at home gradually changed: she was permitted to have friends in the house, and finally when her father became acquainted with them, he even permitted her to go off with them alone.

An understanding of consequences of behavior and the ability to predict consequences of their own and other's actions were other kinds of growth. Although previously these students had seldom projected consequences, toward the end of the year projection was almost automatically a part of their discussions and expressions. "If I refuse to join the gang too many times, pretty soon they won't ask me, and I'll be left out." Or, "If the kids always laugh at one kid or always push him around, he'll end up keeping away from everybody, and he'll be sad. Later he'll get mad and start pushing others around."

Finally, these students developed amazingly in their social relations and group skills. They developed a rather remarkable ability to work in groups and to relate themselves to each other. A series of sociograms given through the year gave tangible evidence of shifts toward broader and more enduring relationships.

The most dramatic change was the reduction of hostility among the peers. From September to May there was a marked decline in rejections, both between individuals and generally between boys and girls. In September the class was characterized by three intimate closed cliques. In April such clusters still existed, but their personnel had changed, and they were no longer closed. The number of unchosen students dropped. The tendency to center hostility on certain individuals also was reduced. At the beginning of the school year, five individuals were rejected so highly that no matter what they did or said it was criticized or ridiculed. At the end of the year there was only one boy for whom life in school had become no more comfortable.

In general these students became capable of, and willing to, work with each other, to support each other, to accept newcomers and deviates, and to put up with a variety of problem behaviors on the part of a number of individuals. It is not easy for adolescents to learn to work together in groups when for many years they have been conditioned to working by themselves. These students had to learn that other people had something to offer them, that it was "all right" to share their knowledge and skills with others, that working together required a consideration of other people's abilities and feelings, that one could get a sense of satisfaction from group achievement. They also needed to learn to settle conflicts on their own, to reach common agreements, and to play an appropriate role in the group. They began to realize that, as a group, they could learn to understand one another.

Once they learned the effectiveness and the wise use of group action, they benefited both in and out of school. One of the students was a virtual orphan, living with strangers who were afraid to let her leave the house unaccompanied. A group of girls visited the home "to let the lady see how nice we are so she'd let Clarissa come with us." Their mission was accomplished.

Students grew in their ability to make democratic procedures work, although they did not describe the process in these terms. For example, early in the year they were completely at a loss to see how the family can make decisions as a group. In several different situations they invariably portrayed the decision as being made automatically by one member. That was true in school, too. If the teacher left the room they expected her to put someone in charge, or else "Who will make us be good?" Working out a way of making group decisions without a teacher or a teacher-substitute was a painful task, but as time went on, the group assumed more and more control and needed less assistance from the teacher in matters of behavior or in making decisions.

While some of these changes may have been due in part to maturation, the fact that similar changes did not occur in other classes suggested that creating situations in which the students worked together in comfort and with satisfaction had something to do with the growth in interpersonal understanding. In this group human relations had been emphasized in all aspects of the program: in the selection of content, in teaching strategies used, and in arrangements for group work and activities. Inclusiveness and belonging were fostered by combining and re-combining students sociometrically into committees, study groups composed of students with heterogeneous levels, skill, and achievement.

What the Teacher Learned about Teaching

The learning that accrues in experimental work in curriculum is not limited to students alone. Teachers also grow and change. The evaluation of what happened to the teacher is better told in her own words:

Perhaps the most dramatic single discovery for me was that an ordinary teacher can cut loose from cherished moorings of textbooks and curriculum outlines and chart a journey of her own. Of course, I had to learn how to study children, how to diagnose needs, how to turn the myriad suggestions from the data and from countless experiences of children into some coherent learning sequence. I found that one secret of an effective sequence lay in using a few basic ideas and objectives as guideposts. With these as a basis I could relate to each other points and ideas from diverse sources, and at the same time develop a fair sequence of content.

Another dramatic discovery was in the use of group work. By finding ways of making children comfortable with each other and with me, by setting assignments so that students could work with each other in small groups, and by allowing them to react to each other's ideas, I had apparently tapped a new source of creative thinking and learning.

I also learned how to construct a learning sequence which progressed according to the psychological principles of learning rather than against them as I had done in my former teaching. I discovered that, to be effective, learning activities must be arranged to develop readiness to take each new step. For example, students had to explore a topic and pool their information before they could discover new ideas. If we eventually wanted them to see why occupations affect the pattern of family living, we first had to discuss at length what happened in each family because of who earned the living. In other words, we first talked about things that the students already knew and could understand.

But students' experiences are too limited to depend on exclusively. To build new ideas required giving them new experiences. A story or a sequence of stories arranged for contrast served that purpose. If the students did not understand that slapping is not an effective teaching device, merely telling them so did no good. Instead, I read them a story in which they could see the results of slapping. Then we compared and contrasted these results with results in stories where there was no slapping. The stories at least raised a question in their minds on the advisability of slapping younger children to teach them.

But reading and analyzing stories is only a preparation. There must be opportunities to observe real-life situations, to select alternative behavior, to predict what will happen if certain types of behavior are used, and to make generalizations about many facts they have examined. And finally, they need to have opportunity to try out those solutions in real-life situations.

It takes a long time for the teacher to learn to plan sequences. It means watching closely the results of each step, getting feedback as to why the expected did not happen, and going back and picking up omitted steps. After the teacher has followed this procedure many times she will recognize the kinds of learning steps that simply cannot be omitted.

The sequences of activities that we planned were based on objectives that would take a long time to reach. I knew we would not see our goals realized tomorrow. Week after week might pass with no sign of change. But day by day I was working to insure change. I also realized that the changes I sought do not come with factual knowledge alone; they do not come with emotional learning alone; the changes I sought required a combination of emotional learnings and factual knowledge.

The method stood up well under the three years of trial. Over and over again I discovered that even the most unpromising starting groups responded to it and came to life. There were, however, variations in reactions to some specific processes. I was surprised to note, for example, how the composition of the group affected reaction to stories I used, and why, therefore, the stories sometimes failed in the purpose for which they were being used. I read, for example, "A Mother in Manville" (Rawlings, 1947) to three groups of students. Sixteen of thirty members of one class who came from broken homes identified closely with Jerry, the orphan boy in the story, while other classes passed over this point.[1] Reactions were also influenced by the emphasis in curriculum content. For example, one year much time was spent on sibling relationships. This emphasis influenced reactions to all stories read that year. In reading and discussing books the class tended to dwell on problems of sibling relationships.

I should not conclude this account without describing some of the conditions that made it possible for me to learn these things.

First of all, I could not have done it without the inspiration, guidance, and direct help of the consultants. Each time they came we talked over our attempts since their last visit. They suggested new ways, criticized, and encouraged. They opened new paths for experimentation and suggested new methods to try out. Their ideas injected new vitality and joy (for both students and teacher) into the classroom. When they left, the feeling of lostness was somewhat alleviated by the knowledge that they could be reached by a three-cent stamp if it was necessary to send an SOS. And sometimes it was! The feeling of discouragement was frequently my companion during the initial period. Many a time I could have turned back gladly if there had been a graceful way of doing so.

Also I doubt if this work could have been done without the help and encouragement of my principal and the school administration. Teachers fear giving up the security of the traditional. Added fear comes from the feeling that they will be

[1] For the record of that discussion, see Staff of Intergroup Education in Cooperating Schools (1949), p. 35.

held to strict account for what facts their children know or do not know. I did not have those fears. My school administration gave me complete freedom to experiment. My principal went so far as to change radically my daily schedule so that after the first year I could have my own class for a longer time each day and generally gave me much direct help.

One other requirement was necessary to carry out this program: Long hours of work at night—recording discussions, tabulating needs revealed by student's papers, devising ways of carrying out a new idea, and keeping a daily log of classroom events. That was long, hard work, and yet these three years unquestionably have been the most satisfying of all the years of my teaching career. In comparison, the other twelve seem deadly and barren for me and for the children who looked to me for guidance.

It is difficult to explain exactly why the years that represented the hardest work should also have been the most gratifying. Perhaps it is because I felt I was learning much even as I taught. I had had courses in education and in psychology many years ago, but actually all I remembered and had to work with were vague notions of "S-R bonds." Whatever else I knew about "what makes children tick" I learned from years of experience with children. Now, I was learning new ideas in psychology, and they actually worked! For example, there was the principle that children learned better in an environment in which they are comfortable. So, we worked out ways to make them comfortable, and as their frustrations lessened the teacher's anxieties eased, too. We worked on the sensible theory that children learn to accept one another's differences and appreciate one another's assets only as they become better acquainted. So, we provided situations in which acquaintances might ripen; the theory proved correct. Sometimes I learned new principles that disproved old ones I had been using. For example, I had been trying to change children's attitudes by teaching facts. This usually ended in frustration. To see children's attitudes changing under my very eyes was very encouraging.

With the new satisfactions of learning new teaching strategies came the gratifying experience of really knowing the students. I thought I had known them before, but I learned otherwise. Now I saw them in a new light against a background of experiences that made them what they were. Each stood out as an unforgettable individual.

Whatever made them so, these three years were a highlight of my life, and I regret only that all this did not happen twelve years earlier when I started teaching.

EVALUATION OF THE SIXTH AND SEVENTH GRADES

The evaluation of the effect of the program in the first group—the sixth and seventh grades—was made in a manner similar to that used for the second group. However, the available data were scantier and less systematic, consisting largely of anecdotal records, taped discussion excerpts, and teacher reports and descriptions.

The evaluation of the work in the first group also needs to be considered in the perspective of the general atmosphere of hopelessness in such schools where teachers often feel that nothing works and that nothing has ever worked. Why therefore, they ask, should any particular innovation bring results? This attitude may explain some of the teacher remarks which may seem to be overoptimistic and to magnify small accomplishments into grand achievements. These reports, therefore, tend to be colored by teachers' surprise at the fact that the new sequences worked as well as they did.

Because reading is such a prestige activity in our society and because schools emphasize it so much, discussion of successes and failures inevitably begins with remarks about reading achievement. As with the second group, these students, most of whom began the school year as functional illiterates with no reading power, not only began to read, but continued to read, on their own, whole books, and turned to books whenever they could. In several classes, pupils began to read a book a week and to vie with themselves rather than with each other. Some of these students advanced as much as three years in one year. Only six of the seventy-odd students progressed so little that their progress could not be measured by a standardized test. Even these students admitted that they had learned more that year than they had learned previously in their whole school life.

What surprised their teachers most, however, was the fact that books from the paperback library they had purchased with their own funds were taken home, and—miracle of miracles—most of them found their way back to school again. In part this happened because finishing a book was a prerequisite to reporting on it or recommending it to other students, and the latter activity was highly prized. In part, books reappeared because other students were usually waiting for them. Thus, keeping the library intact was important in many ways.

The students also began to search actively for books. During the paperback book fair, all but three students bought at least one book, and most bought several. One student bought two dollars' worth every day of the fair. He was the one who, with his pals, made a special effort to gain access to the library more often than the one period a week that the classes were scheduled for the library. He and his group simply "sneaked in" by joining other classes who were using the library. He confessed that one day he had paid another student "a whole nickel" to get him *The Boy Who Stole the Elephant* and *Ben Hur*.

Growth in Thinking

The area that was basically of greatest importance, that of the cognitive powers of the students, and the closely related language powers, also showed surprising growth. Students learned, for example, that stories have events, as do people's daily lives, that these events have order, and that there are reasons for the events and for the order. In the early weeks of the school term, while listing the events in "Spelling Bee" almost all students listed the culminating event, the winning of the spelling bee, as the first one. When the process was repeated later, after listening to "A Mother in Manville," almost all of them were able to place events in their actual sequence and to defend their order.

Tallying and categorizing findings were other fruitful activities in inducing the differentiation and development of concepts. For example, in the sequence on sounds, pupils were asked to identify the happy sounds they heard during one evening. The list contained a wide range of sounds, among them street sounds, uncle's footsteps, church bells, food boiling, little children laughing, people talking, the last school bell, money jingling, my mother laughing, everyone kissing their children.

The task of categorizing such a list was not easy at first, and the class tried a number of schemes, only to discover that they "did not fit enough things." The first scheme classified sounds by the places in which they occurred, such as the home, the school, and the church. The class finally settled on categorizing sounds by *who* or *what* made them: sounds made by older people, teenagers, younger people, things. In other words, these students began to be able to study the specifics, to differentiate a variety of general common characteristics of these specifics, and to discern what might be called a logical fit.

Prediction and hypothesizing were new processes that were learned with some success. Initially, most of the class were unable to predict events and consequences from a given set of facts or conditions. Toward the end of the term when the class was reading *Squanto,* predicting became a regular part of the discussion. "Squanto's friend would steal the white robe, because the story mentioned that the friend refused to go hunting with Squanto pleading need for rest, because he inquired whether anyone knew about the robe, etc., etc." This is progress for students who in the beginning could not even state the sequence of events in a story.

When the students were asked to finish stories, the endings of which were cut off, they were able to use all the available clues, and no student wrote an ending that was not logical to the story. Often this involved comprehension of the subtleties of both the language and events.

A similar consistency was evident when the students were required to describe what might happen after the story ended—next morning, for example. Most newly created sequels were plausible. For students who at the beginning of the program rarely connected consequences with causes and whose language comprehension was insufficient to decipher the simplest story, this represented a great deal of progress. An observer who had been acquainted with these students before the program began commented that if she closed her eyes she could not believe these were the same students.

While even a simple analysis of the causes of behavior was practically an impossibility at the beginning of the year, by the end of the year many students were able not only to explain behavior, but also to compare and contrast behavior in two or three stories. For example, they could compare the ways in which family members protect one another.

As the material to talk about developed, increasingly longer discussions became possible. While class discussions lasted only a few minutes at the beginning of the term, by the end of the year they extended to entire periods.

The students began with such a meager capacity to understand subtleties of allusions or metaphors of any kind that the teachers had to substitute simpler words in reading books to them. Such expressions as "Ellen left one of her lives behind . . ." were completely incomprehensible to them. Later, in reading such stories as "A Mother in Manville," the idiomatic and metaphorical speech no longer hindered them from following the thread of the story.

The volume of writing increased also. Students who had been reluctant to set anything down on paper for fear of earning red pencil marks began to produce two-page reports on such matters as observations of insects. Often they got angry when the bell rang and prevented them from completing their descriptions.

Pooling observations on "life" began to cultivate the capacity to see human behavior in terms of generalizations. This capacity in turn made it possible to project and to practice alternative solutions to problems they once would have handled in a single standard way. For example, it seemed possible to substitute plain talk for fighting.

The process of rank-ordering events in stories, news, and school activities gave an impetus to more substantial as well as longer discussions. When events in a story were rated according to the effect they had on actions of a particular character, many kinds of relationships had to be considered. Comparing and defending the individual rankings created both excitement and involvement—rare phenomena in these classes. Values were expressed and analyzed as, for example, in the debate over whether Mama, in *Mama's Bank Account* (Forbes, 1943), was more courageous when she sneaked into the hospital to see Dagmar than was the mother in "Spelling Bee" who "just had to get there" for the final spelldown.

Teachers reported rather radical changes also in the atmosphere of interpersonal relations. Classes in which initially everyone had been ready to attack everyone else on the slightest provocation, and sometimes even without one, began to show signs of cooperativeness and helpfulness. For example, one teacher reported:

> You know, Raoul is a very poor reader. Well, Janet would finish her work and she'd ask him to illustrate her story because he's a very good artist. Then she thanks him and says, "Want me to be your secretary? I'll write it for you if you tell me what you want me to write."

Evidently, as a result of working in pairs and in small groups on many projects, a sharing of knowledge and talent became an accepted and regular procedure. For example, Jerry, who used to scream when everyone else was quiet just to get attention, became quite interested during the study of insects and developed a knack of drawing them accurately. Other students had to wait their turn to consult him on whether their drawings were "right." And he'd say, "Now, just a minute please. I can only help one at a time."

The class developed an awareness that each person has a different talent and that not all need to be equally successful at everything. This in turn developed their pride in achievement and in taking tasks seriously, an act that formerly earned only ridicule for the most part.

An increasing number of students began to talk about what they wanted to be and to do. Participation and involvement in school activities increased. A substantial number joined groups and activities outside the school, a decided change for students who before had spent their entire leisure time watching "Batman" and "Peyton Place" on TV.

Perhaps one of the most significant gains was in the desire to learn. This showed itself in several ways. Students who were chronic truants and those who developed sudden stomach aches began to appear in school and to perform rather regularly. A significant proportion of students started doing homework. Parents who had never crossed the threshold of the school appeared voluntarily to find out what had happened to their children, and "how you are teaching now, because ———— likes school suddenly." Perhaps for students who have been considered hopeless for years and who have assumed the same view of themselves, this "learning to learn" is the most significant achievement.

CHAPTER XIII

Creating Conditions for Learning

The preceding chapters have described a variety of approaches to teaching the students of two kinds of deprived minorities: Negroes as recent immigrants to urban areas, and white immigrants. The program described represents a restructuring of the curriculum, of teaching strategies, and of approaches to learning in order to make learning relevant to these students. They are also experiments in taking seriously and applying what is known about the motivation, drives, deficiencies in prior experience and education, and of the potential of these students.

Incomplete as these sequences may be, and meager as the evaluation of the results is from the scientific viewpoint, they at least demonstrate that a serious attempt to change the educational program and to bring it into line with the life realities of these students produces some fairly radical changes in their functioning and in their capacity to learn. They demonstrate also that it is possible, even as late as the sixth or eighth grade, to change the course of the educational career of students who have been neglected because of a serious gap between the realities of their lives and development, and what is offered in school.

The main point is that it is necessary to restructure both the content and the process of education to make an impact on these students. This point is emphasized by others who have concerned themselves with the problems of compensatory education. In commenting on the role of Project Head Start, Hechinger (1965) expresses concern about the way of weaving the content and experience of the Head Start program into the fabric of American education.

Dr. Kenneth Clark, professor of Psychology at the City College, along with Dr. Deutsch, one of the pioneers of educational experimentation, has warned consistently that compensatory education for children of deprived minorities is no substitute for changes in the structure of education itself. Merely giving such children an opportunity to begin slightly ahead of the class is of little use if the regular schooling is not, at the same time, made relevant to them. There is little to be gained from surrounding these youngsters with loving and understanding adults in their pre-school taste of learning, if they subsequently are exposed to teachers who approach them with preconceived notions of limited potential. . . . The evidence of prior research, unrelated to the Head Start experiment, shows conclusively that early compensatory education is of very limited short-term benefit unless there is consistent follow-up. Children's pre-school gains have been shown to be spectacular as they entered first grade, but are quick to erode in the next four years unless they are constantly reinforced. If there is a gap between pre-school education and kindergarten or first grade, the gains are minimal. . . .

Perhaps the school can be an island that compensates for or offsets what is lacking outside, a key that unlocks individuals who have been closed to learning. But what are the conditions that would make this possible? These conditions could perhaps be spelled out by commenting on the role of the four chief instruments of the school: the teacher, the curriculum, the way of teaching, and the administrative organization of the school.

THE TEACHER

What kind of teachers are needed; what must they be and know? First of all, students need to see that the teacher cares, that she is a human being who is interested in them personally and cares about what happens to them. Such a teacher finds ways to make a student feel "good about himself." Sometimes these ways amount only to a word of praise for something well done. It can be a small remark such as "Aren't you the handsome one today," as the teacher greets the students in the morning. It can be a written note of praise that goes home to let his parents know how much the student is learning. But above all, the fact that the teacher cares is demonstrated by the effort she makes to shape a program to awaken the students, to help them with their problems of learning, and to share with them their triumphs of achievement, however small they may be.

But often "caring" involves more than that. It means helping students through some crisis. Schools often give children tasks that are utterly impossible for them to face, tasks set by an unknown outside force for a reason they do not understand. In such cases the teacher needs to be ready to "hold the student's hand" through these tasks. City-wide tests are an example of unreasonable demands, and their consequences are described by a teacher who tried desperately to help one student to "hold on."

> During the midterm test I had to sit and hold that child's hand throughout the whole two days of testing. Otherwise, he just wouldn't take them. There's nothing wrong with his intelligence. He's afraid. He looks at the paper and he gasps. And he screams, "Ten papers! I can't do it!" Then he starts to cry. I took him out of class in my free period, and in three quarters of an hour he did four hours worth of testing. We read it together and he did beautifully. But when it came to the math examination, I didn't have time for him. So he didn't do it, and he got a zero. In science I couldn't help him, because I didn't know the answers myself. The topic sentences were incredibly ambiguous so that any answers seemed valid.

The teacher needs also to build self-respect and trust. The teacher has, at least in part, the power to build an atmosphere in the classroom in which individuals have an opportunity to play a role that is self-fulfilling and that develops a sense of worth. She demonstrates overtly her respect for every child; eventually the students begin to do the same for each other. One such instance is illustrated by a young teacher:

> When he is reading the book that he chose for our reading program, it's his book; he feels that it is. I ask his permission every time. "Can we read the book that you're reading?" When I work with him alone, and he doesn't want to read then, he has enough gumption now to say, "No, I'm not in the mood." Fine, OK. Yesterday we read a chapter and he said, "No more." . . . But he's always being kicked out of classrooms. I walk by in the hall, and he knows that I'm going to talk to him. We talk and then he says, "All right, I can go in now."

This teacher accepts feelings as facts: the need to possess a book, the importance of the freedom to say, "I've had it!" She asks a child's permission to use "his" book as she would ask an adult whose possessions she wishes to borrow. She thus demonstrates to the entire class that her respect is real. Perhaps most important of all, she respects the "mood" of the youngster, the need to withdraw. She talks with a student ejected from class until he feels he can return to the classroom and function. However, it is the student, not the teacher, who makes that decision. Giving students a chance to make decisions about things that concern them is one way for teachers to demonstrate respect.

Trust develops also from evidence of sharing feelings. One teacher read *Happiness is a Warm Puppy* (Schultz, 1962) to the class.

> They loved it! It's a beautiful little book. I'd say, "Do you remember this?" and I'd tell them my experience, and then we'd start sharing experiences . . . to the part where he is learning to tie his shoe, and I said, "Well, I can remember learning to tie my shoe"; and then this one would say, "Me, too! Oh, I remember too!" Then they wrote about the things that mean happiness to *them*. And really what they wrote is just amazing.

The result of such experiences is that the teacher and the students have feelings in common—things that make them happy and things that hurt. There is reluctance at first to express feelings, because the students don't trust either teachers or peers. This trust must be developed.

HELPING STUDENTS TO HELP EACH OTHER

Another young teacher found her own ways of achieving a system of self-help in a group with a wide range of ability. At first she had many problems in managing the class, especially the six students of whom she speaks below. What had been achieved a few months later demonstrates that she learned much about these students and about the ways in which they can learn skills and content as well as respect for each other.

> "Some write as well as my first class, but on the other end are those six kids. . . . They collaborated on the worksheets for *Squanto*. . . . Beautiful! I let them. . . . They can help each other because one has a little bit more ability to read the question, another has the answer or knows how to write it. And they all sign names to the sheet.

This self-help can extend to understanding and controlling interpersonal conflict, one aspect of which is the ability to put oneself in the other person's shoes. Name-calling is one frequent cause of fights. How explosive this practice is can be seen in the description of one first-year teacher:

> Another thing that sets the kids off is name-calling. I have one kid who is very sensitive and they call her "a black idiot" so she begins to fight and then they wind up with "Your mother. . . ." She doesn't have a mother; her mother is dead. Then she says, "I know who my mother is" and then they get onto "Your father" and then they begin to go to blows. When you go over to them when they are just about ready to start a fist fight, the rest of the kids start to scream and hoot. Finally you settle the two kids down, and you have the rest of the maniacs running around the room. My other class isn't that way. They aren't as volatile. They don't do as much fighting.

When teachers learn which situations are explosive, what to do to prevent them, and how to help children to examine the ingredients of the situation and the feelings that result, they can cultivate in their students an interest in finding out more about themselves as human beings with feelings. Which feelings are the same? Which are different? What makes them so? How does the same situation look from the opposite side?

During a siege of name-calling, one teacher planned role-playing sessions in which children portrayed how victims feel about aggressors and what the consequences of aggression are. The students tried to help each other become aware that both parties are ultimately losers in explosive interpersonal conflicts.

Teachers' feelings about the potentialities of their students were deeply divided. There were bitter arguments about the state of being and becoming of these unsuccessful learners. One side of the argument tended to fix the becoming according to the current performance—somewhat in line with the following teacher comment:

> How can we raise the aspirational levels of these kids? They're not even average! Is it fair to them to raise their aspirational levels to heights they can never achieve? We used to have bull sessions when they wouldn't learn anything else. Robert said he wanted a lot of money, because then he wouldn't have to worry about reading and writing. Because he knew he couldn't read and write, he figured, well, if he had the money, then it wouldn't matter whether he could read or write.

A different point is expressed by another teacher:

> When you open up some new idea to them . . . this in itself
> makes them want to move on to know more things, and in this
> sense you are raising the aspiration level.

This teacher had learned that since the attention span is short, it is difficult to talk at length and still hold the class. Teaching by talking must be kept to a minimum, for these students do not learn much merely by listening. One first-year teacher found this out the hard way. She also noted that her students became happier and truancy less frequent once she had learned new teaching procedures:

> Believe it or not, when I had so few kids in my room yester-
> day, I gave one book to each two kids—those interesting easy
> paperbacks like *Down the Mississippi* [Bulla, 1954] and *White
> Sails to China* [Bulla, 1955]. They read to each other. It was
> beautiful. I didn't have to try to make them listen to me, and I
> could help the kids who weren't able to read at all, or who didn't
> want to read. . . . They feel you are trying to help each one
> individually and that we are all working together and that I am
> *with* them. . . . Next day more children came to school. They
> heard about the new books and about the tape recorder. Then
> we began to make up plays from the new books and more truants
> appeared next day. . . . This kept them going for over two weeks
> because their success sustained them. Cartooning had the same
> effect. It worked with every single class. They made cartoons
> about the sequences of events in the books they read, making
> sure that they were put in a proper sequence just as they hap-
> pened. The cartoons were good, and we rexographed all of
> them. . . . I had to do the first one before they could try it. I did
> it right on the chalk board. The best thing was that they had a
> sustained discussion about each one and no monkey business
> either. They love to see what others in their class can do, to talk
> about their own, about what they meant to portray, and why
> these events were important. . . . They got into arguments about
> the importance of each, but it was a positive intellectual argu-
> ment. I never expected this of them. Usually they get into a fist
> fight if someone disagrees.

Teachers are divided also on the question of upholding standards. Usually the questions regarding standards are framed in such a way as to becloud the issue. "Are we lowering standards when we accept from our youngsters something that would not be acceptable from the children in the higher academic classes?" It takes a good bit of self-confidence on the part of the teacher to maintain a position that in order to raise standards students must first have some kind of positive self-image. Better still, the two need to be built simultaneously: increasing the ability to learn raises the self-image; this in turn releases the ability to learn. When "standards" are individualized, achievement becomes possible. As the student experiences the thrill of achievement, he begins to regard himself in a new light. When this happens over and over again, he gains the emotional strength to raise his own "standard." The teacher who is insightful enough to know this will perform his functions in such a way that the student will eventually become self-propelling.

However, when the path to achievement is blocked by multiple hurdles, it is difficult even to make a start. One cannot, for example, send students with meager reading skills to the library and expect them to find suitable books. The hurdles of having to go to a library and having to select a book are piled on top of the obstacles of learning to read and of learning to want to read. Students with continued experience of failure will not even make an attempt to jump these hurdles.

The idea that the teacher may need to provide or even to produce resource materials with which students can work is foreign to many junior high and upper elementary school teachers. Instead, the problem of reading levels and of the responsibility of using the texts is debated interminably. Yet, when teachers attempt to produce appropriate learning sequences and materials with which to implement them, such as were described in the preceding chapters, the results are often rewarding to teachers and students alike. A member of one such team summarized the insights he and his colleagues had gained as a result of the team planning and the tryouts of the new learning sequences and materials:

> . . . This looked like miserable stuff to teach, but now it's interesting because it's—it's like putting cauliflower into a machine and then having it come out gold because of the wonderful results with the children.

Of course, to do all this, it is helpful to have a number of understanding adults present in the classroom. For example, student teachers in the classroom provide a second adult who can sit down with a student and help him before an unendurable amount of frustration sets in. He can talk with another student who is in such an emotional state than he cannot contain himself. He can walk the corridors with a third child who cannot bear to "stay in the room with all those dumb kids." He is another adult to whom a student can relate. The presence of additional adults cuts down the burden upon the one teacher who is constantly besieged for attention by a roomful of children who can get it nowhere else. This second person need not be a student teacher; he may be an aide who is compatible with the teacher. A first-year teacher who felt herself to be one of "the fortunate ones" to have had the additional help of a student teacher explains:

> In that class the fact that there are two people made it possible for one to just sit down and talk with a student in trouble while other things are going on in the room. As long as he was there the lesson would go. But with him gone, that class is chaotic at times. . . .

In the absence of additional adult help, teachers have arranged to send to another teacher temporarily the students who cannot contain themselves in a particular classroom. Calhoun was one such child, sent to a colleague who was slated for a preparation period and therefore had no class.

> I was alone. He wouldn't stay with me, and he went out of the room. My kids were in another class, and this was a free period for me. So I went outside and said, "Calhoun, would you like to help me? I'd really appreciate that." When he didn't answer I said, "Either say 'yes' or 'no.' " He still didn't answer me, so I said, "All right," turned my back, and started to walk into the room. Then Calhoun said, "I didn't say 'yes' or 'no,' " So I said, "Well-l-l?" and he replied, "Yes, I want to help you." He came in and helped me. He washed the blackboard and I gave him a commendation card. He was good all period.

Other teachers threw up their hands and cried, "Commendation card? Why? He was bad! Why should he get a reward? He'll only be worse. He'll want to get out again and he'll know this is how you do it. The other kids will begin to act up too. You're only inviting trouble." Somehow, teachers need to be helped to see that the others do not necessarily need the "relief" this child required; that they will not necessarily imitate his behavior; that they can be taken into a teacher's confidence enough to become aware that individuals are different and need to be handled differently.

It should be understood, however, that this type of relief is a temporary makeshift, and that, in classes with disturbed youngsters, there should be adults on hand to forestall impending "danger," to "read the signs" before a student "blows," and to help him reach the point where he can begin to function again in a positive way and "under his own steam."

What can happen when sufficient help is available was demonstrated in a summer workshop. This workshop was composed of a class of would-be teachers in their first professional course, a group of rather disturbed sixth- and seventh-graders from the classes described in this book, and a group of three-year-olds from the same neighborhood. The task of the sixth-graders was to read to the three-year-olds and to collect data about them so that the teachers would understand them better. The task of the potential teachers was to help the sixth-graders in their "teaching" and to observe how they learned. In a way, this was a two-way "each one teach one" system.

There was one potential teacher for every adolescent and an adolescent for every young child. When the sixth-grade "teachers" were called together to discuss the problems they were having in reading to the young children or in helping them understand something, their "very own teachers" sat by their side, encouraging them, helping them write, helping them phrase a response, giving them a quiet word of praise, interpreting them when others could not understand. Each sixth-grader gained faith in his "own teacher" very early in the game. He knew that she was "on his side" no matter what happened, and there was no danger that still another adult would discover his inferior performance. If he wished, he could "test out" his "lesson" on his own teacher before exposing it to the judgment of the group.

What can happen under these conditions is illustrated by two incidents. One of the adolescents, a failing sixth-grader, met the coordinator of the workshop during the first month of the next school year and announced proudly, "You know, I passed!" "That's wonderful! How do you feel you are doing?" "Well, OK, I guess, but you know, I think I could use a little more help in reading." In other words a two-week workshop conducted in a nonthreatening atmosphere enabled this student to begin to learn to read: he felt the thrill of knowing he could learn and now was willing to admit that he needed and wanted more help, a sign of increasing self-confidence and motivation. Conditions that permit these students to feel free to learn will raise their aspirations and thereby increase their potentiality to learn.

The same workshop revealed the hidden intellectual capacity of another highly disturbed and academically unsuccessful student. In school Mark was classified as a "nonwriter" and "very disturbed."

Mark produced a barrage of questions when, in connection with a series of science demonstrations, he was told that the warmth of the hen is responsible for the process of an egg becoming a chicken and when he observed the fetus of a shark in formaldehyde.

1. How does the egg become a chicken?
2. Well, if I eat an egg, and it goes into my stomach where it is warm, why can't a chicken grow in there?
3. Why is the baby shark dead?
4. Why did they kill the mother?
5. Why can't the baby shark live even though the mother was killed?
6. Why couldn't the baby shark be born before the mother dies?
7. If it's just an egg, how do the eyes, nose, ears, and mouth develop?
8. What makes some people grow tall, others short?
9. Then, why don't midgets grow? Why don't their bones grow too, like our bones, grow bigger and bigger?
10. Why do we have dwarfs?
11. Are rats poisonous? If not, why do babies die that have been bitten by them?
12. How does the child get food from the mother inside?
13. What would happen if I dropped a rock on a turtle's back and broke it? Would he die? Is there a Turtle Doctor to fix it and make him well? Who would be able to help the Turtle get well?

Later, back on the campus, the potential teacher remarked, "I'll never forget . . . how he just poured out all these questions . . . how the teacher has to be prepared for anything I wasn't and he just floored me."

PLANNING LEARNING SEQUENCES

It is not easy to plan adequate learning sequences. It requires a fairly thorough knowledge of what students know and can do in order to break the learning down into bite-size pieces appropriate to the student's capacity to master them. Teachers must know how to select these sequences, how to plan for long- and short-range activities, how to translate what they know about children into motivational devices, and, above all, how to make abstractions concrete. Nor is deciding what is concrete or abstract a simple matter, especially when dealing with students with unexpected gaps and deviations in experience and learning.

The errors that can be committed in the name of "making things concrete" are illustrated by a story of a teacher of a class in the first group with fairly high potential who was trying to "put over" the concept of government and its branches.

> We were talking about the state goverment and I was trying to make them realize the reason we need government. We started talking about clubs, but only one person had anything to say, though a lot had been in clubs. That was my motivation—bring it down to the club level and why in clubs you need government. . . . One teacher told me that's not enough motivation, because maybe they don't belong to clubs at all, but I asked them to raise their hand. When I asked, "What do you do in your club?", they did nothing. And I even tried to use visual materials. I had the tree of government on the bulletin, and I tried to show them checks and balances and I had a scale to show them they had to be balanced evenly.

This well-intentioned, hard-working, and earnest teacher failed to understand many things about her students. First, very few of them belonged to clubs. In the whole school only 30 came to an after-school recreational program. Second, she did not sense that these students would raise their hands and say "yes" if that was what they thought the teacher wanted, especially if they liked her. Consequently, she was unable to detect the relationship between the fact that they said they did nothing in clubs and the fact that since they had no experience with them, they did not know what happens in clubs. Nor did she realize that a "tree of government" is a metaphor and an abstraction which means something only after experiences leading up to the concept of the branches of government, rather than as an introduction to it. Her well-intended use of the scale is in the same category. These students knew scales as something to weigh objects with, but had no preparation whatsoever for the concept of a scale as a symbol for balance. She was further unaware of the fact that it was she who did the talking and the thinking. As her record said, "only one student had anything to say." This difficulty followed her throughout the whole lesson. She was in the driver's seat: she did the talking, invented the clubs, asked the questions, and brought in a scale. There was nothing for the students to do, and therefore no involvement. Since students had no comprehension of the role of the three things to be balanced that grew on trees, the teacher offered them three "unknowns" and confounded them still further. Since the success of the whole sequence on government and laws depended upon this introductory session, the failure to activate the students brought about the failure of the lesson. ˙

This lack of meaning applies also to teaching skills per se, apart from the context in which they are to be used, under the mistaken assumption that drill in isolated skills is what the retarded students need. Actually, learning a skill apart from the context and the purpose of using it is both more abstract and less interesting. Since, in addition, the motivation of such students for learning per se is weak, it is practically impossible for them to master the skills taught in this fashion. The careers of many retarded students in disadvantaged areas have fully demonstrated this fact: by the time they reach the sixth or seventh grade they have been "taught" to read and to spell over and over again, but they can neither read nor spell. Evidently a revision of the whole approach to learning skills is needed, and, as the chapters on learning sequences indicate, repetitive practice of the same skill in new context is one promising possibility.

One of the most difficult skills for teachers to learn is how to conduct discussions that are in effect conversations. This involves the art of asking questions that permit a variety of levels of response. This is difficult to learn, especially for teachers who have long defined teaching as telling and practiced it as such. To conduct such discussions productively, teachers need to know when to talk and when to let students talk. Usually teachers also ask questions which require a single right answer or interpretation. Once the right answer is obtained from one student, it is assumed that the conversation on that topic ends, because the emphasis is on obtaining the right answer rather than on enabling many students to cope with the question in their own way. As the excerpt below illustrates, the result is a staccato and discontinuous discussion.

TEACHER: What do you think is the most important thing that happened in the story?

WAYLAND: That the water was clean.

TEACHER: Why was it hard to get water in those days?

LOLA: It might freeze.

TEACHER: Why did the boy and girl like to go to the well?

MALCOM: Like the boy said, "She's lovely."

TEACHER: And what did the girl like?

DENISE: She liked he said, "Can I take water for you?" That's what she liked.

TEACHER: Did she like anything else?

MICHAEL: She likes to look at her face in the water.

It is easy to see the aimlessness and the lack of focus of this type of questioning. To build continuity and interaction in discussion requires a sequential and inductive question strategy that is not easy to develop. Many a consultant has discovered that converting teachers from answer-giving creatures into question-asking ones is one of the most difficult training tasks. Teachers need to learn not only to ask open-ended questions but also to ask them on issues of sufficient latitude. They need to help students listen to each other in order to make possible a productive exchange among them. They need to learn to pick up cues in student remarks and to make them available for the consideration of the entire class. They must find ways of lifting thinking from one level to another by asking questions that induce analysis, such as "Why did Jerry not appear when the woman was leaving?" as one teacher did at a point when the students were going around in circles either accusing Jerry of lying or criticizing the woman for not adopting him. Fiction offers good initial experiences in developing such skills, because it provides concrete and feeling-oriented incidents to stimulate perceptions on which concepts can be built.

Further, when teaching focuses on the development of concepts, especially when disadvantaged students are the learners, it is necessary to allow each student to find his own way to the concept. For example, when students study the growth of cities, and the problems and advantages of cities, there are common concepts to examine, but the specifics that students use to get at these concepts should be different. Each student may read on his own level and gain command of something he can contribute. Both the gaining of command and contributing are of utmost importance, because involvement in what is being learned is absolutely necessary to keep the class going. Participation and contribution are part and parcel of that involvement.

This implies a new concept of individualization: that of diversifying the approach to learning and the materials used while concentrating on a common focus.

A common fear in using such diversified materials is that "if you give them an easy book they won't learn anything." This may be true if students are to read for no purpose other than to remember the content. If used to supply material for discussion, even the simplest books can be used to contribute to fairly sophisticated generalizations, especially when combined with materials from many books read by different students. The same is true of vocabulary. Books are not the sole source of learning vocabulary, and, further, vocabulary without meaning is not worth learning. One must not forget the simple fact that if a student can only read on the second-grade level, he will learn from a book only if it is at that level. He should be permitted to stay on that level till he feels safe enough to step up. Usually, however, when books are used as aids rather than as sole sources of learning—if, for example, the ideas are discussed and clarified first and the questions to answer through reading are clear—half the battle of reading difficulty is won. Students who can read only on the second-grade level without this help may be able to read something more difficult.

Diversification of the sources of learning must go further than just having students read books of varied difficulty. Teachers need to learn to produce and to invent a variety of other materials, such as were described in the chapters on learning sequences. Observations on what different types of people do with their hands is a perfectly good source for comparing and contrasting, as is the interviewing of adults on aspirations or making scale maps and drawings of their apartments.

Using differentiated materials requires the use of new teaching strategies. For example, when each student reads a different book on the same topic, the discussion must be so structured as to permit their varied contributions to be made without creating confusion, e.g., by asking a student to explain how his book clarifies the idea under discussion. In such a structure, individual students serve as resource persons while the class and the teacher extend points they make and relate these points to what preceded. Such a procedure also creates motivation: only an unusually unresponsive student will resist the pull of his peers needing what he has to give and, perhaps, even being proud of it.

In modifying the teaching strategy, teachers must also be prepared to deal with certain unusual problems, some of which arise out of habits and expectations built by previous practices. One teacher, in developing a sequence on "Houses Around the World," had diligently marked for herself and the students the pages in several texts on the geographic factors that influence the types of houses that are built in various parts of the world. She had listed these pages on the board, but the students refused to skip any pages, asking how could they understand what came later if they did not read what came before?

THE NEED FOR A VARIETY OF ACTIVITIES

If one interprets activities as something to initiate the search for making abstractions concrete, to hold on to while struggling with difficulties, then activities are not frills and a waste of time, but a deliberate way of cultivating readiness and upgrading learning. Students with meager background and experience, with short attention span and poor work habits, need to engage in a great variety of overt activities. Making booklets, drawing hands, and pasting advertisements may seem like useless play. But if these activities help hold attention, provide appropriate starting points, and create a sense of accomplishment, they have a place in the program. Pairing students to read with each other extends the reading practice for students who will not read unless someone listens, and, in addition, they read much more frequently than they would if they had to wait for the teacher to listen to them. This arrangement also gives students routine tasks to work at as soon as they enter the room, which prevents them from engaging in the disruptive activities at the beginning of classes that were described in Chapter II. Reading to each other also stimulates them to move faster in the reading because partners usually become interested in each other's books. As a result they also tend to read more and to cultivate such useful habits as using context clues to figure out the meaning of new words. Furthermore, if the students are paired sociometrically, they are likely to accept criticism from their partners without reacting as negatively to criticism as they usually do.

The use of technological aids is another method of providing "holding" activity. For example, for those students who cannot handle any book independently, there is the tape recorder into which stories can be dictated, a book, and a pair of earphones. They read as they listen, and they can do it as often as they need without disturbing anyone else, including the teacher. For students with long experience of frustration with books and with correcting teachers, this experience is a perfect antidote: It cuts out all previous blocks that stand between them and books and gives them a chance to start anew. Besides, for some students, being alone with the sound of the recorder is perhaps their first experience in privacy. Their ears, eyes, and hands are occupied and all distractions are eliminated. Often a student would sit and listen to a story, then repeat the experience, while reading and even writing. New readers seemed to learn to read in a shorter time, probably by seeing and hearing at the same time. Under these conditions, students may get the meaning from reading for the first time in their lives.

Of course the recorder was also used for many other purposes. In some classes sociodrama sequences were recorded to listen to later. In other classes they were used to record the practice of plays for others to listen to when their assigned work was finished. Readings of poetry were recorded for the same purpose. Often teachers played recorded stories so the whole class could read and listen at the same time.

Evidently the tape recorder is useful even for creating an atmosphere of disciplined behavior, as is illustrated in the record of one teacher:

The children came into the room that day, very noisy as usual, not out of bounds, but very noisy. The moment that tape recorder went on, every child sat at attention and the class was absolutely silent. This, by the way, was not their first introduction to the tape recorder. This technique is good only for certain occasions; it cannot be a regular diet. However, it is one way of using the tape recorder in the classroom.

On this day the children, after listening to the full tape which took about 25 minutes, went up to the tray, row by row, and obtained their books. As they were reading the books, I distributed a mimeographed reading chart. When they had had time to browse and see if they liked their book, I introduced the progress charts and explained how they were to be used.

On that first day an interesting thing happened. There were only a few copies of *Caddie Woodlawn* [Brink, 1963], and the students knew who was supposed to try and read it. With no suggestions from me, all moved toward the area in the room where there was sufficient space for five or so to gather together and read to each other. There were no instructions from me to do this. They were reading to each other and enjoying it. I just considered it a natural thing and no comments were made about it. On the second day they came in again noisily. However, as the tape began to talk and ask them to go up—this row first, that row next—they immediately got their books and sat down to read. Again, the children did the same thing, gradually moved to those people who happened to have the same book and gathered in little groups around one of the desks, in the front of the room, or around the teacher's desk—it didn't matter where, and read in this way. No one asked for help. This was the beginning of the training of the children to come into the room, get their book, and sit down to read.

As I went around I asked the students who were reading their own books to read to me. If the student was having difficulty, I read a portion of the chapter, and then left him at a point where he felt he might be able to go on alone.

Apparently playing music on the tape recorder during art work, modeling, cutting and pasting, also has a calming effect on students. One teacher commented that this changed tigers into lambs. However, it is hard to "sell" this practice to administrators. One commented, "The teachers will think I'm crazy." A second was concerned about parental reaction. A third objected on the grounds that "there's enough noise already. We don't need to fabricate any." Still another wanted to know, "Am I running a school or an afternoon recreation center?" Most asked the standard question, "Where do you think we're going to get all those tape recorders?"

THE ROLE OF THE ADMINISTRATOR

It is no easier for teachers to learn new things than it is for children. They need support from teamwork with other teachers and help from administrators as well. Regular team planning, first with a consultant or administrator, and then with other teachers provides a source of strength. Teachers learn not only that two heads are better than one, but also that sharing ideas reduces the amount of research, and dividing the work on production of materials and devices reduces the "chorework": one makes a bibliography, another duplicates a story, and the third makes the preliminary visit to plan for a class trip. For new teachers who have not yet collected appropriate materials, team planning is necessary for survival.

Teamwork also helps teachers to be supportive of each other. Sharing a new process while it is being attempted builds confidence. Further, teamwork reduces fear of failure, for it demonstrates that other teachers also have problems. However, teamwork cannot flourish without administrative support. It requires appropriate scheduling for free periods and appropriate distribution of materials.

Perhaps the greatest contribution administrators can make is to support experimentation. Experimentation always involves some risks and hazards—the risk of making errors, the hazard of replacing "tried and true" skills with new ones. Administrators need to support teachers in such periods of transition, and to allow for the relatively slow pace that it takes to perfect new strategies of learning and teaching. Most teachers, as well as administrators, expect too much too soon and give up before the new practice has had time to ripen and to become fully productive.

Experimentation also involves creating flexible work teams instead of depending on the usual "standing committees" to invent and install innovations. It requires establishing new channels of face-to-face communication, ways of discovering leadership, and new ways of using existing leadership in the school. There is psychological resistance to considering teachers as experts to help other teachers, and to arranging free time for this purpose.

Finally, any innovation requires some outside consultant help, if for no other purpose than to articulate problems that are difficult for insiders to see or to express. Outside consultants also can gather more differences in points of view, perceive more problems and view them more objectively, than can those who have lived with the situation for a long time. An especially useful consultant function is that of establishing a methodological sequence in planning and testing new programs, such as having a careful diagnosis precede plans, and planning precede action.

Bibliography

Adamic, L. *A Nation of Nations.* New York: Harper and Brothers, 1945.

Addington, Sarah. "The Clodhopper." In Becker, Mary L. (ed.), *Under Twenty.* New York: Harcourt, Brace & Co., 1932. (Out of print.)

Allen, Adam. *Dynamo Farm.* Philadelphia: J. B. Lippincott, 1942. (Out of print.) Suggested alternative: Gipson, Fred. *Old Yeller.* New York: Harper and Brothers, 1956. Available from Pocket Books, New York.

———. *New Broome Experiment.* Philadelphia: J. B. Lippincott Co., 1944. (Out of print.)

Allinsmith, W., and Goethals, G. W. "Cultural Factors in Mental Health: An Anthropological Perspective." *Review of Educational Research,* 1956, *26,* 433–438.

Anderson, A. M. *Squanto and the Pilgrims.* "American Adventure Series." Evanston, Ill.: Row, Peterson & Co., 1949.

Anti-Defamation League of B'nai B'rith in cooperation with the Federal Council of the Churches of Christ in America. *About People.* Filmstrip.

Archibald, Joe. *Rebel Halfback.* Philadelphia: Westminster Press, 1947.

Asch, Sholem. *East River.* New York: G. P. Putnam's Sons, 1946. (Out of print.)

Beim, Lorraine. *Triumph Clear.* New York: Harcourt, Brace & Co., 1946.

Beiser, Morton. "Poverty, Social Disintegration and Personality." *Journal of Social Issues,* January, 1965, *21,* 56–78.

Benét, Laura. *The Hidden Valley.* New York: Dodd, Mead & Co., 1938. (Out of print.)

Bennett, Rowena. *Runner for the King.* Chicago: Follett Publishing, 1944. Available from Scholastic Book Services, Scholastic Magazines, Englewood Cliffs, N.J.

Bernstein, B. "Language and Social Class." *British Journal of Sociology,* 1960, *11,* 271–276.

Bird, Dorothy Maywood. *Granite Harbor.* New York: The Macmillan Co., 1963.

Bontemps, Arna. *We Have Tomorrow.* Boston: Houghton Mifflin Co., 1945.

Brackett, Peter. "Double Payment." In Berger, Eric (ed.), *Best Short Shorts.* New York: TAB Books, 1958. Available from Scholastic Book Services, Scholastic Magazines, Englewood Cliffs. N.J.

Brink, Carol. *Caddie Woodlawn.* New York: The Macmillan Co., 1935. Available in paperback from The Macmillan Co., New York, 1963 (an Acorn Book).

Brown, Francis J., and Roucek, Joseph Slabbey. *One America.* 3rd ed. Englewood Cliffs, N.J.: Prentice-Hall, 1962.

Bryant, Bernice. *Trudy Terrill: Eighth Grader.* Indianapolis: The Bobbs-Merrill Co., 1946. (Out of print.)

Buck, Pearl S. *The Big Wave.* New York: The John Day Co., 1947. Available from Scholastic Book Services, Scholastic Magazines, Englewood Cliffs, N.J.

Bulla, Clyde Robert. *Riding The Pony Express.* New York: Thomas Y. Crowell Co., 1948. Available from Scholastic Book Services, Scholastic Magazines, Englewood Cliffs, N.J.

———. *Eagle Feather.* New York: Thomas Y. Crowell Co., 1952. Available from Scholastic Book Services, Scholastic Magazines, Englewood Cliffs, N.J.

———. *Down the Mississippi.* New York: Thomas Y. Crowell Co., 1954. Available from Scholastic Book Services, Scholastic Magazines, Englewood Cliffs, N.J.

———. *White Sails to China.* New York: Thomas Y. Crowell Co., 1955. Available from Scholastic Book Services, Scholastic Magazines, Englewood Cliffs, N.J.

Burgwyn, Mebane H. *River Treasure.* New York: Oxford University Press, 1947. (Out of Print.)

Carmer, Carl. *For the Rights of Men.* New York: Hinds, Hayden & Eldredge, 1947. (Out of print.)

Cavanna, Betty. *Going on Sixteen.* Philadelphia: Westminster Press, 1946.

———. *A Girl Can Dream.* Philadelphia: Westminster Press, 1948.

Chayevsky, Paddy. "Mother." In Vidal, Gore (ed.), *Best Television Plays.* New York: Ballantine Books, 1956.

Chinn, Laurene Chambers. "Spelling Bee." In Berger, Eric (ed.), *Best Short Shorts.* New York: TAB Books, 1958. Available from Scholastic Book Services, Scholastic Magazines, Englewood Cliffs, N.J.

Clark, Ann N. *Secret of the Andes.* New York: Viking Press, 1952.

Clymer, Eleanor. *The Trolley Car Family.* Philadelphia: David McKay Co., 1947. Available from Scholastic Book Services, Scholastic Magazines, Englewood Cliffs, N.J.

Common Ground, 1940–1949. Published quarterly by Common Council for American Unity, 20 West 40th Street, New York 18, N.Y. (Ceased publication.)

Compere, Mickie. *The Wizard of Menlo Park.* Englewood Cliffs, N.J.: Scholastic Book Services, Scholastic Magazines, 1964.

Coté, Phyllis. *The People Upstairs.* New York: Doubleday & Co., 1946. (Out of print.)

Courtright, Eugenie. "Yours Lovingly." In Cook, Luella B., Miller, H. A., and Loban, Walter (eds.), *Adventures in Appreciation*. New York: Harcourt, Brace & Co., 1947.

Davenport, Marcia. *The Valley of Decision*. New York: Charles Scribner's Sons, 1942. Available from Popular Library, New York.

Davie, Maurice R. *What Shall We Do About Immigration?* Public Affairs Pamphlet No. 115. New York: Public Affairs Committee, 1946.

Davis, A. *Social Class Influence on Learning*. Cambridge, Mass.: Harvard University Press, 1952.

Davis, Robert. *Gid Granger*. New York: Holiday House, 1945. Suggested alternative: Aldrich, Bess Streeter. *A Lantern in Her Hand*. New York: D. Appleton & Co., 1928. Available from Pocket Books, New York.

Deasy, Mary. "The High Hill." *Harper's Magazine,* February, 1948, *196,* 128–135.

De Leeuw, Adele. *Linda Marsh*. New York: The Macmillan Co., 1943.

"Democracy Series, The." New York: The Macmillan Co., 1943. (Out of print.) King, Allen Y., and Dennis, Ida. *The Way of Democracy,* 1941. McGuire, Edna, and Rogers, Don C. *The Growth of Democracy,* 1944. Morgan, Edna. *Pioneering in Democracy,* 1945.

Deutsch, Martin. "The Disadvantaged Child and the Learning Process." In Passow, A. H. (ed.), *Education in Depressed Areas*. New York: Teachers College, Columbia University, 1963.

———. "Facilitating Development in the Pre-School Child: Social and Psychological Perspectives." *Merrill-Palmer Quarterly,* July, 1964, *10,* 249–263. (a)

———. "Some Aspects of the Psycho-Social Framework of Teacher-Pupil Relationships with Respect to the Disadvantaged." First draft of paper prepared for the Inner City Schools Project Conference at the Boston University Human Relations Center, July 16–19, 1964.(b)

Devine, James E. *Our New York*. New York: Noble & Noble, Publishers, 1961. (Out of print.)

Dickens, Charles. *Little Dorrit*. New York: William Collins Sons & Co., n.d.

Dickens, Charles. *A Tale of Two Cities*. Available in paperback from Dell Publishing Co., New York, n.d.

Dreiser, Theodore. *Sister Carrie*. Available in paperback from Dell Publishing Co., New York, 1960.

Dwyer, J. F. "The Citizen." In Grady, W. E., and Klapper, P. (eds.), *Reading for Appreciation*. Book 2, Part 1. New York: Charles Scribner's Sons, 1935.

Eberle, Irmengarde. *The Very Good Neighbors*. Philadelphia, J. B. Lippincott Co., 1945. (Out of print.)

Edmonds, Walter D. "Judge." In Lucas, Harriet Marcelia, and Ansorge, Elizabeth F. (eds.), *Prose and Poetry of Today*. Syracuse, N.Y.: L. W. Singer Co., 1941. Available in Agnew, J. Kenner, and McCarthy, Agnes L. (eds.), *Prose and Poetry for Enjoyment*. Syracuse, N.Y.: L. W. Singer Co., 1955.

Eells, K. "Some Implications for School Practice of the Chicago Studies of Cultural Bias in Intelligence Tests." *Harvard Education Review,* Fall, 1953, Part II, *23,* 284–297.

————, et al. *Intelligence and Cultural Difference.* Chicago: University of Chicago Press, 1951.

Eichelberger, Rosa K. *Bronko.* New York: William Morrow and Co., 1955.

Elam, Sophie L. "Acculturation and Learning Problems of Puerto Rican Children." *Teachers College Record,* 1960, *61,* 258–264.

Elkins, Deborah. "Some Factors Related to the Choice-Status of Ninety Eighth Grade Children in a School Society." *Genetic Psychology Monographs,* 1958, *58,* 207–272.

————. *Reading Improvement in the Junior High School.* New York: Bureau of Publications, Teachers College, Columbia University, 1963.

————, and Seifman, E. "Teachers Solve Junior High School Problems in a Summer Workshop." *Journal of Reading,* 1965, *8,* 245–250.

Emerson, Elizabeth. *The Good Crop.* New York: Longmans, Green & Co., 1946. (Out of print.)

Emery, Anne. *Tradition.* New York: Vanguard Press, 1946.

Estes, Eleanor. *The Hundred Dresses.* New York: Harcourt, Brace & Co., 1944.

Fast, Howard. *Citizen Tom Paine.* New York: Bantam Books, 1946. Available from World Publishing Co., New York, "Living Library (L6)." (a)

————. *Freedom Road.* New York: Pocket Books, 1946. (b)

Felsen, Henry Gregor. *Bertie Comes Through.* New York: E. P. Dutton & Co., 1948. (a)

————. *Bertie Takes Care.* New York: E. P. Dutton & Co., 1948. (b)

Fenton, Edward. *Us and the Duchess.* New York: Doubleday & Co., 1947. (Out of print.)

Ferris, Helen. "I Hated the House I Lived In." In *This Happened to Me.* New York: E. P. Dutton & Co., 1929. (Out of print.)

Fessier, Michael. "That's What Happened to Me." In Cook, Luella B., Miller, H. A., and Loban, Walter A. (eds.), *Adventures in Appreciation.* New York: Harcourt, Brace & Co., 1947. Available in Alwin, Virginia, *Short Stories I.* "Literary Heritage Series." New York: The Macmillan Co., 1961.

Fisher, D. C. "Aw, Go Chase Yourself." In Fisher, D. C., and Cleghorn, S. N., *Nothing Ever Happens and How It Does.* Boston: Beacon Press, 1943. (Out of print.) Suggested alternative: Jackson, Shirley. "Charles." In *The Lottery.* New York: Avon Books, 1960.

Fitch, Florence Mary. *One God.* New York: Lothrop, Lee & Shepard Co., 1944.

Forbes, Esther. *Johnny Tremain.* Boston: Houghton Mifflin Co., 1943.

Forbes, Katherine. *Mama's Bank Account.* New York: Harcourt, Brace & Co., 1943. Available from Bantam Books, New York.

Friedman, Frieda. *Dot for Short.* New York: William Morrow and Co., 1947. Available from Scholastic Book Services, Scholastic Magazines, Englewood Cliffs, N.J.

Gale, Martin. *Joan and Michael.* New York: Viking Press, 1941. (Out of print.)

Gates, Doris. *Blue Willow.* New York: Viking Press, 1940. Available from Scholastic Book Services, Scholastic Magazines, Englewood Cliffs, N.J.

―――. *Sensible Kate.* New York: Viking Press, 1943. Available from Scholastic Book Services, Scholastic Magazines, Englewood Cliffs, N.J.

―――. *North Fork.* New York: Viking Press, 1945.

Gould, Kenneth M. "They Got the Blame." In Herrick, Arnold, and Askwith, Herbert (eds.), *This Way to Unity.* New York: Oxford Book Co., 1945. (Out of print.)

Guilford, J. P. "The Structure of Intelligence." *Psychological Bulletin,* 1956, *53,* 267–293.

Haggard, E. A. "Social Status and Intelligence." *Genetic Psychology Monographs,* 1954, *49,* 141–186.

Halper, Albert. "Prelude." In Herrick, Arnold, and Askwith, Herbert (eds.), *This Way to Unity.* New York: Oxford Book Co., 1945. (Out of Print.)

Harrington, Michael. *The Other America.* New York: The Macmillan Co., 1962.

Haskell, Helen. *Katrinka.* New York: E. P. Dutton & Co., 1915.

Hechinger, F. M. "Head Start to Where." *Saturday Review,* December 18, 1965, *48,* 59.

Heyert, Murray. "The New Kid." *Harper's Magazine,* June, 1944, *189,* 21–27.

Hickok, Lorena A. *The Story of Helen Keller.* New York: Grossett & Dunlap, 1958. Available from Scholastic Book Services, Scholastic Magazines, Englewood Cliffs, N.J.

Holmes, Marjorie. "Reflection of Luanne." *Seventeen,* March, 1949. Available in Bennett, Robert A. (ed.), *Mirrors.* Scholastic Book Services, Scholastic Magazines, Englewood Cliffs, N.J.

Hunt, J. McV. *Intelligence and Experience.* New York: The Ronald Press, 1961. Pp. 258–259.

―――. "How Children Develop Intellectually." *Children,* May–June 1964, 83–91. (a)

―――. "The Psychological Basis for Using Pre-School Enrichment as an Antidote for Cultural Deprivation." *Merrill-Palmer Quarterly,* July, 1964, *10,* 212. (b)

Jackson, Jesse. *Call Me Charley.* New York: Harper and Brothers, 1945.

―――. *Anchor Man.* New York: Harper and Brothers, 1947.

Jackson, Shirley, "After You, My Dear Alphonse." In Moon, Bucklin (ed.), *Primer for White Folks.* New York: Doubleday & Co., 1945. Available in Jackson, Shirley. *The Lottery.* New York: Avon Books, 1960.

Jencks, C. "Slums and Schools." *The New Republic,* September 10, *17,* 1962.

Jennings, Helen Hall. *Sociometry in Group Relations.* 2nd ed. Washington, D.C.: American Council on Education, 1959.

Johnson, James W. *Negro Americans, What Now?* New York: Viking Press, 1934. (Out of print.)

Judson, Clara Ingram. *They Came From France.* Boston: Houghton Mifflin Co., 1943. (Out of print.)

————. *Petar's Treasure.* Boston: Houghton Mifflin Co., 1945. (Out of print.) Suggested alternative: Hill, Marjorie Y. *Look for the Stars.* New York: Thomas Y. Crowell Co., 1956. Available from Scholastic Book Services, Scholastic Magazines, Englewood Cliffs, N.J.

————. *Michael's Victory.* Boston: Houghton Mifflin Co., 1946. (Out of print.)

————. *The Lost Violin.* Boston: Houghton Mifflin Co., 1946. (Out of print.)

Kahl, J. A. "Educational and Occupational Aspirations of the 'Common Man's Boys.' " *Harvard Education Review,* Summer, 1953, *23,* 186–203.

Kerr, Laura. *The Girl Who Ran for President.* New York: Thomas Nelson & Sons, 1947. (Out of print.)

Kjelgaard, Jim. "Code of the Underworld." In Berger, Eric (ed.), *Best Short Shorts.* New York: TAB Books, 1958. Available from Scholastic Book Services, Scholastic Magazines, Englewood Cliffs, N.J.

Kreis, Bernadine. "Things Greater than He," *Senior Scholastic,* 1947, *50,* 25–26.

Krugman, J. I. "Cultural Deprivation and Child Development." *High Points,* November, 1956, *38,* 5–20.

Lambert, Clara. "Theresa Follows the Crops." In Association for Childhood Education, *Told Under the Stars and Stripes,* New York: The Macmillan Co., 1947. (Out of print.)

Leonard, Arthur R., and Jacobs, Bertha E. *The Nation's History.* New York: Henry Holt & Co., 1931. (Out of print.)

Lewiton, Mina. *The Divided Heart.* Philadelphia: David McKay Co., 1947. Suggested alternative: Hill, Marjorie Y. *Look for the Stars.* New York: Thomas Y. Crowell Co., 1956. Available from Scholastic Book Services, Scholastic Magazines, Englewood Cliffs, N.J.

Llewellyn, Richard. *How Green Was My Valley.* New York: The Macmillan Co., 1940.

Longfellow, Henry W. "Evangeline." In Grady, William E., and Klapper, Paul (eds.), *Reading for Appreciation.* Book II. New York: Charles Scribner's Sons, 1936.

Lord, Beman. *Quarterback's Aim.* New York: Henry Z. Walck, 1960. Available from Scholastic Book Services, Scholastic Magazines, Englewood Cliffs, N.J.

Lovelace, Maud H. *Betsy Was a Junior.* New York: Thomas Y. Crowell Co., 1947.

Lowe, Florence. *Somebody Else's Shoes.* New York: Rinehart & Co., 1948. (Out of print.)

McNeely, Marian Hurd. "The Horse." In Broening, Angela M., *et al.* (eds.), *Best Liked Literature.* Book III. Boston: Ginn and Co., 1947.

Maltz, Albert. "The Happiest Man on Earth." In Ansorge, Elizabeth, *et al., Prose and Poetry for Appreciation.* Syracuse, N.Y.: L. W. Singer Co., 1942.

Malvern, Gladys. *Jonica's Island.* New York: Julian Messner, 1945. Suggested alternative: Murphy, Frances S. *Runaway Alice. (A Nickel for Alice.)* New York: Thomas Y. Crowell, Co., 1951.

Marx, J., and Marx, A. "The Gift That Mattered." *Ladies Home Journal,* December, 1948, *65,* 38–39.

Means, Florence C. *The Moved-Outers.* Boston: Houghton Mifflin Co., 1945. (Out of print.)

Medearis, Mary. *Big Doc's Girl.* Philadelphia: J. B. Lippincott Co., 1942. Available from Scholastic Book Services, Scholastic Magazines, Englewood Cliffs, N.J.

Merrill, Jean. *Shan's Lucky Knife.* New York: W. R. Scott, 1960. Available from Scholastic Book Services, Scholastic Magazines, Englewood Cliffs, N.J.

————. *The Superlative Horse* New York: W. R. Scott, 1961. Available from Scholastic Book Services, Scholastic Magazines, Englewood Cliffs, N.J.

Miller, Margery. *Joe Louis: American.* New York: Current Books, 1945. (Out of print.)

Miner, J. B. *Intelligence in the United States.* New York: Springer Publishing Co., 1957. Pp. 6–7.

Moore, Eva. *Johnny Appleseed.* Englewood Cliffs, N.J.: Scholastic Book Services, 1964.

National Education Association, Association for Supervision and Curriculum Development. *Building America.* "Illustrated Studies on Modern Problems." Distributed by Americana Corporation.

Neilson, Frances G. *Giant Mountain.* New York: E. P. Dutton & Co., 1946.

Papashvily, George, and Papashvily, Helen. *Anything Can Happen.* New York: Pocket Books, 1961.

Piaget, J. *The Psychology of Intelligence.* Harcourt, Brace & Co., 1950.

Powdermaker, Hortense. *Probing Our Prejudices.* New York: Harper and Brothers, 1944.

Raymond, Margaret T. *A Bend in the Road.* New York: Longmans, Green & Co., 1934. (Out of print.) Suggested alternative: Emery, Anne. *Going Steady.* Philadelphia: Westminster Press, 1950. Available from Scholastic Book Services, Scholastic Magazines, Englewood Cliffs, N.J.

Rawlings, Marjorie K. "A Mother in Manville." In Cook, Luella B., Miller, H. A., and Loban, Walter A. (eds.), *Adventures in Appreciation.* New York: Harcourt, Brace & Co., 1947. Available in Taggart, Ernestine, (ed.), *Twenty Grand Short Stories.* New York: Bantam Books.

Reader's Digest. *Our American Heritage.* Filmstrip. Distributed by Popular Science Publishing Co., New York.

Reissman, F. *The Culturally Deprived Child.* New York: Harper & Row, Publishers, 1962.

Ross, L. Q. "Cemetary Path." In Bailey, Matilda, and Leavell, Ullin W. (eds.), *Worlds to Explore.* Rev. and enlarged. New York: American Book Co., 1961.

Rugg, Harold. *Our Country and Our People.* New York: Longmans, Green & Co., 1934. (Out of print.)

Sawyer, Ruth. *Old Con and Patrick.* New York: Viking Press, 1946. (Out of print.)

Schulz, Charles. *Happiness Is a Warm Puppy.* San Francisco: Determined Publications, 1962.

Seredy, Kate. *A Tree for Peter.* New York: Viking Press, 1941.

Sexton, Patricia. *Education and Income.* New York: Viking Press, 1961. Pp. 38–40, 160–162.

Sigel, I. E. "How Intelligence Tests Limit Understanding of Intelligence." *Merrill-Palmer Quarterly,* 1963, *9,* 39–57.

Sperry, Armstrong. *Call It Courage.* New York: The Macmillan Co., 1940. Available in paperback from The Macmillan Co., New York, 1964.

Staff of Intergroup Education in Cooperating Schools. *Reading Ladders for Human Relations.* Rev. ed. Washington, D.C.: American Council on Education, 1949.

Stegner, Wallace (ed.). *One Nation.* Boston: Houghton Mifflin Co., 1945. (Out of print.)

Stevenson, Augusta. *Squanto.* "Childhood of Famous Americans Series." Indianapolis: The Bobbs-Merrill Co., 1953.

Summers, James L. "Like Son." *Senior Scholastic,* 1949, *54,* 20–21. Suggested alternative: Kleihauer, Lois D. "The Cub." In Berger, Eric (ed.), *Best Short Shorts.* New York: TAB Books, 1958. Available from Scholastic Book Services, Scholastic Magazines, Englewood Cliffs, N.J.

Swift, Hildegarde Hoyt. *The Railroad to Freedom.* New York: Harcourt, Brace & Co., 1932.

Taba, Hilda. *With Perspective on Human Relations.* Washington, D.C.: American Council on Education, 1955.

————. "Cultural Deprivation as a Factor in School Learning." *Merrill-Palmer Quarterly,* 1964, *10,* 147–159.

————, Brady, Elizabeth Hall, Robinson, J. T., and Dolton, Flora. *Elementary Curriculum in Intergroup Relations.* Washington, D.C.: American Council on Education, 1950. Pp. 7–8.

————, and Elkins, Deborah. *With Focus on Human Relations.* Washington, D.C.: American Council on Education, 1950.

————, Brady, Elizabeth Hall, Robinson, J. T. and Vickery, William E. *Diagnosing Human Relations Needs.* Washington, D.C.: American Council on Education, 1951.

————, et al. *Literature for Human Understanding.* "Work in Progress Series." Washington, D.C.: American Council on Education, 1948.

Taba, Hilda, and Hills, James L. *Teacher Handbook for Contra Costa Social Studies Grades 1–6.* Hayward, Calif.: Rapid Printers & Lithographers, 1965.

Thorne, Alice. *The Story of Madame Curie.* New York: Grossett & Dunlap, 1961. Available from Scholastic Book Services, Scholastic Magazines, Englewood Cliffs, N. J.

Tunis, John R. *The Kid from Tomkinsville.* New York: Harcourt, Brace & Co., 1940.

––––––. *All-American.* New York: Harcourt, Brace & Co., 1942.

––––––. *Keystone Kids.* New York: Harcourt, Brace & Co., 1943.

––––––. *Yea! Wildcats!* New York: Harcourt, Brace & Co., 1944.

U.S. Office of Education. "Americans All—Immigrants All." Recordings of the radio programs broadcast under the auspices of the U.S. Office of Education.

Whitney, Phyllis A. *Willow Hill.* Philadelphia: David McKay Co., 1947.

Williams, Chester S. *Religious Liberty.* "Our Freedom Series." Evanston, Ill.: Row, Peterson & Co., 1941. (Out of print.)

Wilson, Hazel H. *The Owen Boys.* Nashville: Abingdon-Cokesbury Press, 1947. (Out of print.)

Worth, Kathryn. *The Middle Button.* New York: Doubleday & Co., 1941.

Yashima, Taro. *Crow Boy.* New York: Viking Press, 1955.

Zuckmayer, Carl. "I Like It Here." In Berger, Eric (ed.), *Best Short Shorts.* New York: TAB Books, 1958. Available from Scholastic Book Services, Scholastic Magazines, Englewood Cliffs, N.J.

Index

PRINTED IN U.S.A.